Native Roads

Native Roads

The Complete Motoring Guide to the Navajo and Hopi Nations

Fran Kosik

Rio Nuevo Publishers
Tucson, Arizona

This book is dedicated to my best friend, Duane, and to my heart, Tai.

Rio Nuevo Publishers®
P.O. Box 5250
Tucson, Arizona 85703-0250
520-623-9558, www.rionuevo.com

Cover design: Larry Lindahl • Front cover photos: "Crow Bride" Hopi katsina doll by Roy Dewangyumptewa of Walpi, 2002 (photo by Larry Lindahl); turquoise beaded necklace (unknown artist, photo by Larry Lindahl); Monument Valley/Agathla Peak photo used with permission of the Cline Library, Special Collections and Archives, Northern Arizona University, PH.96.24.5.

Library of Congress Cataloging-in-Publication Data

Kosik, Fran.
  Native roads : the complete motoring guide to the Navajo and Hopi nations / Fran Kosik.-- Rev. ed.
      p. cm.
  Includes bibliographical references and index.
  ISBN-10 1-887896-68-6 (pbk.)
  ISBN-13 978-1-887896-68-9
  1. Navajo Indian Reservation--Guidebooks. 2. Hopi Indian Reservation--Guidebooks. 3. Automobile travel--Arizona--Guidebooks. 4. Arizona--Description and travel. I. Title.
  E99.N3K67 2005
  917.91'350454--dc22

                              2004027366

Printed in Canada

10 9 8 7 6 5 4 3 2 1

TABLE OF CONTENTS

TABLE OF CONTENTS

The warm winter sun reflected off one of the many water towers that distinguishes the oasis of Tuba City from the rest of the tawny desert as we slowly drove up the town's wide, tree-lined main street. It was exactly the kind of weather I was searching for when I left what my classmates and I referred to as "dreary Erie."

I had just graduated from nursing school, and my father had given me a used powder blue Chrysler Newport, "the tank," to make the drive across country. My sister and my best friend piled everything I owned in the world into that car, wrote the words "Tuba City or bust" all over it, and we started on the adventure of our lives.

I jumped at the chance to work for the Indian Health Service in Tuba City as my first job right out of nursing school. Not fully aware of what we were doing, we decided to take the scenic route over the Rocky Mountains in the dead of winter. We met many friendly people on that trip, but none friendlier than the staff at the Wolf Creek Pass ski resort when "the tank" sputtered into their parking lot completely out of gas. Saved by a five-gallon donation (they wouldn't take any money), we crossed over the highest mountain pass we would encounter and continued on our way.

Arriving at my new job a little wiser about elevation, winter, and distances between gas stations in the West, I realized I knew nothing about the people I would care for or about the beautiful location I was lucky enough to choose for my first nursing assignment. Over the years, I have had many opportunities to learn from "The People" and to wander through this amazing landscape. I hope what I have learned will help you in your travels.

As a visitor, or someone contemplating a trip to northern Arizona, you will want to see all of the scenic wonders: the Grand Canyon, Monument Valley, Lake Powell, and Canyon de Chelly. Distances from one place to another are long, but the beauty remains all around you. Along the way, you may wonder about the people, land formations, and history of the area. That is why I wrote this book: to give you, the road traveler, a better understanding of where you are in the context of the Navajo and Hopi Nations, the geologic formations, and the history of the area. As you drive, each significant mile marker (MM) is explained to give you a snapshot of the important events that helped shape this part of America. For attractions between mile markers, refer to your odometer.

The recommended map of the area is the *Indian Country Guide Map,* produced by the Automobile Club of Southern California and for sale at most tourist stops or bookstores for about $5. To best see many of the sites in this book, take along a pair of binoculars and a compass.

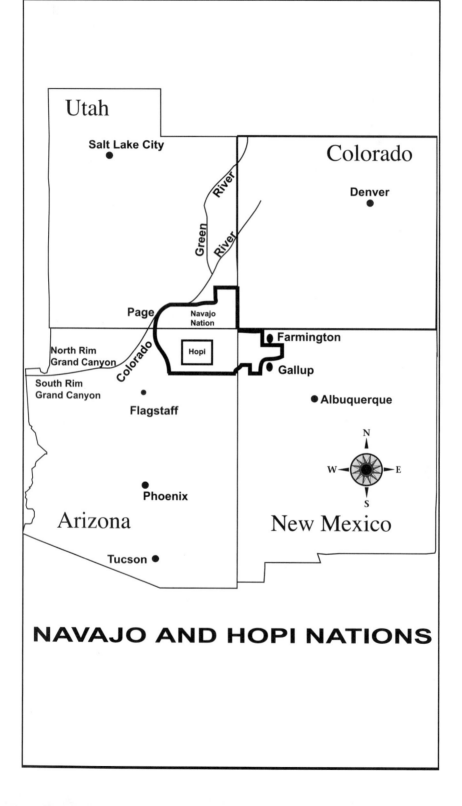

NAVAJO AND HOPI NATIONS

THE COLORADO PLATEAU

In traveling the native roads, you will traverse a spectacular piece of America called the Colorado Plateau. This region covers more than 150,000 square miles (390,000 sq km) and extends from the Mogollon Rim in central Arizona to the south, the Wasatch Range in Utah to the west, the Uinta Range to the north, and the Rocky Mountains to the east.

About 4.5 billion years ago, sediments began to deposit as oceans, seas, lakes, and deserts came and went, laying down one layer on top of another. All the while, forces deep within the Earth were building until powerful plate tectonics began to form mountains and pushed the Colorado Plateau straight up as one unit. This happened 60 to 70 million years ago, about the same time the dinosaur era ended. The Colorado River, up to this time, had meandered across a broad flat plain. As the plateau rose, the river began to run downhill with greater and greater force, eventually forming the Grand Canyon.

During this time, parts of the plateau were affected by folding and buckling of the sedimentary rock layers. Sharply rising rock layers that appear sheared off in mid-air demarcate the edges of an uplift, known as a monocline. There are many striking monoclines to see on your travels. The Echo Cliffs along U.S. 89, twenty-five miles south of Page, mark the eastern boundary of the Kaibab Uplift. Comb Ridge along U.S. 163 marks the southern boundary of the Monument Uplift, which runs all the way from Kayenta, Arizona, to Bluff, Utah.

To become familiar with the many rock formations, try to follow one rock layer as it appears and disappears over different parts of the reservation. The Chinle Formation is a good one to track because its purple and grey colors make it easy to pick out. You see it as the crumbly, round, purple and grey hills along U.S. 89 between Cameron and Tuba City, and south of Chinle near Canyon de Chelly. It makes up the bottom of the Echo Cliffs on U.S. 89 and the Organ Rock Monocline on U.S. 160, and is seen again under Owl Rock on U.S. 163 heading toward Monument Valley.

In addition to sedimentary rocks, there are many igneous formations caused by underground volcanos that failed to break the surface when they erupted. Over eons, erosion wore off the top layers of sedimentary rocks, exposing the harder volcanic plug. Agathla Peak and Shiprock are two primary examples of igneous formations.

TOURIST SEASON ON THE COLORADO PLATEAU

The high season for tourists on the Colorado Plateau is April 1 through November 1. This includes the Hopi and Navajo Nations, north and south rims of the Grand Canyon, Flagstaff, and the Lake Powell/Page area.

TIMELINE OF COMMON ROCK LAYERS

Era / Age	Group	Rock Layer	Location
Age of Mammals **Cenozoic** 65 million years ago		Volcanics	
		Bidahochi Formation	Hopi Buttes
		Chuska Sandstone	Ganado Mesa Chuska Mountains
Cretaceous 135 million years ago	Mesa Verde Group	Yale Point Sandstone	
		Wepo Formation	Black Mesa
		Coal	
		Toreva Formation	
		Mancos Shale	
		Dakota Sandstone	
Jurassic 180 million years ago	San Rafael Group	Morrison Formation	Carrizo Mountains
		Cowsprings Sandstone	Coal Mine Canyon
		Entrada Sandstone	
		Carmel Formation	
	Glen	Navajo Sandstone	
Triassic 230 million years ago	Canyon Group	Kayenta Formation	Echo Cliffs Vermilion Cliffs
		Moenave Formation	
		Wingate Sandstone	
		Chinle Formation	Painted Desert Petrified Forest
		Moenkopi Formation/Shinarump Formation	
Age of Fishes **Paleozoic** 600 million years ago		Kaibab Formation	
		Coconino Sandstone (Monument Valley) De Chelly Sandstone (Canyon de Chelly)	
		Supai Group	
		Redwall Limestone	

TIME ZONES

The Navajo Nation joins the rest of the U.S. in changing to daylight saving time (DST) beginning the first week of April and ending the last week in October. The rest of Arizona and the Hopi Nation stay on mountain standard time (MST) year-round. The Navajo Nation switches because the reservation extends into New Mexico and Utah, states which also move to DST.

Obviously, this causes a good deal of confusion in towns that honor both time zones. In Tuba City, for example, the Tuba Trading Post and the Hopi village of Moenkopi stay on MST, while Bashas' Market and the Tuba City Hospital switch to DST. In some homes, husbands and wives go to work in different time zones.

WEATHER

The Colorado Plateau is classified as arid. It receives less than ten inches (25.4 cm) of rain per year. Most precipitation comes in two seasons: winter, from December to March, and summer, from July through August. Summer thunderstorms, known locally as monsoons, dump about 65 percent of the entire year's moisture. Amazingly, most of these summer storms have a diameter of only three miles.

The average summer temperature depends entirely on your elevation. A good rule of thumb is for every 1,000-foot (305 m) increase in elevation, the temperature will drop about three degrees Fahrenheit (1.7°C). On average, summer temperatures at 5,000 feet (1,524 m) are in the 90s to 100s (32°C–38°C). At 7,000 feet (2,133 m), the daytime temperatures are usually in the 80s (27°–32°C). Nighttime temperatures can drop considerably, especially in the mountains, so carry something warm to wear.

There are a few things you need to keep in mind when traveling in the West (like not running out of gas on a mountain pass) to avoid problems. One of these is flash floods. Because most of the soil is sandy, when it does rain it dumps more than the ground can absorb. Water flows downhill in washes and into slickrock funnels and spouts, collecting runoff from numerous outlets. Along the way it picks up debris and boulders. That's why it's not a good idea to cross a wash under flash flood conditions. The water may be deeper than you think, and your car could easily be whisked away by the powerful water or pummeled by large rocks swept down from the higher mesas. This rule also applies to hiking in narrow canyons, which can flood even when storms are far away.

Lightning

Navajos and Hopis have many taboos and words of warning about lightning. Because this is a common danger in high country, Navajos instruct their children on appropriate behavior in a storm. If you sit down, they say, the lightning will go away. They also say not to yell when it's raining or you'll be struck by lightning. The most appropriate behavior in a thunderstorm is to avoid being in the open on a canyon rim. If you're away from shelter, squat on the ground next to a cliff or beneath an overhang. Do not touch grounded metal objects such as a railing or your camera's tripod. Lightning will also strike the water, so if you are in a boat on Lake Powell, get off the lake and find a cliff or overhang to sit next to or under until the storm passes. In this country, storms don't usually last long.

Dust Storms

The wind is an amazingly powerful force in the desert. Bear in mind that it helped carve this land over millions of years. On a less grand scale, it would take only a few minutes for one of these sand storms to damage the paint on your car or pit your windshield. For the Navajos, the wind is the source of breath as well as the cause of illness. Winds are particularly strong in the spring, blowing generally from February through June.

You will frequently see dust devils cross your path. They are harmless but similar in appearance to a tiny tornado. Some Navajos think of dust devils as wind controlled by evil spirits up to no good. You, too, would be a believer if you saw a large dust devil run through a camp, throwing saddle blankets, harnesses, and buckets into the air to land hundreds of feet away.

Quicksand

If you are interested in hiking, especially around the Little Colorado River, you should be aware of this mixture of sand and water that allows heavy objects, like your body, to sink. You probably learned about quicksand through Western movies but never really believed there was such a thing. Yet it is a real danger and was a major obstacle to pioneers trying to cross the Little Colorado to settle in Arizona.

TRAVEL ETIQUETTE

As you motor through the Navajo, Hopi, and San Juan Southern Paiute homelands, you will have the chance to see many of the mountains, rocks, birds and other animals, and plants that make up the core of the traditional belief system. Consider this: only medicine people may climb a mountain. Mountains are revered as sacred places. Traditional medicine people have been schooled in the appropriate behaviors and rituals that protect them as they travel among the Holy People to collect specific herbs, earth, or rocks needed for ceremonial healing. Failure to maintain harmony through inattention to the laws of nature, they say, will result in illness.

Through one of more than fifty ceremonies, such wrong action and illness can be corrected and harmony restored. Your respect for this belief and your gentleness with all things you touch, walk on, or look at is appreciated. Please do not take anything. Under the Preservation of American Antiquities Act, it is a crime to remove artifacts from federal property. To include natives in your pictures, please ask their permission first. Many will definitely not want their pictures taken. Others, such as models working at Monument Valley or Canyon de Chelly, expect a gratuity. Hopis do not allow any photography at all, so don't even take a camera to a Hopi village.

If you are lucky enough to see a Hopi dance, the appropriate etiquette is to stand toward the back of the crowd, leaving the front for villagers. During the dance, maintain silence and do not ask questions about the names or identities of the masked dancers, especially in front of children. Photography and sketching are prohibited in the villages and at dances. Tape recording and taking notes are also not allowed. If there is a "closed" sign at the entrance to a village, this means the ceremony is closed to outsiders and you may not enter. Please read pages 113–114 before visiting the Hopi Nation.

LAND OWNERSHIP

All Indian reservations in the U.S. are federal land held in trust for tribes for their exclusive use. Homesite leases on the Navajo Reservation were first handed out by the Indian Service, now called the Bureau of Indian Affairs, after the Navajos' release from Fort Sumner in 1868 following the infamous Long Walk. Navajo Reservation land is now under the tribe's control. Navajo tribal members are able to get their own piece of land, or homesite, by applying to their own community, a political subdivision of the Navajo Nation known as a chapter. Everyone in the community gives their opinion on the proposed homesite lease. Frequently, though, families will object to any limitation of their grazing land, making it difficult to secure new homesite leases.

THE NAVAJO NATION

Ask a Navajo elder to tell you a story, and you may be occupied for a while. Often an explanation of a current event must be put into perspective by beginning with the creation. The Navajo creation story involves three underworlds where important events happened to shape the Fourth World, where we all now live.

It takes years to develop a true understanding of Navajo oral history. Diné College offers an excellent cultural orientation program for newcomers to the area. A two-day workshop called "The Winter Stories" features the legends that can only be told "after the thunder sleeps." Summer cultural orientations for health workers and educators offer an overview of the important cultural points needed to work successfully in this society. For more information about these programs, contact: Diné College, Continuing Education, (928) 283-6321.

The Navajo were given the name *Ni'hookaa Diyan Diné* by their creators. It means "holy earth people." The Tewa Indians were first to call them *Navahu,* which means "the large area of cultivated land." Father Alonso de Benavides changed the name to Navaho in a book written in 1630.

According to the Diné, they emerged from three previous underworlds into this, the Fourth, or "Glittering World," through a magic reed. The first

people from the other three worlds were not like the people of today. They were animals, insects, or masked spirits, as depicted in Navajo ceremonies. First Man, or *Áłtsé Hastiin*, and First Woman, or *Áłsé Asdzą́ą́*, were two of the beings from the First or Black World. First Man was made in the east from the meeting of the white and black clouds. First Woman was made in the west from the joining of the yellow and blue clouds. Spider Woman, or *Ná ashjé'ii Asdzą́ą́*, who taught Navajo women how to weave, was also from the First World.

Spider Rock, Canyon de Chelly, courtesy Museum of New Mexico, #6168

Once in the Glittering World, the first thing the people did was build a sweat house and sing the Blessing Song. Then they met in the first hogan made exactly as Talking God, or *Haashch'ééłti'í*, had prescribed. In this hogan, the people began to arrange their world, naming the four sacred mountains surrounding the land and designating the four sacred stones that would become the boundaries of their homeland. (The mountains do not actually contain their symbolic sacred stone.) The San Francisco Peaks (*Dook'o'oosłííd,* the Abalone and Coral Mountain), north of Flagstaff, mark the Navajos' western boundary. Mt. Blanco (*Sis Naajiní,* or White Shell Mountain) in Colorado represents the eastern boundary. Mt. Taylor (*Tsoodził,* east of Grants, New Mexico) is the Navajos' Turquoise Mountain and represents the tribe's southern boundary. Mt. Hesperus (*Dibé Nitsaa*), the Black Jet Mountain, lies to the north in Colorado.

After setting the mountains down where they should go, the Navajo deities, or "Holy People," put the sun and the moon into the sky and were in the process of carefully placing the stars in an orderly way. But the trickster, Coyote, growing impatient from the long deliberations being held, seized the corner of the blanket where they lay and flung the remaining stars into the heavens.

The Holy People continued to make the necessities of life, like clouds, trees, and rain. Everything was as it should be when evil monsters appeared and began to kill the new Earth People. But a miracle happened to save them, personified as Ever Changing Woman, or *Asdzą́ą́ Nádleehé*. Changing Woman grew up around Huerfano Mesa, or *Dził Ná'oodiłií*, in New Mexico. She married the Sun and bore two sons, the Hero Twins of the Navajo people. They are Monster Slayer and Child-Born-of-Water. The twins traveled to their father the Sun, who gave them weapons of lightning bolts to fight the dreaded monsters. Every place the Hero Twins killed a monster, it turned to stone. An example of this is the lava flows near Mt. Taylor in New Mexico, believed to be the blood from the death of *Yé' iitsoh*, or the "monster who sucked in people." All of the angular rock formations on the reservation, such as the immense Black Mesa, are seen as the turned-to-stone bodies of the monsters.

With all of the monsters dead, the Holy People turned their attention to the making of the Navajo clans. *Kiiyaá ą́ą́nii*, or Tall House People, was the first clan, made of yellow and white corn.

For her husband the Sun to visit her every evening, Changing Woman went to live in the western sea on an island made of rock crystal. Her home was made of the four sacred stones: abalone, white shell, turquoise, and jet. During the day she became lonely and decided to make her own people. She made four clans from the flakes of her skin. These were known as the Near Water People, Mud People, Salt Water People, and Bitter Water People. When these newly formed clans heard that there were humans to the east who shared their heritage, they wanted to go meet them.

Changing Woman gave permission for them to travel from the western sea to the San Francisco Peaks. They then traveled through the Hopi mesas, where they left porcupines, still common there today. Then they traveled toward the Chuska Mountains and on to Mt. Taylor. Finally, the people arrived at Dinétah, the Diné traditional homeland, and joined the other clans already living there. Dinétah is located in the many canyons that drain the San Juan River about thirty miles east of Farmington, New Mexico.

Eventually other clans traveled to the area around the San Juan River, bringing their important contributions to the tribe. Some were Paiutes who brought their beautiful baskets. Others were Pueblos who shared their farming and weaving skills. Still others were Utes and Apaches.

Anthropologists believe the Navajos arrived at Dinétah between A.D. 1300 and 1680. Life there was not easy. Constant attacks from Ute raiders, as well as the threat of Spanish invasion during the seventeenth and eighteenth centuries, made life very dangerous. Because of the combination of outside threats, as well as a severe drought in 1740, the Navajos began to move out of their center place in Dinétah.

When settlers and prospectors started to travel across Navajo hunting areas in the late 1800s, they were frequently killed or, at the very least, harassed to scare them away. The U.S. Cavalry came to the rescue of the settlers and tried to negotiate peace treaties with people they designated as "chiefs." In actuality, they were talking to *naat'áanii*, people with great speaking abilities who were respected for their leadership skills. Some were medicine men, or *hataaɫii*, like Manuelito, who was born in 1820 in Utah and was a great warrior known as *Nabaah Jiltaa*, or "Warrior Grabbed Enemy."

When one clan's *naat'áanii* signed a treaty, the military thought peace would reign with all of the Navajo people. This was not the case. Information about a treaty signed by one band was not necessarily shared with other bands. Finally, the military would not tolerate any more "broken" treaties. Because of its 1840 promise to Mexico under the Treaty of Guadalupe Hidalgo and the country's interest in settling the West, Gen. James Carleton commissioned a one-time friend of the Navajos, Kit Carson, and his volunteer soldiers to pave the way for miners and settlers. The plan was to kill or capture the Navajos and march survivors to Fort Sumner in New Mexico, more than four hundred miles away. This became known as the Long Walk.

By 1864, Carson's troops had captured some eight thousand Navajo men, women, and children after slashing and burning their way across the Navajos' homeland. This destroyed all of the Navajos' food and water supplies. Completely subjugated, the Navajos surrendered and lived at a place called Bosque Redondo on the Pecos River near Fort Sumner for four years. When they arrived, there was no housing for them. Most lived in hogans, made out of anything they could find, or holes dug in the earth.

Group of Navajo Captives, Fort Sumner, New Mexico, 1866
Courtesy Museum of New Mexico, #38191

Gen. Carleton's grand idea was to turn the Navajos, and about five hundred Apaches, into farmers on a tiny piece of land only forty miles square (104 sq km). But the land was so barren, finding firewood required searching for miles. Water was so alkaline, it was undrinkable. The soil was so poor, crops wouldn't grow.

At last, in 1868 when news of the starvation conditions reached the ears of sympathetic Americans, and because of the prohibitive cost of feeding thousands of people in what was essentially a concentration camp, the War Department agreed to let the Navajos go. They were given the option of relocating to Oklahoma or going back to their traditional homeland. To the military, the home of the Diné was nothing more than useless wasteland. But to the Navajos, it was the place of their emergence and where their ceremonies have the most power.

Gen. William T. Sherman met with a council of twelve Navajo men, including Barboncito and Manuelito, to negotiate their release. He explained that the treaty would allow for each person to receive rations. To this, one of the Navajo leaders said, "No. All we want you to give us is an old buck goat. We will tie him by his horns to a pinyon tree and let him butt it with his head until he is dead. That will show our young men what it is like to fight against the government." Actually, they got $5 worth of clothing and $10 each year if they were farming. Families could select 160 acres to farm and got $100 in farming equipment and seeds. The tribe was to divide 15,000 sheep and 500 cattle evenly between families. For each group of thirty students between the ages of six and sixteen, a schoolhouse was to be built and a teacher provided.

The first signer of the Treaty of 1868 was Barboncito, known as "Peace Chief." The treaty granted the Navajos a reservation of a little more than 6,120 square miles (15,912 sq km) on land that straddled the boundary between the New Mexico and Arizona territories. But this limited acreage would not support the growth of sheep herds, so families began crossing reservation boundaries, living in sheep camps far from other clans.

Because of the huge distances between camps, the BIA devised the boarding school system to meet their obligation to educate all Navajo children. Navajo parents had no idea that the education their children would receive would be so alien to their way of life and, in effect, be another prison sentence. (More about boarding schools in the chapter on Tuba City, pages 105–106.)

Navajo Legal System

The American judicial system was imposed on the Navajo people in 1882 by the secretary of the interior. Called the Courts of Indian Offenses, these forums were based on a punishment system of justice and ignored ancient Navajo customs and beliefs about concepts of right and wrong.

One hundred years later, Navajo judges began to look for more culturally appropriate ways to deal with disputes. In 1982, the Navajo Peacemaker Court was formed. This court operates on three fundamental Navajo beliefs. First, all people are equal, and no one may coerce another person into a decision or make a decision for him or her. Second, the social system revolves around the belief in *ké*—or respect for one's relatives and responsibility to them—and also maintains a deep respect for tradition and the belief that problems are solved through ancient prayers and ceremonies handed down from one generation to the next.

With these basic principles to guide them, the peacemaker judge brings the disputing parties together to talk out the problem and come to a consensus. The goal is for both parties to walk away with their heads held high. The peacemaker judge is not an authority on the legal system and may not have a college education. But he or she is someone able to speak well and lead the negotiations to a peaceful conclusion.

Navajo courts have jurisdiction over all civil matters on the reservation. In criminal matters, the tribal courts have limited jurisdiction. Navajo and Hopi police are cross-deputized with the Arizona Department of Public Safety and have authority to arrest lawbreakers. In criminal matters, a non-native is transported off the reservation to the closest county jail and courthouse.

Navajo Clan System

A Navajo baby is born into the clan of the mother. The clan name passes on through her to her children. When a young man marries, it must be to someone completely outside of his clan. Even though people in his clan are not all blood-related, it is considered inappropriate to marry within one's own clan. Navajos say the children are "born to" a woman's clan, but also that they are "born for" a man's clan. Navajos precisely know who they are through identification by their mother's, father's, maternal grandfather's, and paternal grandfather's clans.

Whenever one Navajo meets another, the appropriate etiquette is to introduce one's maternal and paternal clans on both sides of the family. In this way, it is possible to find a "mother" or "uncle" in a clan relative living hundreds of miles away and, therefore, a benefactor who will help you on your travels.

Navajo Homes

Most of the newer houses and small subdivisions you will pass on the highway are there to make it easier for Navajo children to catch the school bus. These families probably have a camp in a more remote location where they graze their sheep and cattle. Today, just about every camp has a hogan with a frame or cinder-block house or a trailer close by. The modern homes are for the extended family to live in, with the hogan used by the grandma or reserved for ceremonies. Hogan construction follows a very specific blueprint handed down by the Holy People to maintain the spiritual meaning of the dwelling and its use for curing ceremonies. The male hogan, rarely seen today, has three logs placed in the ground at the northern, southern, and western cardinal positions. Two poles form the entry, and the entire hogan is covered with dirt. Tso Bonito Zoo in Window Rock has a good example of a male hogan.

Forked Hogan ca. 1918–1920
Marie Olson Collection, Cline Library, Special Collections and Archives, NAU 516-30

The more common dwelling is the female hogan, built in a round shape with six or eight sides of logs laid one on top of the other to form a wall. The entire hogan is covered with earth except for the smoke hole in the top. All hogans must have their entrance facing the rising sun, to greet the Holy People in the morning. Traditional hogans have dirt floors to maintain a connection to the earth (Mother Earth) and an opening to the sky (Father Sky).

If you find that you must stop at a Navajo camp, drive up slowly to the front of the hogan and stop. Do not get out of the car. Sit and wait a few minutes. If someone is home, they will come out to greet you and invite you in.

Female Hogan in Canyon de Chelly, ca. 1930–1940
Philip Johnston Collection, Cline Library, Special Collections and Archives, NAU PH 413-194

Navajo Food

Traditional foods consisted of corn, beans, squash, pumpkins, piñon (or pinyon) pine nuts, peaches, apples, prairie dog, rabbit, and other game as it was found. After the Navajos learned sheepherding from the Spaniards in the seventeenth century, mutton became a primary food source. Every part of the sheep is used in some sort of dish. Sheep intestines are completely cleaned and filled with a mixture of sheep blood, potatoes, corn meal mush, and fat to make blood sausage called *dił.* The real delicacy is sheep head, or *'atsíí,* which is slowly baked in the ground for many hours before being eaten. The most common meal found at most social gatherings is mutton stew. The stew is made from every part of the sheep except the intestines and head. The meat is boiled with potatoes, onions, celery, and salt. It is served with frybread or tortillas. Coffee has practically replaced Navajo tea as the national drink.

COMMON VEGETATION

Throughout your visit to the Colorado Plateau, you will travel into and out of numerous piñon-juniper woodlands, known as pygmy forests and found at 4,000 to 7,500 feet (1,219–2,286 m).

These trees are an important element in the Native American lifestyle. For centuries, the native peoples have relied heavily on pine nuts for their survival. The seed of the Colorado piñon (*Pinus edulis*), which dominates this area, is extremely rich (it is about 66 percent fat, 14 percent protein, and 18 percent carbohydrate). For starving people with limited food supplies, the storage of piñon nuts often meant the difference between life and death.

The piñon nut saved the Domínguez-Escalante expedition of 1776 from starvation (see pages 68–69 for an explanation of this historic journey). But the infamous Donner party in Nevada was not so lucky. Ignorant of the secrets of the piñon, they passed right through a forest at the peak of its harvest and felt forced to resort to cannibalism to survive the Sierra Nevada winter.

Piñons are gathered from the end of August through November. A bumper crop comes about every seven years. You can buy small bags of roasted piñon nuts, salted and in their shells, for $1 at most roadside bead stands. But beware: like peanuts, they can be very addicting. (Be sure to take the shell off before eating them.)

Sagebrush, or *Ts'ah*, grows at about 6,500 feet (1,981 m). This wonderful plant has many medicinal properties. It is considered to be one of the "Navajo life medicines" and is said to cure headaches just from smelling it. Perhaps the most classic smell in the West is the wonderful scent of wet sage after a rainstorm.

Other common plants are yucca and Mormon tea. Soap made from yucca roots is used to wash the hair of Hopi brides and grooms, as well as those involved in various Navajo ceremonies. Mormon tea, used by the Mormons and by traditional healers, is brewed into a tea for various remedies to restore health. If you decide to try some, be aware that Mormon tea contains ephedrine, which can accelerate your heart rate.

Sheep Shearing, not dated
Ganado Mission Collection, courtesy Sage Memorial Hospital

ANIMALS COMMON TO THE AREA

Dibé **(Sheep)** Many families continue to raise sheep as their sole means of support. All of the Navajo Reservation is open range. This means that you are responsible if a sheep, horse, or cow runs in front of your vehicle, causing an accident. The water runoff from the road surface acts as an irrigation system, encouraging grasses to grow alongside the road when the rest of the pasture land is barren. Watch your speed and the roadsides for grazing animals.

Tłízí **(Goat)** Most of the goats you see grazing beside the road are Angora. The mohair is spun to make Navajo rugs. Drums made of goat skin are used during healing ceremonies.

Gálgii **(Raven)** Larger than the common crow, ravens can be confused with hawks because they alternate soaring with flapping their wings. Their feathers are used by medicine men in certain ceremonies and were used on the shafts of arrows by warriors and hunters.

Gahtsoh **(Jackrabbit)** Much larger than a rabbit, the jackrabbit has very large, powerful hind legs. The fibula bone is carefully prepared by medicine men and used as a whistle, a necessary piece of equipment in some ceremonies. At one time, rabbit fur was braided with yucca to make blankets. Rabbit-skin blankets over three thousand years old have been excavated at Basketmaker sites in Tsegi Canyon.

Máii **(Coyote)** The average coyote is twenty-four inches tall (61 cm) and weighs about forty pounds (18 kg). It eats smaller rodents, especially prairie dogs. The coyote, also referred to as "the trickster," is the major character in many Navajo stories about right and wrong, with the coyote always on the wrong side. According to Navajo healer Ursula Knoki-Wilson, the coyote itself is not evil. He is just a daring character easily persuaded by evil forces to take impulsive risks that usually have a bad outcome. To some, a coyote crossing your path is warning of impending danger. He is therefore doing you a favor. To avoid the danger, the traveler must stop and think good thoughts before continuing. The Hopis believe Coyote is more gullible than he is evil.

Dlǫǫ **(Prairie Dog)** Once a common food for the Navajos, prairie dogs live in "prairie dog towns" throughout the reservation. They build sophisticated underground tunnels that may stretch for miles, with many entrances and exits.

HEALTH PRECAUTIONS

Prairie dogs sometimes carry fleas infected with the bacteria that causes **bubonic plague.** This was once a highly contagious and deadly disease but is now completely treatable with antibiotics. It's seasonal and generally affects only a small number of people. U.S. Public Health Service officials watch prairie dog colonies for die-offs, which indicate infection with the disease. When this happens, warnings are announced to keep domestic animals from roaming and to avoid contact with dead animals.

Hantavirus: Traditional healers and elders soon deduced what the problem was when two young people mysteriously died from a respiratory ailment within days of each other in 1992. They remembered that in 1918, and again in 1933, there were also many unexplained deaths. And in each of those years, a lot of rain produced a bumper crop of piñon nuts, leading to an explosion in the population of deer mice. This time around, the U.S. Centers for Disease Control and the U.S. Public Health Service were able to pinpoint the virus responsible for causing this potentially fatal pulmonary syndrome. Deer mice and other rodents carry the virus in their saliva, feces, and urine. It's believed the people affected somehow came into contact with the virus by cleaning up mice droppings or by sweeping, raising airborne dust that contained the virus. The best way to protect yourself from exposure is to avoid sleeping near rodent burrows or touching sick or injured animals. If you find mice droppings in your hotel or cabin, do not disturb them. Instead, report them to the caretaker, who will remove them wearing a mask and gloves after spraying them with disinfectant.

NAVAJO RUG WEAVING

Spider Woman, one of the Holy People, taught Navajo women how to weave. Spider Man taught her how to build the loom in a very specific way. The loom that was created is much like the Pueblos' vertical loom. Pueblo refugees came to live with the Navajos after the Pueblo Rebellion of 1680 and were known to weave cotton long before the Spanish arrived in 1540 with three thousand sheep from Spain. The Navajos started to build their sheep herds around 1640 in raids against the Spanish.

What to look for if you want to buy a Navajo rug
The best place to buy a rug is from the weaver. This often takes time, so the next best place is from a roadside vendor or a trading post. Examine the rug closely and use all of your senses to determine if you have an authentic Navajo handmade rug.

Look at the rug. Lay it flat and look at both sides to see if the weaving is straight and the sides are even. Then fold the rug in half to see if the edges match up. Do this both for the length and width of the rug. Next, fold the rug in half and peel it back to see if the two halves mirror each other. Look at the colors. They should be the same throughout the rug.

Many weavers leave a "spirit line," or a single line exiting the rug across one of the borders, to prevent their spirit from being trapped in this living entity they have just created. Today, some weavers do not put in the line. It's left to the weaver's discretion and may mean that this particular weaver did not feel a need for a spirit line.

Smell the rug. If it smells like goat or sheep, this is a good indication the rug is Navajo. However, many exceptional Navajo rugs are made from commercial yarn and won't have this smell.

Touch the rug. Feel how tight the weave is. Imitation Navajo rugs made in Mexico will have a loose weave and feel soft to the touch. A good Navajo rug will have a consistent weave throughout. Two characteristics of almost all Navajo rugs are: (1) there are no exposed warp threads (the strong thread running the length of the rug), as found in Mexican or East Indian rugs, and (2) a Navajo rug will have double cotton warp threads on the selvage edges (top and bottom edges of the rug). Mexican rugs will have only one, but you will have to gently separate the colored threads on the edge to see the selvage warp.

Talk to the weaver. If at all possible, meet the weaver and ask her what type of wool she used and whether the colors are natural or commercial dyes. If this is not possible, most reputable trading posts will know quite a bit about each weaver and her rug. Her name and what part of the reservation she's from should be on the rug.

If you know what you are doing, one of the best places to get a good price on a rug is the Navajo Rug Auction at the Crownpoint Elementary School in Crownpoint, New Mexico. Throughout the year on the third Friday of the month, the auction offers more than two hundred rugs from all regions of the Navajo Nation. Viewing is from 3 to 6 p.m., with the auction starting at 7 p.m. For more information, call (505) 786-5302.

Rug weaver at her loom, ca. 1930s
Fred Harvey Collection, Museum of Northern Arizona Photo Archives, MS 301-3-18

48 miles (77 km) from Flagstaff to Cameron

U.S. HIGHWAY 89

Highway 89 was called Lees Ferry Road before 1931. It was a wagon road that connected Flagstaff with Tanner's Crossing over the Little Colorado at Cameron and continued north along the Echo Cliffs to Lees Ferry.

San Francisco Peaks from the north, 1905
Detroit Publishing Co. Collection, Cline Library, Special Collections and Archives, NAU PH 90.10.1

MM 425 SAN FRANCISCO PEAKS (West)

Rising to a height of 12,643 feet (3,831 m), the San Francisco Peaks are Arizona's highest mountains. Franciscan missionaries living in the Hopi village of Oraibi in 1629 named these mountains to honor their founder, St. Francis of Assisi.

The peaks, or *Dook'o'oosłííd*, are one of the four sacred mountains of the Navajos and the winter home of the Hopis' katsinas, *Nuvatu kya' ovi*. They also mark the western boundary of traditional Hopi lands, or Hopi *tutskwa*. These mountains hold meaning for everyone living in northern Arizona. You will see them dominating the southern horizon throughout your travels on the Hopi mesas.

Vermilion Cliffs

Lees Ferry

To Page/Lake Powell

89A

89

Antelope Pass

To Jacob Lake and
the North Rim of
the Grand Canyon

Tanner Wash

Bitter Springs

Limestone
Canyon

Cedar
Ridge

89

ECHO CLIFFS

Hamblin Wash

N
W   E
S

Colorado

River

Little

Hamblin Ridge

To Tuba City

The Gap

Willow
Springs

Moenave

160

Hidden
Springs

Dinosaur
Tracks

To the
South Rim
of the
Grand Canyon

64

Colorado

Shadow
Mountain

Colorado River
Gorge Viewpoint

WARD TERRACE

Cameron

Little

U.S. HIGHWAY 89 North
Flagstaff
to
Cameron

Grey
Mountain

Colorado

River

89

SP Crater

Spider Web Ranch

Wupatki Nat'l Mon.

ANTELOPE HILLS

Sacred Mountain
Trading Post

O'Leary Peak

San Francisco
Peaks

Flagstaff

Sunset Crater
National Monument

GRAY MOUNTAIN

The group of peaks that make up the center of this extinct volcanic range includes Agassiz, Fremont, and, the tallest, Humphreys. Despite having blown its top a millennium ago, the peaks today rise from the high plain at about six thousand feet (1,818 m) in elevation to more than twice that. Mt. Humphreys was named for Andrew Atkinson Humphreys, a surveyor for the railroad. Mt. Agassiz was named in memory of Jean Louis Rodolphe Agassiz, a famous geologist and zoologist who developed the theory of the Ice Age, and Mt. Fremont commemorates John Charles Frémont, governor of Arizona from 1878 to 1882. Frémont was also a well-known botanist who started his plant collection in the 1840s. The Fremont cottonwood, named for Gov. Frémont, is one of the most common trees you will see along streams and washes in the Southwest.

Basque shepherds are an interesting yet little-known group of people who lived and worked on the San Francisco Peaks from the late 1800s to the 1980s. Originally from an area between France and Spain in the Pyrenees Mountains, the Basques emigrated to the West to seek their fortunes when life in their own country became too difficult. Some sailed to the New World with Christopher Columbus in 1492 and with Coronado's expedition in 1540.

Some people think the word Arizona is actually the Basque phrase "arriz ona," meaning the good or valuable mineral ore. Another variation may be "arrtiza ona," meaning the good or valuable rocky place. Either definition is appropriate.

Life in America was not easy for the "Amerikanuak," or Basque living in America. This was especially true during the Gold Rush of 1848, when thousands of Basques emigrated to California. Most would not find their fortune in precious metals but instead offered their services to landowners interested in developing large sheep herds.

Basques were soon in demand, renowned throughout the West for their successful and productive management of sheep. They accepted four-year contracts with landowners, taking their salary in sheep. At the end of his contract, the shepherd would venture off on his own as a private sheep rancher.

It was not an easy life to care for animals that must constantly graze on less than ideal grassland. To get the most nutrition from available grasses, shepherds moved their sheep to the San Francisco Peaks from summer through early fall. Before winter, the flocks moved to low country, where the ewes dropped their lambs in the spring. Navajo shepherds also follow this pattern of cyclical migration, known as transhumance.

One of the more beautiful times of the year to visit northern Arizona is when the band of aspens that encompasses the middle of the San Francisco Peaks changes colors, usually at the end of September or beginning of October. It is also when many of the wildflowers are in bloom.

Surrounding the peaks are more than 2,200 square miles (5,720 sq km) of volcanic remnants and more than 400 extinct volcanos. The most prominent and most recent volcanic cone is Sunset Crater.

MM 425 SUNSET CRATER

Northeast, the volcanic cone with the red rim

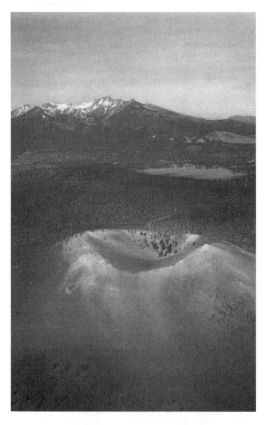

Known to Navajos as Yellow Top Mountain and to Hopis as Red Hill, this cinder cone was given its name because of its sunset colors by John Wesley Powell, the famed explorer of the Colorado River and Grand Canyon. The Hopis believe their wind god, *Yaponcha,* lives in a crack in the black rock near the crater.

Sunset Crater is the last of numerous volcanos that developed in this area and is thought to have erupted around 1064. Two lava flows created this volcanic cone: Kana-a Flow, which headed northeast toward the Little Colorado, and Bonito Flow, which traveled northwest.

Aerial View of Sunset Crater with the San Francisco Peaks
Fronske Studio, Cline Library Special Collections and Archives, NAU.PH.85.3.1.117

*NOTE: If you are continuing north on U.S. 89 without visiting
Sunset Crater/Wupatki National Monuments,
turn to page 27 to continue your tour.*

SCENIC DETOUR

Mile 430.5 *SUNSET CRATER VOLCANO / WUPATKI NATIONAL MONUMENT*

One entrance fee covers both Sunset Crater Volcano and Wupatki National Monument. If you plan on visiting the Grand Canyon, purchasing a National Park Pass here is a good idea. It is $50 and can be used at any national park requiring an entry fee. The pass is good for one year and will admit you and accompanying passengers in your vehicle.

The road through the monument is a thirty-five-mile (57 km) winding road with no gas stations and no food aside from that in the snack machines in the visitors centers at Sunset Crater Volcano and Wupatki. To see everything in both parks, plan at least four hours and bring a lunch. Both visitors centers open at 8 a.m. and close at 5 p.m. (MST). All of the trails and ruins close at dusk.

The volcano became a national monument in 1930, due in part to a movie company's interest in dynamiting Sunset Crater to simulate a volcanic explosion. Here you can explore and learn about volcanism, cinder cones, and lava flows. The visitors center has exhibits on these topics, and a self-guided tour through Bonito lava flow is available. Even though Sunset Crater is off limits to hiking, you can climb Lenox Crater, .25 mile (.40 km) south of the visitors center. Impressive lava flows and scenery can be viewed from the many overlooks.

Mile 33.5 *BONITO PARK (South)*

Beautiful views of the San Francisco Peaks to the west and Sunset Crater Volcano to the east.

Mile 32.7 *BONITO CAMPGROUND (North)*

Located directly across from the Sunset Crater Volcano visitors center, this forty-three-site campground operates on a first-come, first-served basis. Maximum vehicle length, thirty-five feet; no RV hookups. Closed in winter. For more information call (928) 526-0866.

Mile 32.6 *SUNSET CRATER VOLCANO VISITORS CENTER (South)*

The center has interpretive displays about volcanism and the Sunset Crater area. It also has an earthquake monitoring system that records earth movements all over the world. Open from 8 a.m. to 5 p.m. (MST).

Mile 31.3 *BONITO LAVA FLOW (North)*

Flowing from the base of Sunset Crater, the molten lava cooled very quickly to form the hard outer covering seen here to the north. Inside, the lava continued to flow as a liquid, spreading over a wide area. Because the lava flows look much like the surface of the moon, NASA sent Neil Armstrong (the first man to walk on the moon) and other astronauts to train at Sunset Crater. They practiced how to walk on the jagged rocks in space suits to collect moon specimens. Outside the park, craters were blasted into a volcanic cinder field to duplicate the Sea of Tranquility, where Apollo 11 would land. Ice caves are found throughout this flow. In the 1880s, Flagstaff saloon owners harvested the ice for their restaurants.

Mile 31 *SELF-GUIDED WALKING TOUR THROUGH LAVA FLOW*

Mile 29 *CINDER HILLS OVERLOOK (South)*

You can see the beginning of the Kana-a Flow that follows the road all the way to Wupatki. *Kaná* is the name for the Hopis' friendly katsina that lives here. The Hopis lived on the southern edge of Black Mesa when Sunset Volcano erupted around 1064. There is a story in their oral history about a Hopi community destroyed by a cloud of ash. People saw a strange light in the mountain moving toward them and warned the villagers to get out of its way. Some who were pursuing pleasures and did not follow the Hopi teachings were destroyed, but the good people who carried out their responsibilities and duties were saved.

Mile 25.3 *PAINTED DESERT VISTA AND PICNIC AREA (West)*

Mile 24 *STRAWBERRY CRATER WILDERNESS (West)*

The jagged, sharp-looking lava found here is a good example of *aa* lava. A Hawaiian word, it is pronounced ah-ah. *Pahoehoe* (pronounced pa-hoy-hoy), also Hawaiian, is smooth lava.

Mile 14 *WUKOKI PUEBLO (East)*

Meaning "Big House" in Hopi, this three-story dwelling was home to ancient Sinagua people from shortly after A.D. 1100 to 1210. For more information about the Sinagua people, see pages 249–250.

Mile 13.6 *WUPATKI NATIONAL MONUMENT (West)*

NOTE: Wheelchair accessible to the upper pueblo.

The ruins were named Wapatkikuh, or "Tall House Pueblo," by anthropologist Dr. Jesse W. Fewkes, who completely mapped the area in 1896.

Wupatki plays an important part in the Hopi Snake Clan legend. The Zuni Parrot Clan was said to have traditionally stopped here. The Havasupai people claim knowledge of these ruins through their ancestors. And like so many ruins in the Southwest, this one also bears a Navajo name, Anasazi Bikin, or "House of the Ancient Ones."

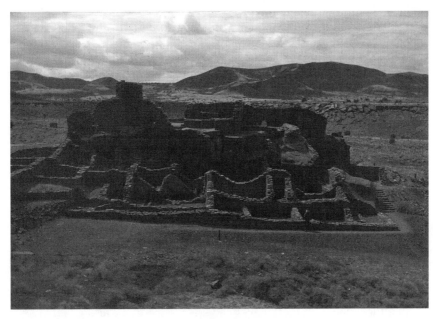

Wupatki Pueblo (A.D. 1100–1200), May 1954
Cline Library Special Collections and Archives, NAU.PH.5.109

The ballcourt is the most unusual feature at the ruins. It's thought to be similar to ballcourts built by the Aztecs and Mayans. Next to the ballcourt is a blowhole that acts like a barometer. When the atmospheric pressure is low, air is forcefully blown out of the hole; when it is high, air is sucked into the hole.

Mile 12.4 *CLYDE PESHLAKAI'S HOME (East)*

This rock house north of the monument headquarters is closed to visitors. Clyde Peshlakai was a custodian of Wupatki National Monument in 1936. His father, Peshlakai Etsidi, traveled in 1902 and again in 1904 to Washington to advocate for an increased land base for the Navajos. Protestant minister William Johnston from Tuba City accompanied him to meet with President Theodore Roosevelt. Roosevelt was sympathetic to the needs of the Navajos and added the Leupp area, about twenty miles (32 km) south of Wupatki, to the Navajo Reservation.

Mile 10.5 *PAINTED DESERT VIEWPOINT*

As you come down off Woodhouse Mesa, the vegetation changes to desert scrub dominated by sagebrush and saltbush. The names and characteristics of these plants are identified at the Wupatki visitors center.

Mile 9.4 *DONEY PICNIC AREA (South)*

Ben Doney was a fortune hunter who lived here from 1883 to 1930 and spent most of his time looking for the Lost Padre Mine. He believed this area was the site of a lost Spanish mine from the seventeenth century. The story described the mine's location as being in a red hill forty miles (64.5 km) west of the Hopi villages. Doney sunk many shafts looking for the mine but never found anything.

The large and small volcanic cinder cones here bear his name. **Doney Trail** leads to the top of one cinder cone and takes about one-half hour to climb. It offers a great view of the Painted Desert, Sunset Crater, and the San Francisco Peaks Volcanic Field. Keep your eyes open for golden eagles, which nest on Doney Mountain. Not wheelchair accessible.

Mile 4.1 *CITADEL PUEBLO (West)*

Built in the late 1100s, this pueblo offers a 360-degree view. It's called the Citadel because its design suggests the builders wanted protection from attack, although there is very little evidence that warfare was a serious threat. Behind the ruin is a large limestone sink originally thought to have provided the community with water, but it is too porous to hold water. Cisterns and drainage systems were built to collect rainwater during the wet years. When it didn't rain, the closest source of fresh water was the Little Colorado River, about ten miles (16 km) away.

Sitting below the Citadel is **Nalakihu Ruin,** which means "House Standing Alone" in Hopi. The Museum of Northern Arizona excavated the ruin in 1933 and found many owls buried here, as well as pottery sherds that came from as far away as Prescott, Arizona, about 150 miles (242 km). Archaeologists do not know if the rather large pots were obtained through trade and carried all the way from Prescott, or if a group of people migrated to this area, bringing the pots with them.

Mile 3.8 *TURNOFF TO LOMAKI PUEBLO (North)*

The name of this pueblo, built in the 1100s, means "Beautiful House" in Hopi. The .25-mile (400 m) trail that leads to it passes by **Box Canyon Ruin.** Both ruins sit on the edge of earth cracks that are found throughout Wupatki and Sunset Crater Volcano National Monuments. Earth cracks are thin vertical openings in the Kaibab Limestone caused from the movement of the earth.

END SCENIC DETOUR

OR: Begin scenic detour if you are traveling south. This is a thirty-five-mile (57 km) road through Wupatki and Sunset Crater Volcano National Monuments that connects back with U.S. Highway 89. Attractions at mile markers 433–443 can be seen only if you do not take the scenic tour of Wupatki and Sunset Crater Volcano National Monuments.

MM 433 O'LEARY PEAK (East)

Named for Dan O'Leary, a guide for the military during the Indian Wars of the 1800s, this volcanic dome is more than 200,000 years old and is part of the San Francisco Peaks Volcanic Field.

Mile 436.5 SACRED MOUNTAIN TRADING POST (West)

Built in 1915, this trading post was once known as Deep Wells. Bill Beaver bought the post in 1960 and renamed it Sacred Mountain Trading Post. Today it is an operating post, supplying native craftspeople with materials for beadwork and jewelry in exchange for finished jewelry, rugs, and artwork. Beaver speaks Navajo and was influential in assisting local Navajo artists develop their roadside businesses, which you will see along U.S. 89. He also is credited with encouraging the San Juan Paiutes to revive their basketmaking traditions.

ROADSIDE VENDORS

The first automobile to travel from Flagstaff to the Grand Canyon made the trip in 1902. Traveling over a rutted wagon road, it took the tourists three days to make the seventy-mile journey from Flagstaff to Grandview Point on the South Rim of the canyon. Encouraged by the increase in tourism, the first Navajos to set up vendor stands were probably those living close to the wagon trail. Today vendors typically congregate in large groups of bead stands. Many sellers are related and from the same area. Outside vendors are not welcome to participate in this lucrative method of direct selling to tourists. For many vendors, roadside selling is their only means of support, and the entire family, including children old enough to make change, will participate in running the stand.

The typical roadside stand is a variation of the traditional Navajo shade house, or *chaha'oh*. The shade house has four forked wood posts with a cross-beam on each side. Long boughs of juniper or piñon, dried reeds, or a blanket cover the top of the cross-beams for shade.

Navajo Shade House, not dated
Brown, Bahl and Watson Collection, Cline Library, Special Collections and Archives, NAU PH 92.14.114

Among the more common items sold at the stands are necklaces called "ghost beads," made of juniper seeds. Navajos believe these beads offer protection in unfamiliar places and protect children from nightmares.

Ghost bead necklaces
Photograph by Christine Stephenson

SINAGUA TRADING POST (East)

This trading post has an RV park with full hookups (no shower) and a AAA 24-hour towing service; (928) 679-2331.

Mile 442.5 ANTELOPE HILLS

You will see herds of wild antelope on both sides of the road around this area. Truly a New World animal, the antelope has roamed the prairies of this continent for more than 12 million years. Hunted almost to extinction like the Plains buffalo, antelope were killed by sharpshooters from coach windows of passing trains, then slaughtered en masse to supply meat for hungry gold and silver miners. Standing only three feet high (1 m) and weighing about 125 pounds (57 kg), the antelope's only defense is its keen eyesight. Watch for them in early morning.

Antelope at Indian Gardens, Grand Canyon, Arizona, ca. 1930s
Fred Harvey Collection, Museum of Northern Arizona Photo Archives, #301-3-118

Mile 443.2 PAINTED FACES (East)

Don't miss this...if you can find it. Three faces painted in the style of Hopi katsinas decorate these fenceposts. In 1997 a local newspaper, *The Navajo-Hopi Observer,* offered five dollars to the person with the best explanation for the highway folk art. The winner, Teddy Goldtooth from Tuba City, says in 1938, his father, Frank Goldtooth Sr., and another Navajo man were commissioned by Hubert Richardson, owner of the Cameron Trading Post, to place the posts along the road between Flagstaff and the Grand Canyon. Three sets in all were erected: one here at MM 443, another at the old Grand Canyon Road intersection at Cameron, and the third on the Navajo Reservation Boundary on the Old Grand Canyon Road. But the artist who painted the faces remains a mystery.

MM 445 JUNCTION WITH FOREST SERVICE ROAD 545

This is the north entrance to Wupatki and Sunset Crater Volcano National Monuments. See pages 23–27 for more information.

Three Faces
Photograph by Fran Kosik, 1994

MM 446 HANKS TRADING POST

Directly behind Hanks to the west is **SP Crater.** Like Sunset Crater, SP is a cinder cone and has an extensive aa lava flow that traveled northward. This is the closest gas station before you enter Wupatki National Monument, if you are traveling south.

Mile 450.5 SPIDER WEB RANCH (East)

This is the headquarters for the CO Bar Ranch, owned by the Babbitt family of Flagstaff. The five Babbitt brothers moved to Arizona from Cincinnati, Ohio (hence the "CO" Bar cattle brand), in 1886. The first thing the brothers did when they arrived in Flagstaff was purchase 864 head of cattle. To buy their first herd, they used most of the $20,000 from the sale of their home and business in Cincinnati. Over the next forty years, they built a cattle empire of more than one hundred brands, with a grazing area covering most of northern Arizona from the Mogollon Rim south of Flagstaff, north to Tuba City, west to the Grand Canyon, and east almost to the New Mexico border.

The Babbitt family still owns most of the grazing land on both sides of U.S. 89 to Gray Mountain. If you are lucky, you will see real cowboys rounding up the herd to take them to market or to transfer them to another grazing area.

Mile 452.5 WAUNETA TRADING POST (West)

MM 458 GRAY MOUNTAIN (West)

This looming gray expanse to the west rises to an elevation of 7,500 feet (2,286 m) and extends all the way to the Grand Canyon, about seventy miles away. The Navajos shared this plateau with the Havasupais for almost 150 years.

Former Navajo tribal chairman Peter MacDonald—in his autobiography, *The Last Warrior*—tells a story about Apollo 15 astronauts Jim Irwin and David Scott, who were training on the moon-like landscape of Gray Mountain in 1971. Wearing space suits, the two astronauts practiced driving the moon buggy over the rocky terrain, gathering specimens and traveling to and from a mock-up of the lunar landing module.

Seeing these strange creatures, a medicine man who was grazing sheep in the area came over to MacDonald for an explanation. When MacDonald told him the astronauts were practicing to travel to the moon, the elder asked if he could send a message with them. MacDonald explained to the astronauts that Navajo legend describes the Diné stopping on the moon on their way to visit their father, the Sun. The message was for any Navajos still living on the moon. Happy to oblige, the astronauts gave the medicine man a tape recorder for his message. When he was finished, MacDonald interpreted the tape for the astronauts. In essence, the medicine man had warned the moon-dwelling Navajos to beware of these two men, because they will want to make a treaty with you.

SERVICES AT GRAY MOUNTAIN

Lodging
Anasazi Inn at Gray Mountain: Reservations (928) 679-2214, (800) 678-2214

Dining
Gray Mountain Trading Post: Serves breakfast, lunch, and dinner. Summer hours: 6 a.m–10 p.m. Because the town is off the reservation, it is legal to purchase alcohol here. Possession of alcohol on the reservation, however, is illegal.

The Navajo Nation changes to daylight saving time (DST) with the rest of the country from April to October. The Hopi Nation and the rest of Arizona stay on mountain standard time (MST) year-round.

MM 460 - ENTERING THE NAVAJO NATION

Diné Bikeyah—Navajoland—has had many boundaries decided for it by the federal government. But to the Navajos, four sacred mountains enveloping the land mark their territory. The San Francisco Peaks, or Abalone and Coral Mountain, north of Flagstaff, forms the Navajos' western boundary. Mt. Blanco, or White Shell Mountain, in Colorado, represents the eastern boundary. Mt. Taylor, east of Grants, New Mexico, is the Navajos' Turquoise Mountain and represents the tribe's southern boundary. Mt. Hesperus in Colorado represents the Black Jet Mountain and lies to the north.

MM 466 NAVAJO ARTS AND CRAFTS ENTERPRISE (West)

This business in the hogan-shaped building is owned and operated by the Navajo Nation. It offers quality handmade Navajo jewelry, rugs, and pottery, as well as unusual T-shirts and sweatshirts. Open from 8 a.m. to 6 p.m. (observes DST).

MM 466 CAMERON VISITORS CENTER (West)

If you are planning to camp or hike on the Navajo Reservation you must obtain a permit. Camping permits are $5 per person per night. A backcountry permit for hiking is $5 per person, $10 for 2–10 people, and $20 for more than 10 people. The permit is good for 14 days. For more information, contact Navajo Nation Parks and Recreation, P.O. Box 308, Window Rock, AZ 86515. (928) 871-6645, www.navajonationparks.org.

JUNCTION U.S. 89 WITH ARIZONA HIGHWAY 64
TO THE GRAND CANYON

If you are continuing north on U.S. 89 and not going to the South Rim of the Grand Canyon, turn to page 51 to continue your tour. For information about services available in Cameron, see pages 51–52.

57 miles (92 km) from Cameron to the South Rim

⚙ MM 290 GRAY MOUNTAIN (South)

Gray Mountain is part of the Kaibab Monocline, formed when the Earth uplifted about 250 million years ago. This gradual uplift caused the meandering Colorado River to run at a steeper gradient, giving it more power to cut through the less resistant rock layers. It eventually led to the creation of the Grand Canyon. The elevation at the South Rim is 7,000 to 7,500 feet (2,135–2,287 m), with an average gradient on the Colorado River of 7.8 feet per mile (2.38 m per km).

Because of the elevation, temperatures are moderate in summer, averaging in the 70s and 80s (21–27°C). Winter can be very cold, and snowstorms are frequent. The average temperature during the day will be in the 30s to 40s (0–5°C). Average rainfall annually is about 11 inches (28 cm).

⚙ MM 286 LITTLE COLORADO RIVER GORGE (North)

Rimmed with Kaibab Limestone, this 1,200-foot (366 m) gorge is a Navajo tribal park with tremendous scenic views. Many local artists sell jewelry, pottery, and rugs here. There are port-a-potties but no water.

Little Colorado River Gorge, ca. 1930s
Fred Harvey Collection, Museum of Northern Arizona Photo Archives, MS 301-5-78

ARIZONA HIGHWAY 64 West
Cameron
to the
South Rim
of the
Grand Canyon

To Hermits Rest

Kolb Studio

Grand Canyon Village

Look-Out Studio

Bright Angel Lodge

KAIBAB

Santa Fe Rail Station

El Tovar

GRAND

West Entrance Station

Hopi House

Yavapai Obs Station

To Williams

64

Tusayan

Mather Point

COLORADO

Desert View Information Plaza

Yaki Point

NATIONAL

Grandview Point

CANYON

Moran Point

NATIONAL

Lipan Point

FOREST

RIVER

Tusayan Ruin and Museum

64

Desert View

PARK

East Entrance Station

Little Colorado River Gorge

GRAY MOUNTAIN

Colorado

W

N

S

E

To Flagstaff

89

Little

Cameron

To Page/ Lake Powell

160

To Tuba City

⚙ MM 275 KAIBAB NATIONAL FOREST

At this point you enter a pygmy Utah juniper-piñon pine forest, found at elevations of 4,000 to 7,000 feet (1,200–2,135 m). You can camp anywhere in the forest without a permit.

East entrance to the Grand Canyon: $20 per vehicle for a permit valid for seven days at both the South and North Rims. Visitors on foot or bicycle pay $10. National Park passes cost $50 per year and are good at all National Park Service sites. Golden Age Passports for people over 62 cost a one-time lifetime fee of $10. But don't lose your card or you'll have to pay again. Golden Access Passports for handicapped individuals are free. Buying the National Park Pass is a bargain if you want to visit any of the other national parks in the area such as Wupatki and Sunset Crater Volcano National Monuments or the Petrified National Forest.

Fred Harvey Bus at Desert View, ca. 1930s
Fred Harvey Collection, Museum of Northern Arizona Photo Archives, MS 301-4-480N

⚙ DESERT VIEW POINT

From this vista you can see the Painted Desert and where the Colorado River has cut through the Kaibab Plateau. To the east is Cedar Mountain.

You can see the Desert View Watchtower all the way from Highway 160 just outside of Tuba City—if you know what to look for. You will, after you see it up close on the edge of the South Rim for the first time. Mary Colter designed and built the watchtower in 1932. An architect for the

Fred Harvey Company, she designed and supervised the construction of many of the buildings at Grand Canyon.

Desert View Watchtower, aerial view ca. 1930s
Fred Harvey Collection, Museum of Northern Arizona Photo Archives, 301-4-4

Despite the obstacles women faced in the late 1800s, Mary Colter was not one to let life pass her by. Her parents immigrated from Ireland to Pittsburgh, Pennsylvania, where Colter was born in 1869. She graduated from the California School of Design as an architect and in 1902 was hired by the Fred Harvey Co. to decorate the Alvarado Hotel in Albuquerque. Three years later she designed the Hopi House next to El Tovar on the South Rim.

Colter was in her sixties when she developed the concept of the watchtower for the Fred Harvey Co., which wanted a rest station for passengers traveling from Cameron to the Grand Canyon. Colter used the watchtowers of Mesa Verde and Canyon de Chelly as her prototypes. To accomplish the effect she wanted, stones for the exterior of the building had to be naturally shaped. This required picking each stone by hand from a local quarry.

Colter commissioned famous Hopi artist Fred Kabotie from the village of Shungopavi to paint murals in the Hopi Room in the watchtower. He used the theme of the Snake Dance as his subject. The Snake Dance is an important Hopi ceremonial held in August to bring rain for the maturing of the crops. Other Kabotie murals are in the Painted Desert Inn at Petrified Forest National Park.

Standing on top of the 1932 watchtower, you are at the highest point on the South Rim, 7,522 feet (2,279 m) above sea level. The 360-degree view includes the Colorado River, the Painted Desert to the east, and the San Francisco Peaks in the south.

One of Mary Colter's famous buildings you can't see from the rim is the beautiful and remote **Phantom Ranch,** built by the Fred Harvey Co. in 1921. Colter named the ranch for the nearby Phantom Creek and designed the main building and cabins to blend in with the rustic environment. Later buildings added by the U.S. Geological Survey followed her design.

When the ranch was completed in 1922, it attracted wealthy politicians, movie stars, and artists because of its remote and quiet location. Now the ranch caters to anyone who can get a reservation. The waiting list is some-times as long as two or three years, but it is worth the wait. A little-known fact about the ranch is that at one time it had a beautiful swimming pool, hand dug by the Civilian Conservation Corps of the Roosevelt New Deal era. Cool, clean water was piped into the pool from Bright Angel Creek and flowed over a manmade waterfall. It was truly a wonderful way to end what can be a long, hot hike or mule ride. The National Park Service filled in the pool in 1972 because of maintenance and sanitation problems.

Dining hall at Phantom Ranch with pool, not dated
Emery Kolb Collection, Cline Library, Special Collections and Archives, NAU 568-4690

Phantom Ranch can be reached only by foot or mule. To make a reserva-tion, or for any other accommodations within the boundaries of the canyon, contact: Xanterra Parks and Resorts (303) 297-2757 or toll free (888) 297-2757; www.grandcanyonlodges.com.

DESERT VIEW CAMPGROUND

First-come, first-served; no hookups; closed during the winter. A maximum of two vehicles, six people, three tents allowed per site. In summer, most canyon campgrounds are full by noon.

LIPAN POINT

From here you can see a great expanse of the canyon, including the **Inner Gorge, Vishnu's Temple, Cape Royal,** and the **Colorado River,** as well as **Echo Cliffs,** the **Painted Desert,** and **Navajo Mountain** in the distance.

TUSAYAN RUINS AND MUSEUM

About eight hundred years ago, thirty Anasazi Indians lived at this small site near the canyon's edge. The museum offers interpretative displays of pre-historic life here. Take a self-guided tour through the ruins with a 25-cent brochure. Guided tours are also offered. Open daily 9 a.m.–5 p.m. (MST).

MORAN POINT

From 1867 to 1879, the United States conducted the great surveys of the American West. John Wesley Powell's 1871–1872 trip through the Grand Canyon on the Colorado River was one of these surveys. The government hired Thomas Moran to document the landscape encountered on this trip. He did this by making hand drawings from photographs taken by E. O. Beaman and Jack Hillers, who traveled down the river with Powell. Some experts consider Moran's work at both Yellowstone and the Grand Canyon to be some of the most important and definitive drawings of the newly explored land.

Thomas Moran, Grand Cañon of the Colorado, ca. 1874
John Wesley Powell Collection, Cline Library, Special Collections and Archives, NAU PH 268-35

GRANDVIEW POINT

Directly below this viewpoint, in the Redwall Limestone on Horseshoe Mesa, is the long-defunct Last Chance Copper Mine. Peter Berry and Ralph and Niles Cameron developed the mine during the 1890s. Burros carried the ore out of the canyon on the Grandview Trail, which Berry hand-built for about $12,000. The mine never broke even because of the high cost of transporting the ore. By 1895, Berry realized that the mother lode he sought was in the pockets of tourists, so he built the Grandview Hotel at the head of his trail, the first hotel at the Grand Canyon. Grandview became the most popular place for tourists to get an unobstructed view of the canyon.

Grandview Trail: While beautiful, this six-mile round-trip trail is considered strenuous. It drops 2,600 feet (793 m) quickly to Horseshoe Mesa, where you can see the remains of Berry's and the Camerons' copper mine. Hopis use the flecks of green copper from here to paint their katsina masks and dolls. There is no water on this trail. Each hiker needs at least two quarts of water, but during the summer a gallon (four liters) per hiker is a necessity.

DUCK ON ROCK VIEWPOINT

A plaque here shows the topographic features of the canyon. This viewpoint got its name because the formation looked like a duck until its bill fell off.

YAKI POINT

Here you will find the head of the South Kaibab Trail, which leads to Phantom Ranch. The ranch can also be reached via the Bright Angel Trail.

Turn right at the junction of Arizona Highway 64 with East Rim Drive.

Wonderful changes are happening at the Grand Canyon, the most-visited national park in the United States. Construction is underway to eventually eliminate cars from the park, using a combination of mass transit and pedestrian/biking trails.

The first phase of the new transit plan is the **Canyon View Information Center,** completed in 2000. The transit/orientation center is the primary hub for the multi-modal system. Open from 8 a.m. to 5 p.m., this center offers exhibits providing a variety of information about what to do and see in Grand Canyon National Park. The center is only accessible by free shuttle bus, or on foot or by bicycle via the new **Greenway Trail.** Follow the directional signs to a parking area and then take the free shuttle to the center. The **Canyon View/Mather Point Route** operates from 7:30 a.m. to 6:30 p.m. every day. Buses run about every fifteen minutes from a half hour before opening to a half hour after closing of the visitors center.

The Greenway Trail system currently connects Desert View to Mather Point, but future plans include a total of seventy-three miles of wheelchair-accessible bicycle and pedestrian trails both on the South and North Rims. Leading the effort to bring back the serenity and natural quiet of the canyon is the Grand Canyon National Park Foundation. To contribute to this worthwhile undertaking, please call (928) 774-1760 or contribute online at www.grandcanyonfoundation.org.

🌀 MATHER POINT

Stephen Mather was named the first director of the National Park Service in 1916. From Mather Point the North Rim is ten miles (16 km) away and a thousand feet (305 m) higher in elevation than this point on the South Rim.

🌀 YAVAPAI OBSERVATION STATION

Located one mile east of Market Plaza, here you'll find viewing tubes with sites that point out geologic features. An interesting exhibit is the geologic clock. Based on a three-minute geologic cycle to create one rock layer, each tick on the clock represents 11 million years. Open daily from 8 a.m. to 5 p.m. (MST). The **Rim Trail** starts here and follows the canyon edge through Grand Canyon Village, ending at Hermits Rest. The trail is paved from Yavapai Point to Maricopa Point, 3.5 miles (5.6 km). Shuttle buses run from 6:30 a.m. to 10:30 p.m. (MST) during the summer at approximately fifteen-minute intervals so you can walk as far as you want and then catch a shuttle bus back to where you started.

🌀 SOUTH RIM VISITORS CENTER

Open 8:00 a.m.–6:00 p.m. (MST) every day, the center offers information about the services and educational programs offered within the park.

🌀 MATHER CAMPGROUND

Located one mile (1.6 km) south of the visitors center. Requires reservations from March 1 through November 30; you can make reservations up to five months in advance on a first-come, first-served basis. Toilets, showers, and phone; open year-round, with 320 campsites, seven-day limit, no hookups. Wheelchair accessible. For online reservations, visit http://reservations.nps.gov/ or call (800) 365-2267.

🌀 TRAILER VILLAGE

Adjacent to Mather Campground, Trailer Village offers RV sites with hookups. Advance reservations (888) 297-2757; same-day reservations (928) 638-2631. A dump station is available but closed during winter months.

Turn right to El Tovar and Hopi House.

🌀 EL TOVAR

This national historic landmark takes its name from Don Pedro de Tovar, an officer in Coronado's expedition of 1540. He never actually saw the Grand Canyon. His charge was to explore the Hopi villages and report back to Coronado, who was waiting in Zuni. When he returned, he told Coronado of a great river farther west that the Hopis had described to him. Coronado dispatched Capt. Don García de Cardeñas to find the river.

No expense was spared in 1904 to build El Tovar. Designed by an architect from Chicago, the famous hotel cost $250,000 to build. Native Arizona stone makes up the foundation of the building, but Oregon logs were used for the walls. Water, always a problem on the South Rim, came every day by train from more than 120 miles (193 km) away. In 1932, a pumping station brought fresh water up from Indian Gardens. Today, water is pumped from Roaring Springs on the North Rim.

Guests staying at El Tovar had only the best food prepared for them by an Italian chef. Dinner was served on antique plates and silverware, and the hotel had its own garden, dairy cows, and chickens to assure the freshest food for its patrons. It even had its own greenhouse to grow fresh flowers for the tables.

Fred Harvey was an entrepreneur with an uncanny ability to see the future and the services that people would be willing to pay for. Born in England in 1836, he came to this country as a teenager and earned money washing dishes in a New York restaurant. By age twenty-one, he was a successful restaurateur in St. Louis but lost his business during the Civil War.

He moved to Kansas and landed a job working for the Chicago, Baltimore & Quincey Railroad, traveling extensively on the train. It didn't take him long to see the potential in providing eating and sleeping accommodations to the increasing number of rail travelers. Around 1886, he presented a proposal to the Atchison, Topeka & Santa Fe Railroad to manage restaurants and hotels at each of the company's major stations. At the time of Fred Harvey's death in 1901, his company managed forty-five hotels and restaurants from Cleveland to Los Angeles.

Probably his most famous restaurant and tourism concept was "the Harvey Girl." The topic of many movies, these wholesome young ladies from the East received free chaperoned travel to the Wild West, plus room and board. In return, they had to promise not to marry for one year—often referred to as the most frequently broken promise in history.

The Harvey Girls, in their starched white aprons, learned how to make tourists feel welcome and comfortable. El Tovar was one of the hotels that used Harvey Girls to wait on its exclusive clientele. Reservations: Xanterra Parks and Resorts, (303) 297-2757 or toll free (888) 297-2757; www.grandcanyonlodges.com.

A Harvey House, 1926
The Kansas Historical Society, Topeka, Kansas

HOPI HOUSE

Across the parking lot from El Tovar stands Hopi House, designed by Mary Colter. The Fred Harvey Co. wanted a building to sell Indian arts and crafts that represented the local history and fit in with the canyon scenery. Built primarily by Hopis, it was patterned after authentic dwellings in Old Oraibi. Mennonite missionary H. R. Voth, who lived in the Hopi village of Oraibi, played an important part in obtaining ceremonial objects displayed here when Hopi House opened in 1905. (See page 123 for more about Voth.)

MULE AND HORSE BARNS

Lending the Western scent of manure to the character and charm of the South Rim are these historic barns, built in 1907, on the south side of the railroad tracks. The mules used to transport visitors to the bottom of the canyon and back are cared for here.

If you want to ride a mule into the canyon, you need to plan ahead. Trips are booked one year in advance, but you can place your name on a waiting list for cancellations at the Bright Angel Transportation Desk in Bright Angel Lodge, when you arrive at the canyon. To make reservations, call Xanterra Parks and Resorts, (303) 297-2757.

⚙ YAVAPAI LODGE (Left)

Reservations: Xanterra Parks and Resorts, (303) 297-2757 or toll free (888) 297-2757; www.grandcanyonlodges.com.

⚙ BRIGHT ANGEL LODGE

The lodge sits on the site of the old Bright Angel Camp, which included two historic cabins. Buckey O'Neill built his cabin sometime in the 1890s while part-owner in the Anita Copper Mine located fifteen miles south of here. He talked the Santa Fe Railroad into building a line from Williams to his mine to transport the ore. When the copper ran out, the Santa Fe extended the rail to the rim to take advantage of the growing tourist trade.

The second cabin was Red Horse Station, built here in 1896 by J. Wilbur Thurbern, a stagecoach operator who brought visitors from Flagstaff to Grandview Lookout. The station sits about a hundred yards (91 m) from the corral at the head of Bright Angel Trail. In 1902, Ralph Cameron bought the camp and added a second story to the station, calling it the Cameron Hotel.

Colter built Bright Angel Lodge in 1935 and wanted to keep the designs of the older Red Horse Station and Cameron Hotel, so she used native stone and timber. Truly the first historic preservationist, she understood the irreplaceable value of the handmade cabins, saving and incorporating them into the plans for the Bright Angel Lodge.

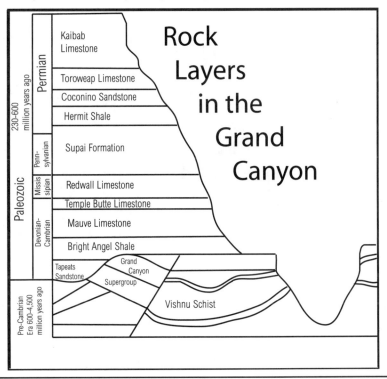

One of the more interesting features as you walk into the lodge is the geologic fireplace in the lobby. Each rock layer of the canyon is represented in the fireplace, with Kaibab Limestone at the very top. Every stone in the fireplace came out of the canyon by mule train. There is also a Fred Harvey Museum in the lodge. Reservations: Xanterra Parks and Resorts, (303) 297-2757 or toll free (888) 297-2757; www.grandcanyonlodges.com.

To see the **Lookout Studio, Kolb Studio,** and **Bright Angel Trail,** you will have to park your car and walk on the Rim Trail behind the Bright Angel Lodge. Take the shuttle bus to see the Orphan Mine, Powell Memorial, and Hermits Rest.

THE LOOKOUT STUDIO

Mary Colter designed the **Lookout Studio** for the Fred Harvey Co. in 1914 to completely blend in with the rim environment. The chimney is almost indistinguishable from a distance, looking like a pile of rocks. Weeds grow on top of the roof so that when looking at the Bright Angel trailhead from a distance, it is almost impossible to see the camouflaged lookout.

Kolb Studio, 1915
Emery Kolb Collection, Cline Library, Special Collections and Archives, NAU PH 568-772

KOLB STUDIO

Open 8 a.m.–5 p.m. daily, year-round. Emery and Ellsworth Kolb were photographers from Pennsylvania who made their way to the Grand Canyon in 1901 and set up a studio on the rim of the canyon. Their idea was to take pictures of tourists hiking down the Bright Angel Trail. But in 1902, the U.S. forester who controlled the canyon refused to allow the brothers to build on the rim. The Kolbs made a deal with Ralph Cameron to set up a temporary studio in a tent beside the Cameron Hotel.

As more and more tourists came to the canyon, attracted by the Fred Harvey enterprise and the newly constructed El Tovar hotel, the photographers' makeshift studio couldn't handle all of the business. Somehow they were able to talk Cameron into giving them a piece of his mining claim at the head of the Bright Angel Trail to build their elaborate studio.

In the early 1900s, photography was a cumbersome and delicate operation. It required clean water not available on the South Rim. After taking the visitors' pictures at the head of the trail, the brothers hiked to their darkroom at Indian Gardens, 4.6 miles (7.4 km) one-way. Emery processed the film with water from the spring and then ran back up the trail to meet the groups as they arrived back from their mule rides.

To supplement their meager earnings from taking tourist photographs, the brothers explored the canyon and sold pictures of areas never seen before. Their most daring and famous adventure was the first filming of a boat trip through the Grand Canyon. Starting out on the Green River in 1911, using specially designed wooden boats, the two brothers began their historic journey and arrived at Bright Angel Trail six weeks later. Taking a few days to develop footage and restock, the brothers continued down the river and after 101 days arrived in Needles, California.

To capture this amazing journey, which included running more than 365 rapids, one brother steered the boat while the other dealt with the bulky motion-picture equipment, shooting from the bow. A dangerous rapid was recorded from the shore by one brother while the other ran the rapid. If you have a chance, see the Imax™ movie *Grand Canyon: The Hidden Secrets* to get an idea of just how dangerous and complex capturing the river on film must have been in 1911.

Imax™ Theatre is located in the town of Tusayan, one mile south of the entrance to the park. The movie is shown in the summer from 8:30 a.m. to 8:30 p.m. and in the winter from 10:30 a.m. to 6:30 p.m., every hour on the half hour daily. (928) 638-2203

In the basement of their studio on the South Rim, the Kolbs built an auditorium to show canyon visitors their amazing film. Because of an ongoing battle with the Fred Harvey Co. and the Forest Service, the brothers couldn't show their film at the canyon. Undaunted, they took their show on the road, traveling to Washington, D.C., to lecture to sold-out crowds at the National Geographic Society. Ohio was to be the brothers' downfall. Emery did not want to go to Ohio, thinking they would lose money on the appearance.

Ellsworth insisted, and when the show did not break even, the brothers decided to split permanently. In a coin toss, Emery won the studio and photography business. Ellsworth moved to Los Angeles to pursue his interest in flying. The brothers never reconciled, visiting each other only on occasion.

An interesting story that involves the Kolbs is the mystery of the fate of Glen and Bessie Hyde. Newlyweds from Idaho, the Hydes traveled to the Kolb studio in 1928 to have their picture taken after traveling 26 days from the Green River to the Bright Angel Trail in their homemade wooden boat. When the Kolbs found out the Hydes did not have life jackets on board their boat, they offered them inner tubes just in case. The Hydes refused, saying they were both very good swimmers. Unfortunately, the Kolbs were the last people to see the honeymooners alive.

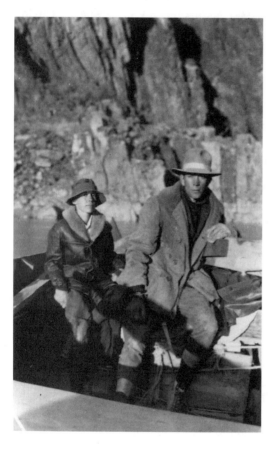

Bessie's father started a hunt for his daughter soon after she failed to show up on schedule in Needles, California. One of the first airplanes to fly below the rim was dispatched from March Air Force Base in California to look for the couple. They found Bessie and Glen's boat below Diamond Creek with their gun, camera, notebook, and a copy of *Through the Grand Canyon,* written by Ellsworth Kolb, lying inside. The search party discovered the couple's footprints seven miles (11 km) above Diamond Creek, and Glen's footprints were found downriver by a rapid.

Glen and Bessie Hyde, 1928 Photographed by the Kolbs before their disappearance. Emery Kolb Collection, Cline Library, Special Collections and Archives, NAU PH 568-5386A

Emery Kolb's theory of what happened to the couple is probably the most likely scenario. Typically, the couple would work as a team, with Bessie leading the boat downriver by rope while Glen scouted the next rapid. It is possible that Bessie fell into the water, her ninety-pound (41 kg) frame pushed by high winds, and Glen may have jumped in to save her, both drowning in the process. No one really knows what happened to the couple, and no human remains were ever found.

An interesting twist to this story occurred forty-eight years later. After Emery and Ellsworth were both dead and buried, someone found a skeleton in Emery's garage. Many people speculated that this was somehow the body of Glen Hyde, and that Emery and Bessie had conspired to kill Glen so that she would not have to continue on this extremely hard journey.

Luckily, Emery kept a diary that explained why he stored this skeleton for so many years. He had found it while exploring an old mine and on occasion would pull it out to entertain his grandson.

Emery is buried in the Grand Canyon Pioneers' Cemetery. In 1974, two years before his death at age ninety-five, he took his last trip down the river to experience the thrill of Crystal Rapids. A flood in 1966 altered this rapid, making it one of the more dangerous sections of water on the Colorado.

BRIGHT ANGEL TRAIL

The Kolb Studio marks the head of the Bright Angel Trail, part of the Cross Canyon Corridor Historic District. This man-made trail follows a fault in the sandstone cliffs. Prehistoric Indians used this pathway, and the Havasupai, who now live downriver from this point in the canyon, lived at Indian Gardens in the early 1900s.

Although the trail is 7.8 miles (12.6 km) long and not recommended unless you have sufficient water and appropriate footwear, a short jaunt to Mallory's Grotto is worth the effort. As you pass through the first tunnel, note the Havasupai pictographs on the left above a ledge.

Ralph Cameron, the miner who owned the Last Chance Copper Mine with his brother and three other prospectors, spent two months making the ancient path passable from the rim to Indian Gardens for pack mules and horses. Peter Berry, one of the trail builders, recorded the Bright Angel Trail as a toll road in the Yavapai County Courthouse in 1891. At that time, it was

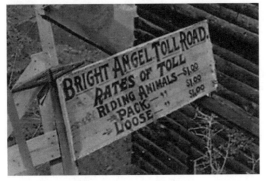

legal for private citizens to build roads on public land and charge a toll for ten years. If the owner did not break even within that time, he could get an extension for five more years.

Detail of toll sign next to the Kolb Studio, 1915
Emery Kolb Collection, Cline Library, Special Collections and Archives, NAU PH 568-772

Cameron established ownership by staking mining claims at every important point on the trail. He filed claims on the rim and at Indian Gardens, the Devil's Corkscrew, and Pipe Creek.

When the Grand Canyon was made a national monument in 1908, the problem of Cameron's toll road was a thorn in the side of the Park Service. The local people sided with Cameron, but the Santa Fe Railroad, which wanted to develop the tourist business at the canyon, viewed Cameron's toll road as an unnecessary barrier to visitation of a national treasure. To get around the problem, the National Park Service built the South Kaibab Trail, a shorter, steeper, but slightly easier route to the river.

In 1920, Cameron, by then a U.S. senator, tried to eliminate funding for the Grand Canyon from the Interior Department's budget, but his colleagues outvoted him. After losing reelection to the Senate, Cameron left Arizona permanently. In 1928, Coconino County took control of the Bright Angel Trail and promptly deeded it to the National Park Service.

The Bright Angel Trail is nineteen miles (31 km) round-trip. Like all canyon trails, it's a strenuous hike, descending 4,400 feet (1,342 m) over well-maintained switchbacks to Indian Gardens and down to the Colorado River. The Silver Suspension Bridge crosses the river to Phantom Ranch. The trip takes most hikers two days and requires a reservation at either Indian Gardens Campground (fifteen campsites), Bright Angel Campground (thirty-one campsites), or at Phantom Ranch. Because of the limited number of campsites, it is necessary to make reservations well in advance of your hike. Contact the Backcountry Reservation Office, P.O. Box 129, Grand Canyon, AZ 86023, (928) 638-7875 (1–5 p.m.).

To generate more revenue to maintain and improve services in the canyon, the National Park Service has instituted a new fee structure. Backcountry permit fee, $20; backcountry camping fee, $10 per permit plus an additional $5 per person per night.

ORPHAN MINE

Daniel Hogan, a prospector and former Rough Rider under Theodore Roosevelt, discovered the Orphan Mine when he noticed copper on the wall of the canyon about a thousand feet (305 m) below the rim. He got a patent for the mine in 1906, but it wasn't until 1956 that the U.S. Geological Survey discovered the true wealth of the mine—uranium. The Western Gold and Uranium Co. began mining more than forty-five tons (40,909 kg) of ore daily from the Orphan Mine, sending it to the Rare Metals Processing Mill outside of Tuba City. (See pages 148–149 for more about rare metals.) There is no mining going on within the Grand Canyon today.

⚙ POWELL MEMORIAL

This memorial lists the names of all of the men who completed the two trips with John Wesley Powell in 1869 and 1871–72. Three men who deserted Powell's first expedition at Separation Canyon are not on the memorial. Seneca and O. G. Howland and William Dunn, not knowing how much farther the river would run and thinking they would surely die of dehydration and starvation, quit the party and attempted to hike out of the canyon, only to be killed by Shivwits Paiute Indians. The Powell party safely completed the journey just a few days later.

⚙ HERMITS REST

Trying to get Ralph Cameron to relinquish his control of the Bright Angel Trail was a slow and tedious process requiring seven trips to the Arizona Supreme Court. Finally, the Park Service and the Fred Harvey Co. developed the attitude that if you can't beat him, go around him. At a cost of $185,000, the Harvey Co. built an eight-mile road to the west end of the canyon, where sightseers could hike down Hermit Trail to get to the Colorado River and Phantom Ranch. Mary Colter designed Hermits Rest in 1914 for the Harvey Co. to look like a haphazardly constructed miner's cabin made of native stones and timbers. Even the entrance arch was crudely constructed with a broken bell from a Spanish mission hanging from the center. Seeing the massive fireplace as you enter Hermits Rest will help you to understand the genius in Colter's ability to bring out the primitive charm and power of a structure through her rustic architectural style.

Hermit Trail is a very strenuous, unmaintained trail that leads to the Colorado River, dropping 4,240 feet (1,293 m). On this seventeen-mile (27 km) round-trip hike there is no safe water to drink. The trip takes at least two days to hike and is recommended for experienced desert hikers only.

Who was the hermit? Prospector Louis Boucher mined this corner of the canyon in the late 1800s. Because this area was so remote from the more popular section of the canyon, people thought of him as a hermit.

To Jacob Lake

COLORADO

Shadow Mountain

Vermillion Cliffs

Lees Ferry

Hidden Springs

The Gap

Cedar Ridge

Tanner Wash

Bitter Springs

Cameron

Painted

89

89A

RIVER

To Kanab, Utah

Desert

Wash

ECHO CLIFFS

Hamblin

Hamblin Ridge

Moenave

Scenic Overlook

89

Ward Terrace

Dinosaur Tracks

Tuba Butte

KAIBETO PLATEAU

89

Moenkopi

264

Tuba City

Preston Mesa

Coppermine

Page

Lake Powell

To Hopi Mesas and Window Rock

Navajo Generating Station

Navajo Mountain

Wildcat Peak

160

Red Lake

Black Mesa & Lake Powell Railroad

White Mesa

98

Elephant Feet

Cow Springs

Inscription House

UTAH

ARIZONA

Shonto

U.S. HIGHWAY 89 North
Cameron
to
Page/Lake Powell

To Kayenta

81 miles (130 km) from Cameron to Page/Lake Powell

MM 467 CAMERON TRADING POST (West)

To adventurers or homesteaders traveling through here in the early 1900s, Mabel's Oasis was a welcome sight. Owners Mabel and Hubert Richardson took great pains to make this a green mecca for travelers to enjoy. In 1911, Mabel planted Chinese elms, apple trees, ivy, and rose bushes behind the trading post and in front of what is now the gallery. Today's remodeled trading post, with its beautiful dark wood floors, display cases, and antique furnishings, is truly an exquisite place to visit. For sale are unusual items like a Spanish silver horse halter, silver jewelry, and concho belts dating back to the 1860s. Every October, the trading post holds an auction of old beadwork, pottery, rugs, baskets, dead pawn, and modern Navajo rugs and jewelry. For more information, call (928) 679-2231.

The Cameron Trading Post, once known as the Little Colorado Trading Post, is now owned and operated by Joe Atkinson, the grand nephew of the Richardsons. He bought the place from trader Gilbert Ortega in 1977 and began remodeling the old sandstone buildings, adding a sixty-five-bed motel.

It is worth a stop just to hear the trading post's wonderful wood floor creak underfoot, get a feel for what old trading days were like, and enjoy a meal looking out onto the Chiquito Colorado, the name for the Little Colorado River in 1854.

Cameron is named for Ralph Cameron, a former U.S. senator and friend of the Richardsons. Before becoming a senator, Ralph and his brother Niles supervised the 1899 construction of the Bright Angel Trail in the Grand Canyon. Originally developed to serve Cameron's mines and others in the Grand Canyon, the trail was first taken over by Coconino County and, finally, by the National Park Service. The trail is now the most popular hiking trail on the South Rim of the Grand Canyon leading to the Colorado River. See pages 47–48 for more on the Camerons and the Bright Angel Trail.

Cameron and other miners used burros to pack equipment and supplies into the Grand Canyon. Many of the burros, or *télii*, you may see on your travels along U.S. 89 North and U.S. 64 are direct descendants of burros set free by miners who gave up on their poorly producing mines in the Grand Canyon.

SERVICES IN CAMERON

Cameron Trading Post and Motel: Rates are based on amenities and season. All rooms in the summer are booked by 4 p.m. (MST). Wheelchair-accessible rooms are available with access to the gardens and the Little Colorado River viewpoint. Check their website for accurate, up-to-date rates: www.camerontradingpost.com. For reservations, call (800) 338-7385, (928) 679-2231.

Burros in Cataract Canyon, ca. 1899
Cataract Canyon Collection, Cline Library, Special Collections and Archives, NAU PH 90.15.15

RV Park: Full hookup includes water, electricity, and dump station, but there are no public restrooms or showers.
Cameron Trading Post Dining Room: Open for breakfast, lunch, and dinner, 6 a.m.–10 p.m (MST) in the summer and 7 a.m.–9 p.m. in the winter.

MM 467 LITTLE COLORADO RIVER

The Little Colorado originates at Mt. Baldy in Arizona's White Mountains and travels northward to Joseph City, Winslow, and Wupatki National Monument before reaching the Colorado River in the Grand Canyon.

At Cameron, the river, known by river guides alternately as the "LCR" or "Little C," can no longer meander as it has on most of its journey. It builds up within this solid rock canyon, where it begins to make a very rapid 2,000-foot (610 m) descent in elevation in just thirty miles (48 km) to the Colorado River. See pages 239–240 for more information about this unusual river.

MM 467 TANNER'S CROSSING

Until 1912, the only way across the dangerous Little Colorado River in this area was Tanner's Crossing, six miles (9.7 km) upriver from Cameron. The name for the crossing comes from Seth Tanner, one of the original Mormon settlers of Tuba City and an incessant explorer. Used mostly by Mormon pioneers traveling from Utah to settle in Arizona, Tanner's Crossing was dangerous because of hidden pockets of quicksand and the river's seasonal flash floods. In 1911, the Bureau of Indian Affairs hired the Midland Bridge Co. to build a one-lane iron suspension bridge over the Little Colorado's gorge.

The original bridge still stands directly west of the modern highway bridge along U.S. 89 at Cameron. Today it carries only the Four Corners Pipeline owned by the Atlantic Richfield Co., which used it in the 1960s to transport oil from the fields near Farmington, New Mexico, to Los Angeles. Now the direction of the oil is reversed. Since most of the oil is now brought down from Alaska, it is sent through this pipeline from Los Angeles to Farmington.

Little Colorado River Bridge at Cameron, 1912
Arizona Historical Society-Pioneer Museum

MM 468 HAMBLIN WASH GORGE (West)

This gorge enters the Little Colorado just north of the bridge.

MM 474 WARD TERRACE (East)

You have followed this ridge since Cameron. It is named for Lester Ward, a paleobotanist who found an extensive fossil field in this area in 1899. One of the dinosaurs he found was the water-dwelling phytosaur. This reptile was about eighteen feet long and closely resembled the present-day crocodile, but with a much longer snout filled with long, sharp teeth. The phytosaur lived in or near lake beds and streams that covered this area during the Jurassic era, so its fossils are predominantly found in the Chinle Formation. Behind Ward Terrace are the Red Rock Cliffs that form the western edge of the Moenkopi Plateau.

MM 474 SHADOW MOUNTAIN (West)

This dark, mysterious-looking mound to the west is a volcanic cinder cone that was called A1 Mountain in the 1890s. The Arizona Cattle Co. used the A1 brand on cattle it raised in this area.

MILE 480.5 JUNCTION OF U.S. 89 AND U.S. 160 EAST TO TUBA CITY

NOTE: Turn to page 95 if traveling to Tuba City.

MM 486 MOENAVE (East)

Set against the backdrop of Moenave Sandstone cliffs, Moenave is a green oasis with springs fed from the Kaibito Plateau. These springs have supported Havasupai and Hopi farms since before the Domínguez-Escalante Expedition passed through this area in 1776. The Navajo Tribe now owns this land. Mormon trailblazer Jacob Hamblin began farming here after making friends with Hopi farmer Tuuvi at Moenkopi. He sold his farm in 1874 to John D. Lee, who used it as a hiding place from authorities wanting to arrest him for his part in the Mountain Meadow Massacre. Lee's stay at Moenave lasted only five months. He was found by lawmen, taken back to Panguitch, Utah, and executed standing in his own coffin. See pages 77–78 for an account of the Mountain Meadow Massacre.

MM 486 HAMBLIN RIDGE (East)

Composed of Moenave Sandstone, these red rocks serve as a backdrop for Moenave. Hamblin Ridge ends at The Gap, where the Echo Cliffs begin.

Badlands of the Painted Desert, ca. 1930s
Fred Harvey Collection, Museum of Northern Arizona, 301-3-145

Mile 486.5 BADLANDS OF THE PAINTED DESERT (East)

The Painted Desert is a swatch of color that runs northwest all the way from the Petrified National Forest near Holbrook, passes to the north of Winslow at the Little Painted Desert County Park, skirts around the edges of Sunset Crater Volcano and Wupatki National Monuments, and extends to the Echo Cliffs on U.S. 89. The same colorful Chinle Formation that makes up most of the Painted Desert is again exposed around Ganado on Arizona Highway 264 and on U.S. Highway 191 around Round Rock.

MM 487 WILLOW SPRINGS (East)

A constant source of water from the Kaibito Plateau made Willow Springs a lush farming area for the Havasupai and a popular water stop for Mormon pioneers and prospectors. One rock near the spring bears the names of many Mormon pioneers who passed through here. The first Mormon name, written in 1873, was that of H. K. Perkins, a member of the Haight Expedition responsible for developing the Mormon wagon trail. More than one hundred Mormons were "called" by Mormon Church leader Brigham Young to settle along the Little Colorado River. Perkins helped build a road from Utah to Winslow, Arizona, to carry supplies and families. A prayer Perkins inscribed on the same rock says, "Oh that men would praise the Lord for his goodness and his wonderful works."

Home at Willow Springs, ca. 1900
Warren Family Collection, Cline Library, Special Collections and Archives, NAU, PH 412.1.44

Trading Post Ruins: A rutted road leads to the trading post, and a Navajo family lives nearby. The best way to see the ruins is through binoculars, from Highway 89. As you look beyond the silver water tank, the ruins blend in with Hamblin Ridge. Keep looking and you'll see it.

George McAdams built this post around 1889 after he sold his Red Lake Trading Post to the unfortunate Sam Dittenhoffer. (See pages 149–150 for more on Red Lake.) McAdams was a famous gambler who believed the Willow Springs location would give him more opportunities to play poker with the constant flow of pioneers traveling the Mormon Trail.

Billy Williams and his brother Ben built a small post here around 1885, before McAdams. But it is really their father, John, who makes an interesting story. John belonged to the fraternity of desperate characters who arrived in this part of the West in the late 1800s. He spent most of his life pursuing lost gold and silver mines. The incident that really increased his addiction was when Jack Carson, a teamster for the military at Fort Defiance, noticed an unusual color in a dry wash bed. He started to dig, easily unearthing about three pounds of gold. Realizing his strike was too big to work alone, he secreted the location of his mine, leaving a lone pole with a marker pointing in the direction of his claim. At Fort Defiance, he enlisted the help of John Williams, then a clerk at the trading post, to start working the mine for a third of its profits while he went to California to get his brother. Williams was too happy to oblige. He closed the trading post and moved his family to the mining site with only a hastily drawn map to show him the location of the gold. When he arrived, the pole marker was gone. Even though Williams eventually found the fallen pole, he could not find the gold. The only person who could, Carson, died on his way to California.

Williams became obsessed with dreams of lost gold mines. After exhausting the possibility of finding the rich deposit Carson promised, Williams moved his family to Blue Canyon near Tuba City, where he opened the first trading post in the canyon. His real reason for choosing this location was to be closer to the lost mines rumored to be somewhere on Navajo Mountain.

Too restless to run a trading post, Williams left Blue Canyon in 1890 to start a company to mine "flour gold" from the San Juan River. He used an ingenious method of staking cowhides to the bottom of the river to catch the gold flakes against the grain on the fur side of the hide. He did manage to collect more than a pound of gold this way but it eventually proved to be too costly, and Williams gave up his hope of ever finding gold in the Southwest.

Mile 488.5 HIDDEN SPRINGS (West)

Hidden Springs is the home of the 240-member San Juan Southern Paiute Tribe, which did not obtain federal recognition as a tribe until 1990, despite having occupied Hidden Springs since before Navajos arrived in this region. The Paiutes' ancestral home included southern California, southern Nevada, southern Utah, and northern Arizona. Traditionally hunters and gatherers, they foraged over a wide area in groups of ten to fifteen people, keeping their material belongings to a minimum. They developed elaborate basketmaking skills to carry the things they needed.

Because of the distance between bands and their relatively small numbers, the Paiutes did not get their own reservation. Instead, they initially became part of the Navajo Tribe for federal administrative purposes. The government figured they had become part of the Navajo clan system through intermarriage. However, the Paiutes kept their own language, culture, and traditions despite their small numbers. Finally, tired of being the stepchild of the larger tribe, the Paiutes launched their long, ultimately successful quest for federal acknowledgment.

The making of baskets, or *yingups,* is one of the San Juan Paiutes' greatest arts. They have supplied the Navajo people with traditional wedding baskets for years.

WHAT IS A NAVAJO WEDDING BASKET?

A Navajo wedding is rich in symbolism, and every action of the bride and groom is steeped in traditional meaning. The basket represents the fundamental beliefs of Navajos. The center is the point of emergence or birth, with the four sacred mountains, sky, and earth all included in the design. As part of the wedding ceremony, sacred blue corn mush is eaten from each of the four directions of the basket by the bride and groom. After they have finished, family and guests share the remaining mush with the couple. Once the mush is consumed, the couple is married. The basket then becomes a gift from the bride to the groom's family.

Sumac twigs are used to make Navajo wedding baskets. They are stripped, dyed, and soaked so they will bend easily for weaving. A good basket can cost from $125 to $250. However, a fine used one can sometimes be found for about $60 at the Tuba City flea market held each Friday. See the map on page 96 for directions to the flea market.

Photograph by Christine Stephenson, 1994

MM 498 THE GAP TRADING POST (West)

"The Gap" refers to the huge break in the Echo Cliffs. In 1957, before completion of Highway 89 through Antelope Pass, the dirt road across from the trading post was the only route to the Glen Canyon Dam site. The road is unimproved, has no directional signs, and so is not recommended. For the intrepid, it travels to the top of the Echo Cliffs onto the Kaibito Plateau and leads to Coppermine near Page. Trader Thomas Keam of Keams Canyon was also a prospector and found copper here around 1880. In 1915, the Pittsburgh Copper Co. began working the area, but because of the poor quality of the copper, the mine is no longer open.

The first trading post at The Gap was housed in buildings left by copper miners who failed to find anything of value in the Echo Cliffs. From 1924 to 1943, the post along the frontage of Highway 89 was owned by Joe Lee, great-grandson of John D. Lee of Lees Ferry fame. Lee was well-known for his talent as a storyteller, horseman, and friend to the Navajos, whose language he spoke fluently. Film producers in Hollywood heard about his knowledge of the area and hired him to recruit three hundred "warriors" for the movie *The Last Frontier,* shot on location at The Gap in 1924. The Lansky Players, now Paramount Pictures, filmed Zane Grey's *Heritage of the Desert* at The Gap, Willow Springs, and Tuba City.

The trading post is open from 7.a.m. to 9 p.m. (DST). (928) 283-8932.

Mile 502.5 MOENKOPI FORMATION (East)

The chocolate-colored mudstone east of the highway is a good example of one of the oldest rock layers, formed more than 230 million years ago during the Triassic era. Iron oxide makes the rocks red, and its particles have an affinity for magnetic north. They aligned facing north when the rock was formed, which helped scientists determine the ancient location of the North Pole. The pole of 200 million years ago was over the northern Pacific Ocean, and Arizona was very close to the equator. This helps explain why northern Arizona had a subtropical climate during the dinosaur age.

MM 504 CEDAR RIDGE (West)

The elevated plateau to the west marks the beginning of Hamblin Wash, cutting through the soft Chinle Formation, draining water south to the Little Colorado River. Heading north is the beginning of Tanner Wash, draining water north to the Colorado River.

MM 504 ECHO CLIFFS (East)

This ancient monocline, running north-south along U.S. Highway 89, is the result of a major uplift rising more than 1,300 feet (396 m) through a vertical fault. The Echo Cliffs expose most of the geologic members of the Glen Canyon Group except the Wingate Sandstone. At the bottom of the cliff is the Moenave Formation, then the Kayenta Formation. At the top is Navajo Sandstone.

The Mormons' famous **Honeymoon Trail,** also called the Mormon Trail, ran along the base of these cliffs. Pioneer settlers used this trail from 1877 through 1890 to travel to St. George, Utah, to be married in the Mormon temple. Most of the honeymooners lived in one of the many Mormon communities settled on or near the Little Colorado River.

St. George

Vermilion Cliffs

Kanab
Johnson
Navajo Wells

Utah
Arizona

Lees
Ferry

Fredonia
House Rock
Navajo Springs

Pipe Springs

Soap Creek

Bitter Springs

Echo Cliffs

Cedar Ridge

Willow
Springs

Moenave

Moenkopi

Colorado

River

N
W — E
S

Cameron

Little Colorado River

The Honeymoon Trail 1877–1890

Black Falls

Grand Falls

Sunset

Because of the great distances of the time, most couples were first married locally in a legal civil ceremony. When time or business permitted, they would travel the three hundred miles (483 km) to seal their vows before God. The trail actually starts at Winslow, goes over Tanner's Crossing in Cameron, runs through the Painted Desert, then along the Echo Cliffs and below the Vermilion Cliffs by Lees Ferry, through House Rock Valley, and around the Buckskin Mountains into what is now Pipe Springs National Monument, and then into St. George.

Mile 507.5 LOMBARDY POPLARS (East)

To mark the trail for others, Mormons planted tall Lombardy poplars, here visible to the east, easily seen for miles on the barren red landscape.

MM 511 LIMESTONE CANYON (West)

Six miles (10 km) north of Cedar Ridge and west of the highway, Limestone Canyon was used by Mormon pioneer Jacob Hamblin as a watering place.

🐐 MM 514 NAVAJO CORNFIELDS (East)

If you don't see a cornfield to the east, keep looking. Because of the changing lifestyle and the need to earn a wage, cornfields are not as plentiful as they once were. See page 157 for a description of Navajo dry farming.

Navajo Farming, Northern Arizona University, Cline Library, NAU. P:H, 2003.11.10.2.A938

🐐 MM 515 VERMILION CLIFFS (Straight ahead)

Vermilion Cliffs is home to a growing population of condors.

🐐 Mile 521.5 TANNER'S WASH

Named for Seth Tanner, a Mormon explorer who lived in Tuba City.

🐐 MM 525 BITTER SPRINGS, JUNCTION OF U.S. 89 AND U.S. 89A (West)

Bitter Springs is a Navajo tribal housing project whose water, despite its name, really does not taste bad.

Bear right and proceed through **Antelope Pass** *to go to Page/Lake Powell.* To build Highway 89 to Page, this three-hundred-foot (91 m) cut was made through the Echo Cliffs at an elevation of 6,533 feet (1,992 m).

If you are continuing on U.S. 89A to Lees Ferry, Jacob Lake, and the North Rim, turn to page 73 to continue your tour.

MM 527 SCENIC OVERLOOK (West)

This is one of several fine panoramic vistas along this route. Looking due west, you can see the **Colorado River Gorge** etched into the **Marble Plateau** of **House Rock Valley.** The cliffs to the north are the **Vermilion Cliffs,** named by John Wesley Powell for their bright red color. For more than a century, ranchers have struggled to raise their stock on the flat table land of the Paria Plateau. Lack of water was always their nemesis until the advent of trucks, which now haul water to the stock.

Just fifteen miles (24 km) north, where the valley narrows, is historic **Lees Ferry,** once the only crossing of the Colorado River for hundreds of miles. On the horizon ten miles (16 km) to the west is the Kaibab Plateau, the land mass that forms the North Rim of the Grand Canyon. While part of Arizona, this huge stretch of territory—known as the **Arizona Strip**—has all but been cut off from the social and political life of the state because of the Grand Canyon. For the past century, Arizona residents here have identified culturally with Utah more than with Arizona for all but elections and taxes. Even today, only Utah newspapers and television reach this isolated area.

The Kaibab Plateau has always been rich in timber and wildlife, making it a popular hunting region.

Navajo Mountain, South Side, 1937
Aerial photograph by E. Beckwith, Museum of Northern Arizona Photo Archives, MV 2238

MM 531 NAVAJO MOUNTAIN (East)

Navajo Mountain, just north of the Arizona-Utah border, has strong spiritual significance to all Indian tribes living on the Colorado Plateau. The Hopi migration stories tell of their travels to Navajo Mountain, and the Hopi Snake Clan has shrines here. Navajo Mountain also plays an important part in the Navajo creation story.

Rising to an elevation of 10,416 feet (3,177 m), Navajo Mountain can be seen throughout the Four Corners area. The Navajos call it *Naatsis'áán,* or "Head of Earth." To them it was also known as the place to hide from their enemies, the refuge for Hoskinnini's band of Navajos who were able to escape Kit Carson's soldiers. (See pages 164–166 for more on Hoskinnini.)

To help Carson in his effort to find and subjugate the Navajo people, the soldiers built a heliograph station on top of Navajo Mountain. Directions were flashed, using mirrors, to troops looking for Navajos in other parts of the reservation.

On his second trip down the Colorado River in 1872, John Wesley Powell climbed out of Glen Canyon, and seeing Navajo Mountain for the first time, named it Mount Seneca Howland. Most people in the area already knew it as Navajo Mountain, so his name did not stick like so many of his other descriptive names. Seneca Howland, his brother O. G., and William Dunn had abandoned Powell's company on the first exploration of the river three years earlier. The three hiked out of the Grand Canyon fearing they would die of starvation, only to be killed by Shivwits Paiute Indians.

Rainbow Bridge, not dated
Warren Family Collection, Cline Library, Special Collections and Archives, NAU P.H. 412.2.18.
Keith Warren and his wife operated the Cedar Ridge Trading Post around 1900. This photograph was taken some time between 1910 and 1945.

RAINBOW BRIDGE

One of the Colorado Plateau's most famous natural Navajo Sandstone bridges is found at the northern base of Navajo Mountain. Rainbow Bridge is the largest natural bridge in the world, with a 278-foot (85 m) span and rising 309 feet (94 m) above the canyon floor. The bridge is thirty-three feet (10 m) wide at the top and forty-two feet (13 m) thick. (See page 72 for information on boat tours to Rainbow Bridge.)

The Paiutes call Rainbow Bridge *Barohoini,* meaning "the rainbow upon which one could travel to the sun." The Navajos know it as *Tsé'naanání'áhí* and have a similar story about the bridge.

The most common modern story about the race to officially "discover" Rainbow Bridge tells of Wetherill's expedition with Dr. Byron Cummings, dean of arts and sciences at the University of Utah, meeting W. B. Douglass, a federal surveyor who was in the region on a competing expedition looking for rumored natural bridges.

1909 Wetherill Expedition to Rainbow Bridge Stuart Malcolm Young Collection, Cline Library, Special Collections and Archives, NAU PH 643.1.130. *Stuart Malcolm Young, the grandson of Brigham Young, photographed the 1909 expedition to Rainbow Bridge with Wetherill and Cummings. From left to right, back row: Ned English, Dan Perkins, Jack Kienan, Vern Rogerson, Neil Judd, and Dan Beauregard. From left to right, front row: Jim Mike (San Juan Paiute guide), John Wetherill, Byron Cummings, W. B. Douglass, and Malcolm Cummings.*

Rivals, but also good sports, the two groups teamed up. On August 14, 1909, Dr. Cummings rounded the bend to become the first non-native to spot their goal. One year later, President Taft signed a proclamation to make Rainbow Bridge a national monument.

After many protests, the family of the Paiute guide Jim Mike, also known as "Mike's Boy," who led the Douglass group, succeeded in having the National Park Service recognize Mike, at the age of 102, as the rightful discoverer of this natural wonder. But according to testimony in a 1972 federal lawsuit brought by the Shonto Chapter of the Navajo Tribe, it is clear that he was not the first man to see the bridge. The chapter brought the lawsuit to oppose the flooding of Forbidding Canyon by the rising water of Lake Powell, fearing it would inundate this sacred site.

Testimony in the suit showed that in 1909, John Wetherill and a Paiute guide, Náashjá Beghay, reported finding a Pueblo shrine dating to A.D. 1270 near the northeastern corner of the bridge. Wetherill also reported that the informant who first told him about the bridge, "Salt People His Eye Alone Man," told him a Navajo altar below the bridge was frequently visited by Navajo medicine men.

What makes a natural bridge? Natural bridges appear when an ancient river cuts its way through sandstone. In some places, like the Goosenecks of the San Juan River (just north of Mexican Hat, Utah), the river rolls in a U-shape. Over thousands of years, as the gorge deepens and the water meets softer sandstone, the river carves a tunnel straight through the side of the U. Water cuts the tunnel deeper and deeper until the overlying rock layer appears to be a bridge standing high above the current level of the water.

MM 537 PANORAMIC VISTA OF LAKE POWELL

NOTE: Leaving the Navajo Nation, change to mountain standard time if traveling between the first week in April and the last week in October, when only the Navajo Nation changes to daylight saving time.

MM 546 NAVAJO GENERATING STATION (East)

Sulfur dioxide emissions from Navajo Generating Station have long been suspected of causing haze over the Grand Canyon. Environmental groups, led by the Grand Canyon Trust, initiated a lawsuit against the power plant to improve visibility in the canyon. An agreement reached in 1991 required the generating station to install $430 million of scrubbing devices on all three smokestacks and to reduce the sulfur dioxide emissions by 90 percent.

The power plant is owned jointly by the U.S. Bureau of Reclamation, the Salt River Project, the Los Angeles Department of Water and Power, and the Arizona Public Service Co.

U.S. 89 LOOP THROUGH PAGE

NOTE: If you are continuing on to Lake Powell, turn to page 66 to continue your tour.

TOWN OF PAGE

Situated atop Manson Mesa at 4,300 feet, Page got its start in 1957 as the staging site for the construction of Glen Canyon Dam. The land was part of the Navajo Reservation, but the Navajos traded the Page site for oil-rich land in Utah. The first homes built in Page were for Bureau of Reclamation employees. It wasn't until 1975 that Page incorporated as a city on 16.7 acres (0.7 sq km) donated by the Bureau of Reclamation. The town is named for John Page, commissioner of the bureau under the Franklin Roosevelt administration from 1937 to 1943.

Powell Museum: At the corner of Lake Powell Boulevard and North Navajo Drive, open noon–5 p.m. (MST) on Sundays and 9 a.m.–5 p.m. (MST) Monday through Saturday from June to September. The museum offers educational displays about Powell's two trips down the uncharted Colorado River. Memorabilia about the founding of Page and the ethnohistory of native cultures are on display. River trips, jeep tours, and boat tours can be arranged here. (928) 645-9496.

INTERESTING SIDE TOUR: ANTELOPE CANYON

One of the rare geologic features of this region is the slot canyon. Sculptured salmon-colored canyons the width of a hallway are formed when a crack in the

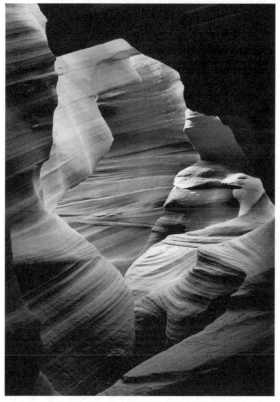

sandstone allows water to flow into and enlarge the crack over thousands of years. As water passes through the irregular crack, racing water places force unevenly, leading to a hollowing effect. This is a wonderful challenge with great rewards for photographers. Slot canyons allow diffuse sunlight to filter through, filling them with pastel hues of incredible beauty. To tour slot canyons on the Navajo Nation, contact Navajo Parks and Recreation at (928) 698-2808. Commercial tours are also available from Antelope Canyon Adventures, (928) 645-5501 or www.jeeptour.com; or Duck Tours, (928) 645-2955.

Photograph by Christine Stephenson

SERVICES IN PAGE

Lodging and Restaurants
Page has an excellent website at www.page-lakepowell.com, or call the Page Chamber of Commerce, (888) 261-PAGE.

Camping
Page-Lake Powell Campground is located on Arizona Highway 98, less than one mile (1.6 km) south of town. Tents and RVs. Showers available.

Health Services
Page Hospital, 24-hour emergency care, (928) 645-2424.

NOTE: Resume travel on U.S. Highway 89 North; turn right to continue to Lake Powell.

GLEN CANYON BRIDGE

This suspension bridge stands seven hundred feet (213 m) above the Colorado River, making it the highest steel-arch bridge in the world. Completed in 1959, the bridge links Highway 89 in Arizona with the Utah side and spans Glen Canyon, named by John Wesley Powell.

The Navajos refer to the Colorado River below as "life without end." It's a female being who marries the male waters of the Little Colorado and the San Juan River.

GLEN CANYON DAM

This was the last dam to be built on the Colorado River and is considered a major engineering triumph. Started in 1956, the dam rises 638 feet (194.5 m) above the Colorado River and produces more than 1,288,000 kilowatts of hydroelectric power per day. Self-guided tours of the dam are available from 8 a.m. to 4 p.m. (MST) every day.

For decades, the dam has been the center of controversy between environmentalists and energy interests. At issue have been the fluctuations of rising and falling water resulting from the release of water from the dam to produce electricity. Those fluctuations have washed away sandy beaches and interfered with aquatic and plant life along the Colorado River. At its peak during summer months, the river would rise and fall thirteen vertical feet (4 m) in a day, often stranding the huge rafts of river runners on beaches until water levels rose again. But those fluctuations were eliminated by the Grand Canyon Protection Act of 1993.

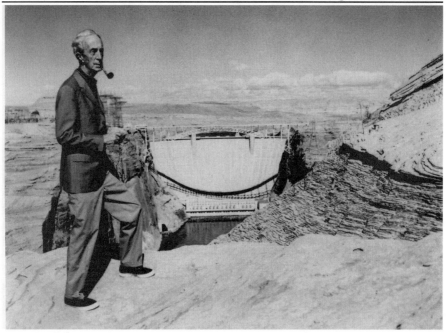

Norman Rockwell overlooking Glen Canyon Dam, 1969

U.S. Bureau of Reclamation, Upper Colorado Region Collection, Cline Library, Special Collections and Archives, NAU PH 90.13.20 *Norman Rockwell was a participant in the Bureau of Reclamation Art Program in 1969.*

CARL HAYDEN VISITORS CENTER

Just over the Glen Canyon Bridge is the visitors center for the Glen Canyon Recreation Area. Perched on the very edge of the cliff, the center's massive windows let you peer down into the canyon for a good view of the lake, Glen Canyon Dam, and the chasm of Glen Canyon. The National Park Service operates the information desk and will answer your questions about boating, camping, hiking, and fishing in the Glen Canyon Recreation Area. Open 8 a.m.– 6 p.m. (MST) in the summer and 8 p.m.–5 p.m. (MST) the rest of the year.

SCENIC DETOUR ON LAKE SHORE DRIVE

Take a right out of the visitors center onto Highway 89, and follow signs to Wahweap Marina. There are no mile markers, so set your odometer to zero. Entrance fees per vehicle: $10 for seven days; if you bring a boat it is an additional $4 for seven days. The National Parks Pass ($50) is accepted here.

Mile .3 (.48 km) *CASTLE ROCK VIEWPOINT (Look north)*

Before the Glen Canyon Dam flooded the land, Cecil B. DeMille filmed the 1923 silent version of the epic drama *The Ten Commandments* below Castle Rock. This famous landmark consists of sandstone, limestone, and mudstone from the Morrison Formation. Ancient rivers deposited the building materials for this formation during the Jurassic era more than 180 million years ago.

Mile 2 (3 km) *NAVAJO MOUNTAIN VIEWPOINT*

There is an interesting plaque explaining the topography of the area and the significance of Navajo Mountain to the Navajo people.

Mile 3 (5 km) *EL VADO DE LOS PADRES (Crossing of the Fathers), THE DOMÍNGUEZ-ESCALANTE EXPEDITION OF 1776*

At six places on your tour around northern Arizona, you will find markers commemorating the Domínguez-Escalante Expedition of 1776. This groundbreaking mission provided the first maps of the area west of Santa Fe, New Mexico. Based on this information, fortune seekers in 1816 opened the Spanish Trail to the gold mines in California.

Domínguez-Escalante Trail of 1776 –1777. . . . .

Father Atanasio Domínguez was in charge of the Spanish missions in New Mexico in 1775. He had been sent here from Spain by his superiors to do three things. First, he was to assess the spiritual and economic conditions of all of the missions in New Mexico and make a detailed report. Second, he was to determine the damage to the historic archives in Santa Fe caused by the Pueblo Revolt of 1680. (See page 112 for more on the revolt.) Third, he was to develop a land route from Santa Fe to the Spanish capital at Monterey, California.

Assisting him in his third task was Father Silvestre Vélez de Escalante, the priest for the Spanish mission in Zuni. Domínguez needed his knowledge about the Hopis and what might lay beyond their villages. Escalante spent a week with the Hopis in 1775 and had learned that there was a gorge to the west so deep and long that it was impassable. Based on this information, Escalante decided that the best route to Monterey would be north over an already well-known Spanish route past Mesa Verde in Colorado. Their plans were to cross the Dolores and Colorado Rivers and then to turn west to cross the Sierra Nevada Mountains at a pass used by earlier expeditions.

Ten men accompanied the two priests on their exploration, but none more important than Captain Don Bernardo Miera y Pacheco, a cartographer. Using an astrolabe—an ancient instrument used to determine the position of the sun, moon, and stars—he made detailed maps of their journey. Leaving Santa Fe on July 29, 1776, which was actually very late in the season for crossing the Sierra Nevadas, they encountered many problems. Thirst, dehydration, and illness plagued the group until finally, on October 11, 1776, just north of present-day Cedar City, Utah, lots were cast to decide if they should continue on to Monterey, facing the possibility of being snowbound in the Sierras, or return home. A return to Santa Fe was chosen, but the route was to be over territory never before charted and without a local guide to help them. One attempt to cross the Colorado River was made at the mouth of the Paria River, close to where Lees Ferry is today, but it was found to be too difficult and dangerous. Trapped, the padres' only hope was to climb out of Glen Canyon and find another crossing. On November 6, 1776, after many failed attempts and nearly starving, they crossed the Colorado River at this site. They continued on through the Hopi villages to Zuni and arrived in Santa Fe on January 2, 1777. They had covered more than 2,000 miles (3,226 km) over some of America's most difficult terrain.

In 1976, the Domínguez-Escalante Bicentennial Expedition retraced the fathers' route by horseback to commemorate the spirit of the 1776 expedition.

The Crossing of the Fathers was well-known by Navajo and Paiute traders. Jacob Hamblin crossed here, at what is also called Ute Ford, on his first journey to the Hopi villages in 1858. It is believed that sometime between 1870 and 1880, the Mormons dynamited this ford to keep the Paiutes and Navajo from raiding Mormon communities in Utah.

 LAKE POWELL

The result of building Glen Canyon Dam was, of course, the birth of Lake Powell, named after John Wesley Powell, the one-armed Civil War hero who in 1869 became the first to navigate the entire length of the uncharted Colorado River. He repeated the feat in 1871, and ten years later he became the director of both the U.S. Geological Survey and the Bureau of Ethnology. Even though Powell was responsible for naming the Grand Canyon (almost named "Big Canyon" by another surveyor) and other landmarks on the Colorado Plateau, he did not place his own name on anything.

There is irony in the Bureau of Reclamation's decision to give Lake Powell his name. Powell did not agree with the proposed remaking of the West into a mirror image of the green farming communities of the East. But the popular notion in the late 1800s was that water follows human settlements. Knowing this faulty thinking was not going to work in the arid West, Powell fought expansionist politicians who were hell-bent to open this land to farmers. He was only one voice against many, and today the huge cities of Phoenix and Los Angeles testify to his failure to persuade policymakers to take a slow, cautious approach to settling the West.

Lake Powell is more than 180 miles (290 km) long and has more miles of coastline than California. The flooding of Glen Canyon led to the inundation of many ruins, natural coves, bridges, caves, petroglyphs, and historic sites, as well as the natural beauty of a magnificent canyon. Archeological projects completed between 1950 and 1970 saved many of the known historic artifacts.

An interesting story about a rare petroglyph found in Navajo Canyon involves the supernova of July 4, A.D. 1054. According to Mt. Palomar Observatory researcher William Miller, a petroglyph of a crescent moon with a round circle below it is one of only four recordings of the supernova found in the world. Other recordings were found in the archives of Japanese and Chinese astronomers.

The supernova was so bright in the eastern sky, lying just below the crescent moon, that the rising sun did not block its light. For ancient people known for their understanding and reverence of the night sky, it is surprising that there are not more recordings of this major astronomical event. Miller describes the exploding star of 1054 as the "brightest object, other than the sun and moon, ever to appear in the sky during the recorded history of man."

Supernova Petroglyph, not dated
Photograph by Robert Euler, Museum of Northern Arizona Photo Archives, NA 5653.9a

Today the lake dazzles the eye with its combination of blue water, white clouds, and red rocks. Fishing for striped bass is popular. Rainbow trout do not survive in the warm lake water. They live below the dam in the Colorado River. It is still possible to enjoy many of the back canyons of Glen Canyon via the lake. Some ruins and petroglyphs can be seen if you rent a boat or take the Wahweap tour boat.

Hole-in-the-Rock: The fastest and safest way to see this historic site, located sixty-five miles uplake, is by tour boat. Alternatively, you can drive to Escalante, Utah, and take the unpaved Hole-in-the-Rock road to the edge of the Kaiparowits Plateau, but it is a very long trip. Just below the junction of the Colorado and Escalante Rivers is testament in the rock to the industrious and tenacious nature of the early Mormon pioneers. Sent by Brigham Young to settle the San Juan Valley, a group of Mormon settlers thought they could take a more direct route from Cedar City, Utah, to their destination than the crossing at Lees Ferry. Once they arrived at the edge of the Kaiparowits Plateau, they could find no descent to the river suitable for wagons. Instead of turning back, the pioneers blasted a road three-quarters of a mile long with a vertical descent of a thousand feet (305 meters). Even more amazing, they hitched up their teams and drove their wagons down the incline without any loss of human or animal life.

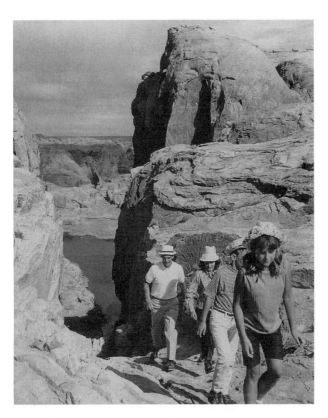

Charles Hall drove the first wagon down the precarious route. He later found a better crossing about twenty miles (32 km) upriver, where Halls Crossing Marina is located today. (See page 180 for a map of the Hole-in-the-Rock route.)

Hole-in-the-Rock
1969, U.S. Department of the Interior, Bureau of Reclamation, Upper Colorado Region, Cline Library, Special Collections and Archives, NAU PH 90.13.18

NOTE: At the intersection of Shoreline Drive, turn right to Wahweap Marina, Lodge, and Restaurant.

LOCAL SERVICES

Boat Tours

Make arrangements at Wahweap Lodge, or for advance reservations contact Lake Powell Resorts and Marinas, 2916 N. 35th Avenue, Ste. 8, Phoenix, AZ 85017-5261, (800) 528-6154. All tours have water, coffee, and lemonade, and restrooms. No pets allowed. **Paddle wheeler cruise around Wahweap Bay** (one hour); **dinner cruise on Canyon King paddle wheel** (2.5 hours); **all-day tour to Rainbow Bridge** (7.5 hours, includes lunch); **Navajo tapestry tour of Navajo Canyon** (3 hours); **Antelope Canyon** (1.5 hours); **Colorado River Wilderness float trips from Glen Canyon Dam to Lees Ferry** (approximately 6 hours).

Lodging

Wahweap Lodge: Luxurious accommodations with views of Wahweap Bay and Castle Rock from your room. Reservations: (800) 528-6154, or in Page, (928) 645-2433. The lodge has an excellent restaurant called **The Rainbow Room,** which overlooks the lake. Open from 6 a.m. to 11 a.m. for breakfast, 11 a.m. to 3 p.m. for lunch and 5 p.m. to 10 p.m. for dinner. Reservations are not accepted. (928) 645-2433

Lake Powell Motel: Past the Glen Canyon Dam on U.S. 89 north, four miles (6.5 km). Moderately priced. Reservations: (928) 645-2477.

Boat Rentals at Stateline Marina

Drive five miles (8 km) north on Stateline Drive. Ski boats sixteen to twenty feet (5–6 m) long and wave runners can be rented at Stateline. It is a good idea to make reservations at least one or two days before you arrive at Lake Powell during the high season from May 15 through October 14. Houseboats 36 and 44 feet (11–14 m) long are available to rent for two, three, or five days. Prices vary depending on size and time of year. Reservations for houseboats are recommended at least six months in advance. Call Lake Powell Resorts and Marinas, 2916 N. 35th Ave., Ste. 8, Phoenix, AZ 85017-5261, (800) 528-6154.

Fishing

The best fishing is for large mouth, small mouth, and striped bass, but you can also find northern and walleye pike, catfish, crappie, and carp. Depending on where you want to fish, you may need a license for both Arizona and Utah. The southernmost part of the lake is in Arizona and the rest is in Utah. If you rent a boat at Stateline Marina, you are in Utah. Fishing licenses are sold at Wahweap, Stateline Marina, or any sporting goods store in Page.

Camping

Wahweap Campground and RV Park: First-come, first-served; drinking water; no showers or hookups. **RV Park:** Coin showers and laundry with hookups. Reservations (800) 528-6154.

Lone Rock: (On U.S. Hwy. 89 North at Mile 556.5) Considered a party area by most locals, this primitive camping area is loud and crowded on weekends during the summer. No running water, outhouses only. Nearby hills make this an attractive place for all-terrain vehicles, which sometimes run all night.

END SCENIC DETOUR

56 miles (90 km) from Bitter Springs to Jacob Lake

MM 525 BITTER SPRINGS (West)

Bitter Springs is a Navajo tribal housing project whose water, despite its name, really does not taste that bad.

MM 525 ANTELOPE PASS (East) From here you can see where

Highway 89 cuts through a pass blasted out of the Echo Cliffs.

MM 527 VERMILION CLIFFS (West)

Capped by Navajo Sandstone, the sheer and imposing Vermilion Cliffs were named by John Wesley Powell for their vermilion, or bright reddish orange, color, particularly at sunrise and sunset.

MM 539 NAVAJO BRIDGE AND THE COLORADO RIVER

The older of these two bridges was the first bridge to span the Colorado River. It was constructed in 1929 by the Kansas City Structural Steel Corp., financed by a cooperative effort between Arizona and Utah. All of the steel was made in Kansas City and shipped to Flagstaff by rail, then carried by truck over 145 miles of primitive roads to the bridge site. Steel was driven

Navajo Bridge with the Vermilion Cliffs in the background, 1929
Cline Library, Special Collections and Archives, NAU PH 114.2

Native Roads

KAIBAB PLATEAU

To Kanab, Utah

Jacob Lake

North Rim Campground

Kaibab Lodge

FR 429

67 The Meadows

Warning: road closed in winter

Jacob Lake Campground

Grand Canyon Lodge

DeMotte Campground

KAIBAB

PARIA CANYON-VERMILION CLIFFS NATIONAL MONUMENT

U. S. HIGHWAY 89A (North, then east) Bitter Springs to Jacob Lake

89A

FR 1049

NATIONAL

VERMILION CLIFFS

House Rock Buffalo Ranch

HOUSEROCK VALLEY

San Bartolome Hist. Site

FOREST

Cliff Dwellers Lodge

COLORADO

Vermilion Cliffs Lodge

Marble Canyon Lodge

RIVER

Soap Creek

Badger Canyon

Paria River

The Gap

Bitter Springs

Marble

89

89A

Canyon

Navajo Bridge

Lees Ferry

To Cameron Flagstaff

ECHO CLIFFS

To Tuba City

HAMBLIN RIDGE

160

W

S

N

E

89

To Page/ Lake Powell

down Lees Dugway and carried across the Colorado River on the ferry to build the western side of the bridge. Once completed, it was the highest bridge of its type in the world, standing 467 feet (142 m) above the Colorado

River with a span of 834 feet (254 m). The historic bridge is now a pedestrian walkway with a view of the imposing canyon and river below.

In 1997 the Arizona Society of Civil Engineers named Navajo Bridge "one of the most historically significant bridges in Arizona." There are three other projects in the state with this designation: a prehistoric Hohokam canal system in the Phoenix area, Theodore Roosevelt Dam/Salt River Project, and the Hoover Dam.

A plaque commemorating the Navajo Bridge as a National Historic Monument is located at the Interpretive Center.

The Colorado River, not dated
Philip Johnston Collection, Cline Library, Special Collections and Archives,
NAU PH 413-605

Navajo Bridge Interpretive Center: On the west side of the new bridge is a native stone visitors center that provides information about the area. The gift shop sells books and maps specific to the area. The building is open from 9 a.m. to 5 p.m. daily (DST) from mid-May to mid-October. The restrooms are open year-round. On the east side of the bridge are Navajo arts and craft vendors.

*NOTE: As you leave the Navajo Nation, change to
mountain standard time if traveling between
the first week in April and the last week in October.*

LEES FERRY

(You may wonder why Lees Ferry doesn't have an apostrophe. According to the *Sixth Report of the United States Geographic Board: 1890 to 1932,* the name was officially changed from Lee's Ferry to Lees Ferry.)

Lees Ferry, ca. 1900
Warren Family Collection, Cline Library, Special Collections and Archives, NAU PH 412.1.2

Turn north past the bridge, just before Marble Canyon Lodge. Along the five-mile (8 km) winding road to the Colorado River are interpretive sites where you can read about the area's geology. Among the interesting features are "balancing rocks"—examples of the forces of erosion wearing away the soft underlying sandstone faster than the harder rock on top.

At the bottom of the hill, just before you cross the Paria River, turn west onto a dirt road to the **Lonely Dell Ranch Historic District.** You can purchase a walking tour guide at the ranch. To the east is a **river drive,** or you can continue straight down the entrance road to the launch ramp, or "Mile Zero" of the Colorado, where commercial river-rafting trips begin. Just past the launch ramp is the **Lees Ferry Historic District,** where a primitive Mormon fort still stands.

The most important point for colonization of the Southwest was this very remote section of the Colorado River. Because of the near impossibility of crossing the river for three hundred miles (480 km), the ferry allowed for the rapid Mormon settlement in Arizona.

In 1860, Jacob Hamblin was the first Mormon to see the possibilities for a ferry site at this location. After several failed attempts to cross the fast-moving Colorado, he was finally able to cross in a raft in 1864. As more and more settlers needed to use the ferry, the Mormons built a fort to protect them from attacks by local Navajos. It wasn't used very much for fighting and eventually turned into a trading post.

John D. Lee and his wife, Emma, were sent here in 1872 by Mormon leaders as punishment for Lee's involvement in the Mountain Meadows Massacre. Mountain Meadows, located in Utah on the pioneer trail to California, is where reportedly twenty-three men, ten women, and thirty-four children of the Fancher wagon train were slain by Paiutes and Mormons.

The Mormon involvement in something so out of character with their religious conviction is a complex topic to discuss. In a nutshell, the massacre stemmed from a background of persecution that forced the Mormons to leave Missouri in 1838. When hostilities between townspeople and the Mormons turned violent, the governor forced them to leave, saying, "The Mormons must be treated as enemies and must be exterminated or driven from the state if necessary for the public peace."

From there they moved to Nauvoo, Illinois, where they prospered. Their leader, Joseph Smith, managed to secure a charter for the town, making it almost independent from the state, with its own army for protection. At the same time, Smith was running for president of the United States. This led to dissension among members of his own faith, and Smith excommunicated many of his critics. To voice their opposition to their former leader, the banished group started a newspaper called the *Nauvoo Expositor.* An enraged Joseph Smith ordered the paper's headquarters destroyed. This violence, and growing anti-Mormon sentiment in the area, led to the arrest of Smith and his brother in 1844. Gov. Thomas Ford was called to mediate between the "Gentiles" and Mormons, but he arrived too late. An angry mob had pulled Joseph and Hyrum from their jail cells and murdered them. This was the final straw for Brigham Young, Joseph Smith's successor. Knowing that the Mormon people needed a place where they could worship in their own way, he sent a Mormon scouting party west. In 1847, Brigham Young declared the Great Salt Lake Valley to be their new home.

Non-Mormon settlers, on their way to the gold fields in California, were soon on the heels of the Mormons, some hurling taunts and insults as they passed through Mormon communities. One group named their team of oxen "Joseph Smith" and "Brigham Young" and shouted that they hoped someone would kill Brigham Young as they had Smith. The Mormons began to resent outsiders. With each passing day there were fresh rumors of 2,500 federal troops traveling west to destroy the Mormon people.

A kind of frenzy began to possess the Mormon communities. Often fueled by inaccurate reports and rumors, this resentment and fear finally surfaced in the attack on the Fancher wagon train in 1857. Why the Mormons picked this particular train to attack is not clear. One explanation was that it was an attempt to maintain good relations with the Paiutes, who outnumbered the Mormons four to one. By cooperating in an attack on the wagon train, it would show solidarity with the Indians trying to discourage the unending flow of white settlers through their traditional hunting area. The supplies and, allegedly, gold carried by the Fancher party were also speculated by some as being an attractive incentive for attacking the train.

The Fancher party was able to hold off the first wave of Indian attackers for about a week. Then John D. Lee got the job of persuading the besieged survivors to lay down their weapons and come out from the protection of their wagon train. Not realizing the Mormons were also their enemy, the group did as requested. The men led the way, and the women and older children followed behind. When Lee gave the command to halt, the Mormons began shooting and killed anyone old enough to talk.

Because of his insidious role in tricking the settlers out of their relatively secure place, Lee became the scapegoat for the entire affair. To hide from federal authorities, and as punishment from the church for his involvement in this crime, he fled to this Colorado River crossing with his wife, Emma, in 1872.

One of the colorful stories about Lee while he was living at the ferry concerns his many opportunities to explore the canyon for gold. Around 1885, a prospector found a large deposit of gold in the canyon near Vulcan's Throne (a volcanic cinder cone in the western section of the Grand Canyon). Lee prospected in this area many times, and locals think he had his own mine or gold dust buried somewhere in the Grand Canyon. If he did, he never told anyone, not even his wife.

After Lee's arrest and subsequent execution in 1877 for his part in the massacre, Emma married miner Franklin French, known for his building of the Tanner-French Trail in the Grand Canyon. Emma believed Lee had found gold and told French all that she knew about where Lee might have hidden it. French searched for the gold many times but without success.

Warren Johnson and his two wives, Permelia Jane Smith and Samantha Nelson, ran the ferry after Lee's arrest, from 1875 to 1895. Three of Johnson's children died of diphtheria within three months of each other. They are buried in the cemetery on the Lonely Dell Ranch up the Paria River, very close to the ferry. Across the street from Marble Canyon Lodge is a memorial to the efforts of the Johnson family.

To many Mormon settlers, the thought of crossing the Colorado River caused more fear than the thought of all of the other dangers that lay ahead as they traveled through Navajo territory. Mormon leader Daniel Wells and Bishop Lorenzo Roundy fell off the ferry when the bow dipped under high waves in 1879. The bishop's body was never recovered. Once across the river it was then necessary to climb Lee's Backbone, a two-mile (3 km) ascent out of the canyon, followed by a sharp descent once on top.

The dugway was built in 1898 so travelers could avoid the arduous climb up Lee's Backbone. The Grand Canyon Cattle Company bought Lees Ferry in 1909, and in 1916 Coconino County purchased the ferry and ran it until 1929, when Navajo Bridge opened.

Lees Ferry Dugway, not dated
Emery Kolb Collection, Special Collections and Archives, NAU #568-6473

Lees Ferry Campground: A U.S. Fee Area operated on a first-come, first-served basis. Campsites have shade provided by metal awnings. No trees. Community bathrooms, running water. Public showers and laundry are located at Marble Canyon Lodge on U.S. 89A by the post office. Telephone, RV dump site. Information: Glen Canyon National Recreation Area's Lees Ferry Ranger Station, (928) 355-2234.

Fishing at Lees Ferry: Lees Ferry is well known for excellent fishing for rainbow trout year-round, with artificial bait and fly only with barbless hooks. No trout between sixteen and twenty-two inches (40–56 cm) may be kept. The limit is two fish in your possession. No live fish may be kept. You may take a boat sixteen feet (5 m) or larger with at least a 25-horsepower engine on the river upstream 14.5 miles (23 km) to the Glen Canyon Dam. No boating is allowed downriver from Lees Ferry without a permit.

River Trips on the Colorado River

Please contact each company for complete details on the type of trip offered. Some companies offer motorized or oar-powered trips. Others offer dory or paddle trips. Each company offers its own schedules and prices.

Arizona Raft Adventures, Inc. (800) 786-7238

Canyon Explorations, Inc. (800) 654-0723

Canyoneers, Inc. (800) 525-0924 outside Arizona, (520) 526-0924 in Arizona

Colorado River & Trail Expeditions, Inc. (800) 253-7328

Diamond River Adventures, Inc. (800) 343-3121

Grand Canyon Expeditions Company (800) 544-2691

Hatch River Expeditions, Inc. (800) 342-8243

Hualapai River Runners (928) 769-2419

Moki Mac Expeditions, Inc. (800) 284-7280

O.A.R.S., Inc. (209) 736-4677

Outdoors Unlimited (800) 637-7238

Tour West, Inc. (800) 453-9107, (801) 225-0755

Western River Expeditions, Inc. (800) 453-7450

Wilderness River Adventures (800) 992-8022

MARBLE CANYON LODGE AND TRADING COMPANY

Just past Navajo Bridge after the turnoff to Lees Ferry. Built in 1926 by "Buck" Lowry in anticipation of the completion of Navajo Bridge, this lodge offers a restaurant open from 6 a.m. to 9 p.m. (MST). For room reservations, call (928) 355-2225.

DOMÍNGUEZ-ESCALANTE TRAIL MARKER (North)

South, across the street from the Marble Canyon Lodge, is where the famous Spanish expedition passed on October 26, 1776. It spent five days near the present-day Lees Ferry, where its members attempted to swim across the river. When this failed, they built a log raft, but this too failed. Near starvation, they ate the last horse in their expedition and decided to climb out of Marble Canyon through an "impassable" notch in Echo Cliffs. Once on the rim of Glen Canyon they were able to work their way down to the river again and find the Crossing of the Fathers near what is now Wahweap Marina. (See pages 68–69 for more on this expedition.)

MM 542 LEES FERRY LODGE AT VERMILION CLIFFS (North)

Constructed in 1929 of native stone, Lees Ferry Lodge served the needs of uranium miners working in the area. Each room opens onto a garden patio. About one-tenth of a mile (160 m) from the lodge, heading west on 89A and on the south side of the road, are two markers for the **Honeymoon**

Trail. You will see these markers as you drive to the North Rim. There are two more on the way to Cliff Dwellers Lodge. (See pages 58–59 for more about this trail.)

The **Vermilion Cliffs Bar and Grill** offers 150 different kinds of cold bottled beer. Even though the food is good in the summer, in the winter it gets even better to satisfy the gourmet demands of the world-class fishermen visiting Lees Ferry. Open 6:30 a.m.–10 p.m. (MST) every day. No TV or telephone in rooms. Reservations: (928) 355-2231.

 MM 542 BADGER CANYON AND SOAP CREEK

Directly across from Vermilion Cliffs Lodge. According to an old story, Badger Canyon and Soap Creek got their names because a couple of sheep herders, left to watch the sheep with limited food, wanted a change in their diet. It was going to be a long time before the next supply wagon came through. Even though they could eat mutton any time, the shepherds longed for something different. One day one of them was lucky enough to trap and kill a badger. To make it edible, they boiled it all day and all night. In the morning when it was time to move camp, the badger was still too tough to eat, so they took it with them. Arriving at their next campsite, they took water from the new stream and continued to boil the badger. To their surprise, the fatty badger mixed with the plentiful gypsum in the water, turning it to soap.

 MM 547 CLIFF DWELLERS LODGE

The lodge was built in 1949 by Glen Canyon guide and entrepreneur Art Greene. It is now owned by the Lees Ferry Anglers Guides and Fly Shop, which was formerly located next to Vermilion Cliffs Lodge. The owners bought this resort to "be able to handle guide services, fishing, and lodging accommodations with one phone call." In addition to the twenty-one motel rooms, there is an 1,800-square-foot fishing lodge that anglers can rent for group retreats. There is also a restaurant-bar, store, and gas station. Reservations: (800) 962-9755.

Why are there huge boulders lying beside the road? These boulders once rested at the top of the Vermilion Cliffs. They are from the much harder Shinarump layer. They fell to the valley floor when the softer Moenkopi Sandstone underlying the Shinarump eroded away.

VERMILION CLIFFS SCENIC HIGHWAY/NATIONAL MONUMENT

Watch for **California condors** as you drive along this scenic road. In 1996 ten condors weighing about twenty-five pounds with wingspans of

9.8 ft.(3 m) were released into Vermilion Cliffs National Monument from the San Diego Wild Animal Park and Los Angeles Zoo. There are now a total of fifty-one California condors in Arizona, and in 2003 the first baby was born to captive-produced parents at the Grand Canyon. Since the beginning of the reintroduction effort, there have been twenty-three fatalities, primarily caused by lead poisoning from the large carcasses of deer and other game the birds eat. The birds can travel up to 150 miles (240 km) a day in search of food, so Arizona Game and Fish, along with various wildlife organizations, is asking for cooperation from hunters to use lead-free ammunition when hunting.

Photograph courtesy of Arizona Game and Fish

Vermilion Cliffs was designated as a national monument in 2000 by President Clinton. The monument covers 294,000 acres of some of the most remote and unspoiled landscape in the country. It includes the Paria Plateau, Paria Canyon, Vermilion Cliffs, and Coyote Buttes.

Mile 557.8 SAN BARTOLOME HISTORIC SITE (North)

An interpretive site that explains the natural history and geology of the Arizona Strip. It also explains the near starvation of the Domínguez-Escalante Expedition when they reached this spot.

WHAT IS THE ARIZONA STRIP?

It is the most remote and isolated area of Arizona, separated from the rest of the state by the 279-mile-long (449 km) Grand Canyon. Back in the early 1900s, Utah wanted to acquire the strip because most of its residents identified more closely with Utah than with Arizona. To investigate if the annexation of the strip was in the best interest of Arizona, well-known poet and travel writer Sharlot Hall took a two-month history tour to explore the region. Named state historian in 1909, she believed it was her duty to visit every part of Arizona and accurately record its history. For seventy-five days, she and her wagon driver, Allen Doyle, visited most of the strip country and recorded much of its history, natural resources, and the people who lived there. When she returned, she wrote articles about the importance of keeping the Arizona Strip a part of Arizona. In 1912, she retired as state historian and in 1928 moved to Prescott, where she founded the **Sharlot Hall Museum,** housed in the renovated Old Governor's Mansion used when Prescott was the first territorial capital of Arizona.

MM 548–MM 566 HOUSE ROCK VALLEY

Running from Cliff Dwellers to House Rock Junction, where Highway 89A starts to climb up the Kaibab Plateau, this valley was named by Mormon settlers after they found shelter under two large boulders that had fallen together. Jacob Hamblin had a home here. Between 1870 and 1880, he traveled the Mormon Trail, taking settlers across the Colorado at Lees Ferry to their new homes on the Little Colorado River in Arizona.

SCENIC DETOUR FOR THE WELL PREPARED

MM 560 *HOUSE ROCK BUFFALO RANCH*

It is twenty-one miles (34 km) to the ranger's home on a graded dirt road. Poor ground clearance can be dangerous for passenger cars. Use caution: washes fill when it rains on the nearby Kaibab Plateau. Without help from the ranger, your chance of actually seeing one of the ninety buffalo living here is minimal because of the size of the preserve. This 60,000-acre (244 sq km) ranch is home to Arizona's largest buffalo herd, managed by the Arizona Game and Fish Department. Buffalo hunts are held once a year by lottery. One buffalo is allowed per hunter's lifetime, and permits cost around $700.

Buffalo are not indigenous to Arizona, but eighty-seven were brought here from Texas in the early 1920s by "Buffalo Jones." Charles Jesse Jones was hired by the National Park Service to determine whether the area around the North Rim of the Grand Canyon could accommodate a buffalo herd. To do this, he contacted Edwin Wooley, who ran a stage coach from Kanab, Utah, to Bright Angel Point on the North Rim. Wooley was also the owner of one of the largest cattle ranches in the Kanab-Fredonia area.

After Jones was assured that the buffalo would thrive in this area, he tried to convince Wooley of the economic value of cross-breeding buffalo with Galloway cattle to develop "cattalo." Wooley agreed to the experiment and delivered one hundred head of Galloway heifers for breeding. But when the resulting offspring were too large for the heifers to give birth

Buffalo in House Rock Valley, not dated
Grand Canyon Pioneer Society, Metzger Collection, Special Collections and Archives, NAU PH 90.9.57 *Art Metzger lived at the Grand Canyon in 1913, ranching with his brother. In 1928 he became postmaster at the Grand Canyon.*

without assistance, the idea was scrapped. In 1926, one hundred buffalo were sold to Arizona Game and Fish for $10,000 and moved from the North Rim to this preserve.

Struggling Ohio writer Zane Grey became a Western writer because of his meeting with Buffalo Jones in New York in 1906. Jones was a famous hunter who led the slaughter of many wild animals almost to extinction. Realizing the error of his ways in his later life, he became a champion of endangered species. Grey came to the Southwest to write about Jones's transformation from hunter to protectionist. He spent weeks with Jones and learned how to be a cowboy. This experience became the material for his first successful Western novel, *The Last of the Plainsmen,* written in 1908.

END SCENIC DETOUR

MM 566 SNOW CHAIN-UP AREA

Here is a subtle reminder that the Kaibab Plateau is more than 9,000 feet (2,745 m) in elevation and receives an average of twelve feet (3.6 m) of snow each year. A record twenty-five feet (7.7 m) of snow covered the plateau in 1985. In this high country the snow can start as early as September. The National Park Service closes the North Rim on October 21, but the park remains open for day use until December 1. There is no lodging, food, or gasoline in the national park from October 21 until its final closing on December 1. The park may close earlier depending on the weather.

KAIBAB PLATEAU

Kaibab means "mountain lying down" in the Paiute language. It is a good name for this extensive plateau that rises to an elevation of 9,100 feet (2,775 m). Mormons called it Buckskin Mountain because it has the largest population of mule deer in the world. The plateau also contains the country's largest virgin forest, and it is the only place on earth you will find the **Kaibab squirrel.**

The Kaibab squirrel became separated from its cousin, the South Rim's Abert squirrel, when the Kaibab Plateau was rising and the Colorado River cut its way through the plateau to make the Grand Canyon. Over millions of years, this squirrel got caught on the northern side, adapting to the colder environment. These tassel-eared squirrels adjusted very well to the climate by developing a thick coat that blends well with the surrounding trees to hide it from predators.

MM 568 SCENIC VIEW (West)

To the west you can see House Rock Valley, Vermilion Cliffs, Echo Cliffs, and the Colorado River. There is also a Domínguez-Escalante marker across the highway from the viewpoint.

MM 572 PONDEROSA PINE FOREST

This is where you leave the piñon-juniper woodland and enter ponderosa pine forest, found between 7,000 and 8,000 feet (2,135–2,440 m).

JACOB LAKE Junction of U.S. 89A and Arizona Highway 67

Jacob Lake Inn: This and the Kaibab Lodge (25 miles) are the only motels in the North Kaibab National Forest, so be sure to make your reservations well in advance because they fill up quickly. Jacob Lake Inn is open year-round. Reservations: (928) 643-7232; www.jacoblake.com.

Jacob Lake Campground (National Forest Service): Open May 15 to November 1 (depending on snowfall), the campground has fifty-three campsites with picnic tables and fire grills, paved roads, running water, toilets, wheelchair access. Tents, trailers, and motor homes less than twenty-six feet (8 m) are welcome. No hookups. Reservations are handled by the National Recreation Reservation Service, a one-stop reservation service for the Forest Service, Army Corps of Engineers, National Park Service, Bureau of Land Management, and Bureau of Reclamation outdoor recreation facilities and activities. (877) 444-6777; www.reserveusa.com

Kaibab National Forest Visitors Center: South of Jacob Lake Inn; open 8 a.m.–5:30 p.m. daily; closed in winter. The center offers information and interpretive displays about the Kaibab Plateau and the North Rim. (928) 643-7298; www.fs.fed.us

Allen's Trail Rides, also south of the inn, offers a chance to enjoy the Kaibab National Forest on horseback. You can go for a couple of hours or spend two to five days on horseback. For reservations, call (435) 644-8150.

44 miles (71 km) from Jacob Lake to the North Rim

NOTE: Arizona Highway 67, the Kaibab Plateau-North Rim Highway, is usually open May 15 through October 31; Arizona Department of Transportation warns visitors every year that after November 1 the road could be closed on short notice because of heavy snowfall.

Arizona Highway 67 is a National Forest Scenic Byway and an Arizona State Scenic Parkway. It is the same route formerly used by the stagecoach to transport visitors to the North Rim. It parallels the Kaibab Plateau Trail, which makes up part of the 750-mile (1,209 km) **Arizona Trail,** a primitive, nonmotorized way to traverse Arizona from the Mexico border to Utah. The trail uses old stagecoach routes, logging trails, and some new trails. Once finished, the Arizona Trail will be used by hikers, mountain bikers, horse enthusiasts, and cross-country skiers. Help is needed to complete the trail. If you are interested in donating your time or money, contact the Arizona Trail Association, P.O. Box 36736, Phoenix, AZ 85067.

 KAIBAB CAMPER VILLAGE and JACOB LAKE (One mile south of Kaibab Visitors Center)

The park has forty-three RV sites with full hookups and twenty-four sites with only electricity and water. There are fifty tent sites. Reservations: (928) 643-7804. Closed October 15 to May 15.

Named for Mormon explorer Jacob Hamblin, tiny Jacob Lake is an example of a sinkhole formed through the Kaibab Limestone. The water on the Kaibab Plateau runs through underground limestone passageways and most of the "lakes" formed on the surface of the plateau are formed when the underlying limestone layer collapses. Directly across from Jacob Lake is a historic ranger station, built in 1910, listed on the National Register of Historic Places.

FOREST ROAD 429 (West)

This primitive road leads to Big Springs, where President Theodore Roosevelt stayed while hunting with "Uncle" Jimmy Owens, a famous hunter and guide of the Kaibab Forest and a participant in the failed attempt to develop the "cattalo" in House Rock Valley. (See pages 83–84.)

In the early 1900s, cattlemen used the Kaibab Plateau to graze their herds but did not like cougars eating their calves. To accommodate these interests, the U.S. government hired Owens to rid the plateau of cougars. He alone may have shot more than five hundred of them. Unfortunately, it was not

KAIBAB PLATEAU

To Kanab, Utah

Jacob Lake

FR 429

North Rim Campground

Kaibab Lodge

Grand Canyon Lodge

DeMotte Campground

67

The Meadows

Warning: road closed in winter

Jacob Lake Campground

KAIBAB

ARIZONA HIGHWAY 67 South
Jacob Lake
to
North Rim
Grand Canyon

89A

FR 1049

PARIA CANYON-VERMILION CLIFFS NATIONAL MONUMENT

NATIONAL

House Rock
Buffalo Ranch

HOUSEROCK VALLEY

San Bartolome Hist. Site

VERMILION CLIFFS

FOREST

Cliff Dwellers Lodge

COLORADO

Vermilion Cliffs Lodge

RIVER

Soap Creek

Badger Canyon

Marble Canyon Lodge

Paria River

Bitter Springs

Marble

The Gap

89

ECHO CLIFFS

89A

Canyon

To Cameron
Flagstaff

HAMBLIN RIDGE

Navajo Bridge

Lees Ferry

To Tuba City

160

W

N

S

89

E

To Page/
Lake Powell

long afterward that the mule deer population began to skyrocket because of the elimination of its only predator, leaving the deer to die off from mass starvation. To fix the problem, the cattlemen decided that 75,000 Kaibab Plateau mule deer should move to the South Rim. The government offered

Old Road, Kaibab Plateau, North Rim, ca. 1920s
Emery Kolb Collection, Cline Library, Northern Arizona University, NAU PH 568-7014

$5 per relocated deer, but how does one lead a herd of wild animals to its new homeland? One cattleman came up with the idea of staging a "deer drive." According to his plan, cowboys would round up deer on the Kaibab Plateau and herd them down one of the trails on the North Rim into the Grand Canyon. The herd would then swim across the Colorado River and travel up the trail to the South Rim.

Cowboys came from all around with guns and pots and pans to scare the deer, but when they got to the rim, they didn't have one deer to herd down the trail. Wild animals do not behave the way domesticated animals do, and so the effort failed. Eventually the government stopped listening to the cattlemen and reintroduced the cougar into the delicate balance of life on the Kaibab Plateau.

MM 604 MEADOWS

Different types of grasses and wildflowers compose this biotic community, making this an excellent grazing area for cattle and, at one time, buffalo. Along the edge of the meadows are short blue spruce trees that look out of place next to the large trees of the Kaibab National Forest. These "baby trees" are smaller clones of the larger blue spruce that normally grow to heights of eighty to one hundred feet (24–31 m). The smaller trees are attempting to colonize the meadow, but because of the high water table caused by the spring snowmelt and twenty-two inches (55.9 cm) of rainfall annually, the meadow is usually too wet for the spruce to thrive.

MM 605 KAIBAB LODGE (West)

It is thought by locals that David Rust, famous for promoting tourism to the Grand Canyon in the early 1900s, may have built the Kaibab Lodge around 1926. Regardless of its history, it is a charming place to relax and enjoy the beauty of the Kaibab Plateau. Reservations: (928) 638-2389. **Kaibab Lodge Dining Room:** Breakfast buffet served 6–9:30 a.m., dinner 5–9:15 p.m. Reservations recommended but not required.

The North Rim Country Store across the street sells the only diesel fuel available on the North Rim.

MM 605 KAIBAB NATIONAL FOREST DEMOTTE CAMPGROUND (West)

25.8 miles (41.6 km) from Jacob Lake, just past the Kaibab Lodge on the west side of Arizona Highway 67. This campground bears the name of a member of John Wesley Powell's 1872 survey team. Harvey DeMotte was a professor at Illinois Wesleyan University at the same time Powell was a professor of geology. The campground is open June 1 to November 1 (depending on snowfall) and has twenty-three camping sites with picnic tables and grills, drinking water, and toilets. Reservations: (877) 444-6777; www.reserveusa.com.

NORTH RIM ENTRANCE STATION

The entrance fee is $20 per car and is good at both the North and South Rims for seven days. National Park Passes are accepted. It is a good four-hour drive and over 216 (348 km) highway miles from the South Rim to the North Rim of the Grand Canyon. For those who do make the trip, the canyon view and surrounding vistas make the additional travel well worth the effort. The North Rim is 1,000–1,500 feet (305–457 m) higher than the South Rim and gets much more precipitation, usually in the form of snow.

The culture of the earliest-known people to live on the North Rim, some four thousand years ago, is referred to as the Archaic. These people created mysterious, animal-shaped split-twig figurines, some of which were found in Luka Cave by a Civilian Conservation Corps work crew in the 1930s while building a trail from Phantom Ranch at the bottom of the Grand Canyon to Clear Creek on the North Rim.

Archaeologists think these caves were shrines for hunters of the Archaic period. In their rituals and prayers, the people may have used the figurines to bring success and good fortune to their hunts.

Around A.D. 500, the Anasazi moved into the canyon and built pueblo homes of stone, mud, logs, and brush. They lived in the canyon as farmers for almost seven hundred years but may have left the area because of severe drought and poor soil conditions. Some anthropologists think they may have relocated to the Hopi mesas, along with other Southwestern people, where they farmed around the spring-fed terraces.

Around A.D. 1300, the Cerbat Indians, whose descendants may be the Havasupai Indians who still live in the Grand Canyon, came to live here. These people adapted to the harsh living conditions by farming in the canyon in the summer and hunting and gathering on the rim during the fall and winter. Around the same time, the Southern Paiute Indians began making visits into the canyon to hunt deer but continued to roam throughout the Colorado Plateau.

GRAND CANYON LODGE

Perched on the very edge of the canyon, this beautiful old log lodge was built around 1926 by the Union Pacific Railroad. Stephen Mather, the first director of the National Park Service, commissioned Union Pacific to build a hotel to accommodate the increasing number of tourists. Gilbert Stanley Underwood, the architect who designed the Ahwahnee Hotel in Yosemite, designed this lodge. Constructed of native limestone during the harsh winter of 1927, the lodge was finished in 1928 at a cost of $350,000. But in 1932 a fire destroyed the original lodge. Four years later, the Utah Parks Co. rebuilt the lodge, again under the direction of Underwood, but it did not replace the original second story or the three-story tower.

Grand Canyon Lodge, North Rim, no date
Emery Kolb Collection, Cline Library, NAU PH 568-5616

A bronze statue of **Brighty,** the famous burro that lived and played on the North Rim in the 1930s, used to stand in the corner of the sun room, but Brighty now appears in front of the new visitors center. Marguerite Henry chronicled Brighty's exploits in her book *Brighty of the Grand Canyon,* written for children in 1953.

Rooms in the historic lodge are no longer available, but you can sleep close by in a cabin or motel room. A few cabins have a view of the canyon. The motel units are in the forest. Rates vary depending on the view and room amenities. Call for current pricing. Contact Xanterra Parks & Resorts (888) 29-PARKS, (888) 297-2757. Some cabins are wheelchair-accessible, and a wheelchair lift connects the dining room and lower patio.

Mule and Horse Rides: North Rim trail rides do not go to the river. One-hour rides along the rim and all-day rim or inner-canyon trips are usually available on a daily basis from mid May to mid October. Full-day trips into the canyon include lunch. Register in the lobby of the Grand Canyon Lodge at the Grand Canyon Trail Rides desk; open 7 a.m.–5 p.m. daily. For reservations call Grand Canyon Trail Rides, (435) 679-8665.

The Grand Canyon Lodge Dining Room: It is difficult to get a reservation for dinner unless you plan ahead. Call 928-638-2611, ext. 160, 10–11:30 a.m. and 2:30–4 p.m. daily to make reservations. Reservations can be made two weeks prior to opening, May 10. The dining room hours are:

breakfast 6:30–10:30 a.m.; lunch 11:30 a.m.–2:30 p.m.; dinner 4:45–9:45 p.m. Should you find yourself without a restaurant reservation, there is also a snack bar that serves pizza and fast food 6:30 a.m.–9 p.m. daily.

North Rim Campground: Located 1.5 miles (2.4 km) north and west of Grand Canyon Lodge. Open from mid-May to mid-October. Operated by the National Park Service; no hookups; dump station available. Laundry and showers located near the campground for a fee. Reservations are required; (800) 365-2267. Reservations may be made up to, but not more than, five months in advance.

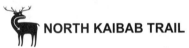

BRIGHT ANGEL POINT

This vista is a half mile (0.8 km) from the corner of the east patio behind Grand Canyon Lodge. At an elevation of 8,153 feet (2,487 m), this is the best vantage point to see and hear **Roaring Springs,** one of the most prominent places where water filtered through the Kaibab Limestone empties into the canyon.

NORTH KAIBAB TRAIL

You must have a permit for all overnight hiking in the Grand Canyon. Contact the Backcountry Reservations Office, (928) 638-2125, for a permit well in advance of your trip to the North Rim. There is a nonrefundable fee of $10 per permit plus $5 per person per night if camping below the rim.

The North Rim, like the South Rim, has had its share of business tycoons interested in developing the tourist trade. E. D. Wooley established the Grand Canyon Transportation Co. in 1903 to bring tourists from Kanab, Utah, to the canyon. To make trips possible from the North to South Rim, Wooley invested $5,000 in the Bright Angel Trail, and his son-in-law, David Rust, built a cable car across the river. This is the site of the present-day Kaibab Suspension Bridge that makes it possible for hikers to cross the river.

Rust set up some tents, built buildings, and planted trees at a site close by the river, but tourists never really used the site during his lifetime. Teddy Roosevelt stayed in the campground in 1913 while cougar hunting, and so everyone began calling it Roosevelt Camp. Mary Colter renamed it Phantom Ranch in 1922 when the Fred Harvey Co. took over the campground. (See page 37 for more on Phantom Ranch.)

To get to Phantom Ranch, the Colorado River, and the Bright Angel Trail, you must take the North Kaibab Trail. It is fourteen miles (22.5 km) one-way to the river, and the trail descends more than six thousand feet (1,830 m), making this a very difficult climb back up. *Do not* attempt this in one day. Take adequate water—about a gallon (4 liters) per person—and wear appropriate clothing and footwear. This is a very arduous trip and should not be approached lightly. Several people die every year in the canyon from dehydration, hypothermia, or falls.

Rust Camp, 1913
Emery Kolb Collection, Cline Library, Northern Arizona University, #526-4689

11 miles (22.5 km) from the junction of U.S. 89 and U.S. 160 to Tuba City

Mile 480.5 JUNCTION OF U.S. 89 AND U.S. 160

This desolate stretch of road is wavy because the earth under the asphalt is a soft layer of ancient silts and volcanic ash, which combine to form bentonite. When bentonite gets wet, it expands, causing the road to heave.

MM 312 HAMBLIN WASH (North)

Usually a dry streambed, this wash follows the base of the Echo Cliffs north along U.S. 89. It is named for Jacob Hamblin, a well-known Mormon explorer and missionary who first came to the Tuba City area in 1858. Hamblin explored this region at the request of Mormon Church leader Brigham Young, who wanted to colonize northern Arizona and develop a good relationship with the local natives. Hamblin Wash became part of the first route south from Utah's Mormon enclaves.

In 1870, Hamblin served as a guide for John Wesley Powell, the renowned explorer of the Grand Canyon and the Colorado River, taking him over the Mormon settlers' route from Lees Ferry, south along Echo Cliffs, then east to the Hopi mesas. After visiting the Hopis, Hamblin and Powell traveled on to Fort Defiance, where Hamblin met with Navajo leaders to negotiate a peace treaty between the Navajos and Mormons.

Mile 312.5 TUBA CITY AIRPORT (North)

This airport is little more than a paved airstrip, used primarily to transport Navajo and Hopi patients for any emergency medical care not available at the Tuba City Regional Health Care Center eleven miles (22.5 km) up the road. Its inconvenient and improbable location is the result of a compromise reached by the Navajo and Hopi tribes, which spent more than twenty-six years disputing ownership of thousands of acres surrounding this site.

MM 313 BADLANDS OF THE PAINTED DESERT

Topping the multicolored, banded plateau at 5,500 feet (1,677 m), the highway opens to a vast, treeless expanse. Here the land changes from tawny whites to burnished red. The soil's ancient silts and volcanic ash were formed during the dinosaur age. Once wet, the resulting bentonite clay swells and then cracks as it dries, making it easily eroded and unable to support any vegetation.

The Navajos call the Painted Desert *halchíítah*, or "Among the Colors." An incredibly beautiful place, especially at sunrise and sunset because of the bright shades of pink, gray, and green, this colorful collection of siltstone

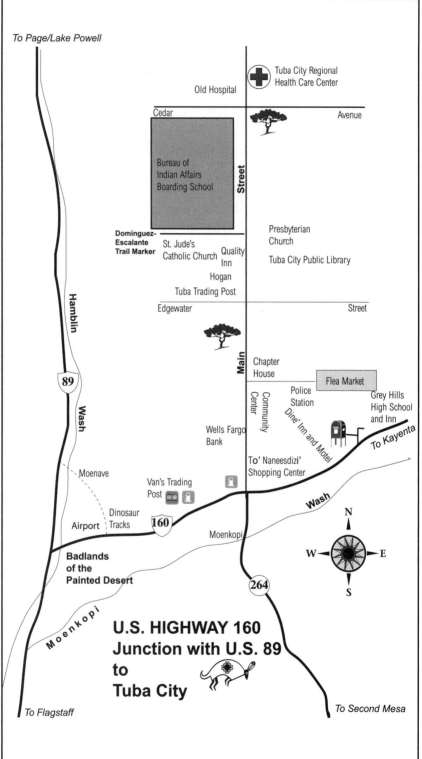

To Page/Lake Powell

Tuba City Regional
Health Care Center

Old Hospital

Cedar   Avenue

Bureau of
Indian Affairs
Boarding School

Street

Domínguez-
Escalante   St. Jude's   Presbyterian
Trail Marker   Catholic Church   Quality   Church
                                    Inn   Tuba City Public Library

Hamblin   Hogan

                  Tuba Trading Post

                  Edgewater   Street

Main

Wash   Chapter
                  House
                                    Flea Market
89   Police   Grey Hills
                  Community   Station   High School
                  Center   and Inn

                  Wells Fargo   Dine' Inn and Motel
                  Bank   To Kayenta

                  To' Naneesdizi'
Moenave   Shopping Center

                  Van's Trading   Wash
                  Post
Dinosaur
Airport Tracks   160

                  Moenkopi   N

Badlands   W   E
of the
Painted Desert   264   S

Moenkopi

**U.S. HIGHWAY 160
Junction with U.S. 89
to
Tuba City**

To Flagstaff   To Second Mesa

and shales is from the Owl Rock member of the Chinle Formation, formed more than 150 to 250 million years ago.

Mile 313.5 PHOTO OPPORTUNITY (North)

Decide quickly! The road rises up between the narrow sides—a huge gully, really—of the eroded edge of the plateau and quickly bends to the east. By then, you've probably missed the undeveloped turnoff (a left turn if traveling east) that takes you off the road onto the top of an isolated mesa, a "little sister," at the top of the hill. This is a great place to pull off, explore the desert, and take pictures of the lunar-like vistas of the northern Painted Desert.

MM 314 TUBA BUTTE (North)

An igneous intrusive formation.

Mile 316.25 BALANCING ROCKS (North)

About 200 million years ago, a warm-water ocean covered most of the western United States. On the edge of the water were marshes, swamps, and jungles. Dinosaurs thrived here until about 65 million years ago, when the western mountain ranges formed, blocking most of the moisture. The balancing rocks are the result of wind and water erosion of the softer sandstone.

Mile 316.5 DINOSAUR TRACKS (North)

Follow the signs to the roadside stands. Usually, an enterprising local Navajo will come to your car to offer services as a guide. Shake hands, introduce yourself, and the guide will show you to the tracks. A small gratuity of a couple dollars is appropriate. These tracks found in the Tuba City and Kayenta area in 1942 and other found in China in the 1980s are the world's only evidence of "running dinosaurs," which lived during the late Triassic/early Jurassic eras. The Dilophosaurus was a medium-sized dinosaur weighing approximately a thousand pounds (453 kg) and standing eight to ten feet (2.4–3.1 m) tall. It had powerful hind legs for running, with forefeet that resembled a bird's foot with four toes. The front arms were short with clawed fingers used for grasping. Although it had very sharp teeth, it probably used its hind legs and front claws to rip its prey.

The Dilophosaurus was depicted in the movie *Jurassic Park* as a venom-spitting creature that poisoned its victims before eating them. There is no evidence that the Tuba City Dilophosaurus poisoned its prey like its Hollywood cousin.

Dinosaur Tracks, ca. 1930s
Fred Harvey Collection, Museum of Northern Arizona Photo Archives, #301-3-149

Mile 316.5 MOENAVE (North)

Looking north from the dinosaur tracks you can see a green oasis at the base of Hamblin's Ridge, made up of Moenave Sandstone. More than a hundred years ago, the abundant springs here supported generations of Hopi farmers and, before them, prehistoric people. Between 1870 and 1904, a few Mormon settlers occupied the little canyon and developed its irrigation system. Since then, Navajos have lived and farmed here.

Mormon trailblazer Jacob Hamblin began farming here after making friends with Chief Tuuvi at the Hopi farming area of Moenkopi, today the Hopis' westernmost village. In 1874, Hamblin sold his homestead to John D. Lee, who used it to hide from authorities because of his part in the Mountain Meadows Massacre. Lee's stay in Moenave was only a short reprieve. Five months later lawmen caught him on a trip to Utah to visit his family. Taken back to Panguitch for trial, he was executed by a firing squad while standing in his own coffin. (For more information about the massacre, see pages 77–78).

Mile 318.5 IGNEOUS RIDGE AND SAND DUNE (South)

The ridge indicates that at one time there was some volcanic activity in this area, pushing lava to the surface to create this igneous formation.

MM 319 KAYENTA FORMATION (North)

The red rocks to the north are part of the Glen Canyon Group, formed during the late Triassic and early Jurassic eras around 180 to 230 million years ago. It consists of bright red sandstone, mudstone, and some limestone. Most of the dinosaur tracks in northern Arizona are preserved in the Kayenta Formation.

Mile 319.5 VAN'S TRADING POST (North)

The Vankeurens are one of the oldest trading families still operating a store in the Tuba City area. This location, at the foot of the mesa, is known to locals as Kerley Valley, named for John Kerley, another trader who was a partner in the Babbitt Bros. Trading Post in Tuba City. Finding the community of Tuba City too large for his liking, he moved to the "valley." Built in 1921, the old post sits right next to the gas company behind the new Van's Trading Post.

Kerley Trading Posts Bus, 1925
Warren Family Collection, Cline Library, Special Collections and Archives, NAU PH 4 12.2.88

HISTORIC DETOUR THROUGH TUBA CITY

Turn left at MM 322 and travel up Main Street. Just past the first stoplight is the Tuba Trading Post. The first Mormon settlers of the area gave this little town its moniker, naming the place after the Hopi called Tuuvi. He was from the village of Oraibi and a leader among the Moenkopi Hopi farmers. Tuuvi and his wife were the first Hopis to venture to Salt Lake City, meet Brigham Young, then-president of the Church of Jesus Christ of Latter Day Saints, and convert to the Mormon religion. It was Tuuvi who gave the first fourteen Mormon families a place in the area Hopis knew as "white sands" to build their town, away from the Hopi village, on the condition that they protect the Hopis and their fields from Navajo and Paiute raids. In his honor, the Mormons named it Tuba City.

Relations between the Mormons and natives were not always placid, especially after one of the dams built by the Mormons in 1877 broke, flooding the Hopis' crops. With the increased number of settlers moving into the area, Tuuvi told the Mormons that his people wanted to live in peace but that the settlers must stop building farms next to every available spring.

Tuba City was also a half-way station for Mormon settlers traveling south from Utah to develop communities along the Colorado River. In 1871, John D. Lee was "called" by LDS church president Brigham Young to establish a crossing on the Colorado. Situated sixty miles (97 km) north of Tuba City, Lees Ferry became the only reliable river crossing for hundreds of miles in either direction, easing an already hazardous journey for Mormon pioneers and other travelers.

In 1878, Erastus Snow platted the town of Tuba City, patterning it after a typical Mormon community, with wide streets lined by Lombardy poplars. By 1900, there were 150 settlers living in the community. Farming was the Mormons' primary interest, and much of the area where the hospital sits today, north of Cedar Avenue, was an apple orchard.

Mormon occupation was short-lived, however, after the Tuba City area was added to the Navajo Reservation. The government pressured the Mormons to sell their homes, farms, orchards, and other improvements for a total of $48,000, and in 1904 they left for good. They reestablished themselves in places like Snowflake and Woodruff, Arizona, and Farmington and Gallup, New Mexico.

A NATURAL OASIS

The Navajo name for Tuba City is *Tónaneesdizi,* which means "Many Springs" or "Tangled Water," for the desert rivulets discharging from an underground aquifer.

The most famous water source in the area is a spring named for Mr. Charlie Day, whose hogan was next to the spring and who once served as an Army scout. In 1928, Bureau of Indian Affairs superintendent Walker ordered the development of the spring. While digging, the construction crew found fossils that the University of Pennsylvania and the American Museum of Natural History identified as extinct mammals. Among the skeletons recovered were camelops, similar to the South American llama; bison larger than those of present day; *Equus,* a type of horse that became extinct in North America during the Ice Age; and *Elephas columbi,* a mammoth about the same size as an African elephant.

Why are there springs in the desert?

Rainwater falls on the porous sandstone and seeps into the underlying clay layers. Tuba City is especially blessed because it is south of the Kaibito Plateau, a large mass of sandstone that collects water and carries it through natural underground clay layers to Tuba City, where it bubbles up as cool, naturally pure drinking water.

TUBA CITY TRADING POST

This famous landmark was first opened in 1870 by Charles Algert, who hired store clerk Samual Preston to run the post for him. Preston later became a partner with the Babbitt brothers, who bought out Algert in 1902. Preston built the big, beautiful, hogan-shaped portion of the post after becoming a partner. It's constructed of locally quarried blue limestone, with logs hauled in from the San Francisco Peaks near Flagstaff.

The Babbitt family, which also owns the CO Bar Ranch on U.S. 89, has played a major role in the Indian trading business for more than a century. They got into Indian trading inadvertently, acquiring ownership of the Red Lake Trading Post in 1891 after its previous owner was shot and killed by a jealous lover. (See page 149 for more about Red Lake.)

Tuba Trading Post, ca. 1930s
Fred Harvey Collection, Museum of Northern Arizona Photo Archives 301-3-328T

Like other traders, the Babbitts were attracted to the reservation because of the country's need for wool. In exchange for one sackful worth about $3 to $4, they traded food, clothing, tobacco, medicine, tools, and kerosene to Navajo sheep herders.

Teddy Roosevelt stayed at the Tuba Trading Post with the Prestons in 1913 on his return from a mountain lion hunt on the North Rim of the Grand

Canyon. Zane Grey also was a frequent visitor, and several films based on his books were shot in and around Tuba City.

Still a working trading post, it offers many items traded or bought from local artists: silver jewelry, sandpaintings, katsina dolls, and Navajo rugs. The post also has a wonderful assortment of T-shirts and books about the Southwest. The trading post is now owned and operated by the Navajo Nation Division of Tourism and honors daylight saving time from the first week in April to the last week in October. Hours: Monday through Friday 8 a.m.–6 p.m. and weekends 8 a.m.–5 p.m. (928) 283-5441.

NAVAJO HOGAN (Just north of the trading post)

Hooghan, pronounced in Navajo as "HO-whan," is the word for "home" and has come to also mean the traditionally round or octagonal dwelling used for living or ceremonies. Whether mud-covered, built of logs or stone, or made from 2 x 4s and plywood, a hogan is a hogan to Navajos. Common to them all, however, is that their doors always face east to the rising sun.

Inside the hogan, life is organized in a specific way. Food is prepared and stored in the northeast corner. Tools for making a living are on the southeast corner. Spiritual paraphernalia are kept in the northwest corner, and beds are stored in the southwest corner. Today, many Navajo families live in modern houses or trailers, using the hogan primarily for ceremonial purposes.

Most trading posts had guest hogans available for Navajo families who traveled long distances to trade at their particular post. To encourage business, many traders sponsored horse races, chicken pulls, and ceremonials. In the past a "chicken pull" was exactly what its name implies. A rooster is buried in the sand up to its neck, and two horsemen, riding bareback, compete to see who can pull the rooster out of the sand first. Since the 1920s this practice has been replaced with the more humane use of a gunny sack instead of a rooster.

ST. JUDE CATHOLIC MISSION

Turn left past the Quality Inn, and the church is on the left about a half mile (.8 km) down the road. John Kerley sent a request in the early 1900s to the Franciscan friars at St. Michaels, located west of Window Rock, to start a mission in Tuba City. The reason he gave was that "they are tired of preachers." At the time of the request Kerley was still a partner with the Babbitt brothers, who offered an acre (.004 sq km) of land and $50 to cover the friars' travel expenses. Kerley and his partners felt that the community of Tuba City needed a more liberal-minded religious leader who smoked and would not condemn "drinking, picnics, card parties, picture shows, etc."

Kerley further explained that this restrictive approach to Christianity had "put the so-called Christian workers to the bad with the Indians and most of the whites on this part of the reservation." The Franciscans couldn't honor the trader's request at the time because of the cost of housing a priest in such a remote location. It wasn't until 1951 that Father Elmer Von Hagel, superior at St. Michaels, made the 330-mile (532 km) roundtrip journey over dirt roads to deliver mass once a month. Finally, in 1962 funds were made available to build a permanent church.

Next to the rectory is a Domínguez-Escalante Trail Marker commemorating those priests' historic trip through Tuba City. (See pages 68–69 for more information on the Domínguez-Escalante Trail.)

Historic Krenz-Kerley Trading Post (now the Tuba City Public Library)
Photo ca. 1917, courtesy of Lindell Cornelison, former Tuba City Postmaster

KRENZ-KERLEY TRADING POST/TUBA CITY PUBLIC LIBRARY

On the east side of Main Street, across the street and north of the Quality Inn, is a historic trading post built by Fred Krenz, an accomplished builder who played a part in constructing many of the BIA schools on the reservation. But when he decided to try his hand at trading, he was described by the *Coconino Sun,* which frequently wrote about Indian traders' social lives, as "the ubiquitous Indian trading poster of Tuba City." It seems that Fred was never at his post, always traveling to Flagstaff, Phoenix, and Albuquerque. According to Fred's four sons, who are alive and well living in various parts of California, John left his post frequently to court their mother. Once he won her hand, he sold his post to the Babbitt brothers and took up the life of a rancher in southern Arizona.

John Kerley gained control of the post in the early 1920s as part of the Babbitt company and used it while the Tuba Trading Post was being refurbished. Because Kerley was such an outgoing and likeable guy, everyone began refering to the Krenz building as "Kerley's Trading Post." The building now houses the Tuba City Public Library.

MOVIE LOCATION

Fictional Navajo police officer Jim Chee, one of mystery writer Tony Hillerman's two principal protagonists, transfers to Tuba City from Shiprock at the opening of *The Dark Wind.* His assignment is to determine who is vandalizing an important windmill. Through his legwork, he comes to learn how important desert springs are to the Hopi people, as well as the motives behind the murder of a Navajo and the burglary of the Burnt Water Trading Post. The basis of the story centers around the Anglo concept of revenge, which is foreign to Navajos. It is this "dark wind" that makes the white men behave in illogical ways, out of harmony with the natural order of things.

The Dark Wind was Robert Redford's first attempt to bring a Hillerman novel to the screen. For authenticity, Redford filmed the production in the Tuba City/Red Lake area. Redford's Wildwood Productions leased the Krenz Building from the BIA to house a papier mâché set of a Hopi village. When the film was wrapped, the crew left the set behind, complete with a lifelike fireplace. Children got into the building and started a fire in the fireplace, burning off the second floor and roof. Tuba City Cultural Projects, Inc., a local historic preservation group, renovated the building for reuse as a regional public library.

FIRST PRESBYTERIAN CHURCH

Just past the library is the first of six Presbyterian churches built on the Navajo Reservation. Located right across from the boarding school, this limestone block church was part of the 1869 Grant Peace Policy. The government assigned the Presbyterians to the reservation to provide religious instruction and to "civilize" the Indians. The boarding school wasn't built until 1905, but in 1896, the Presbyterians established a mission in Kerley Valley.

The San Juan Southern Paiutes have set up a health department in the basement of the church annex. Because they do not have a land base of their own, the Paiutes are forced to lease space from existing agencies. Their administrative offices are in Grey Hills Academy High School. (See pages 56–57 for more on the San Juan Southern Paiutes.)

BUREAU OF INDIAN AFFAIRS BOARDING SCHOOL

The compound starts to the north of the Quality Inn and extends all the way to Cedar Avenue. Construction of this large school began in 1905, one year after the federal government bought the homes, farms, and improvements of the first Mormon settlers and forced them to leave.

Navajo and Hopi stonemasons quarried sandstone from the nearby Moenkopi Wash and hauled it to the boarding school site for fifty cents a load. When finished, the school accommodated only seventy-five students because the design included space for classrooms, a cafeteria, an infirmary, and a place for the staff to live.

The BIA's educational philosophy of the early 1900s emphasized Christianizing and assimilating Indians into mainstream America. Students had to wear uniforms, cut their hair, march military style, and work at manual labor. They were ordered never to speak their own language nor to use corn pollen to pray to the Holy People, the Navajo deities. Students were taught how to farm and master skills such as carpentry to enable them to work successfully in the "Anglo" world once they graduated from school.

By 1910, the Tuba City Boarding School was completely self-sufficient. It operated a two-hundred-acre (0.8 sq km) farm with cows and chickens, a bakery, a laundry, and a carpentry shop. Students attended school half the day and worked in the fields for the remainder. Days were very long and joyless, with the bugle waking them in the morning and announcing the end of the day at sunset.

By 1911, more than 1,500 Navajo families were living in the Tuba City area, but only one hundred students enrolled in school. In 1912, approval came from Washington to build the assembly hall in the center of the campus so more students could attend.

Understandably, many Navajo families hid their children from school authorities in an attempt to keep them at home. Methods used by the BIA to enroll students were less than honorable. At times, school agents kidnapped children found away from their parents. To many children, living in a huge, sterile room with high ceilings, far from the warmth and security of their large families and womb-like hogans, school was not at all a positive learning or living experience. Dorm aides and teachers were no replacement for their own parents, aunts, and uncles. Many children grew up in boarding school without nurturing or knowledge of their traditional heritage. Some could no longer speak Navajo by the time they were released from school.

In 1920, the country's attitude about the education of American Indians began to change. The Indian Citizenship Act of 1924 gave them the right to vote. The Meriam Report, commissioned by the secretary of the interior to study the quality of education and health care provided to Native Americans, urged the involvement of family and community in education. The report, prepared by the Institute for Government Research, now known as the Brookings Institution, was published in 1928. For the first time, the Indian point of view became important in the classroom.

The federal commissioner of Indian affairs, John Collier, attempted to implement the suggestions of the Meriam Report in the 1930s. His goals were to provide a modern, scientific education to every Indian, and to replace the boarding-school system with day schools so students could go home to their families at night.

In 1950, the Johnson O'Malley Act made it possible for Navajo children to attend public school with funding from the BIA. It is because of this law that Tuba City and other communities on the reservation have both BIA day and boarding schools as well as state-funded public schools.

Tuba City Boarding School student sitting in front of dormitory, ca. 1918–1920 Marie Olson Collection, Cline Library, Special Collections and Archives, NAU 516-105. *Marie Olson was a nurse in Tuba City from 1918 to 1920. The historic dormitory in the background was torn down in 2004.*

TUBA CITY REGIONAL HEALTH CARE CENTER

Just past the four-way stop sign, a half-mile (.8 km) north of the trading post, on the west side of the road is the "old" Tuba City Hospital, which today houses a tribally run alcohol rehabilitation program. Behind that building is the oldest Tuba City hospital, which in 1914 began to serve the boarding school students. It was an eight-bed hospital with no electricity. The first physician was Dr. Campbell, who frequently made hogan visits on horseback or by wagon.

In 2000, the Indian Health Service, under the United States Public Health Service, turned the operation of this hospital over to an all-volunteer Native American board of directors under Public Law 98-638. This is an eighty-five-bed hospital with a service population of approximately 26,000 people. It operates a very busy ambulatory care and emergency room department as well as a large community program promoting health and disease prevention.

All Indian Health Service (IHS) clinics and hospitals on the Navajo and Hopi Reservations are strictly for the care of tribally enrolled Native Americans with census numbers, as well as IHS-commissioned officers and their dependents. Non-natives may be seen on an emergency basis only. Health insurance is accepted. In an emergency, non-natives are admitted to the intensive care unit until they are stable enough to be transferred by airplane or ambulance to the nearest private hospital. The emergency room number is (928) 283-2661. There is also a 911 number in the Tuba City, Kayenta, and Chilchinbito areas.

STORM PATTERN RUG DESIGN

Storm Pattern, ca. 1920–1940
Photograph by Gene Balzer, Museum of Northern Arizona

The "storm pattern" design, developed in the Tuba City area, is a vivid representation of the region's weather. Its design holds symbolic meaning for the Navajo people. The center of the rug represents the center of the universe or the hogan. The squares or triangles in the four corners of the rug are the four sacred mountains, and the zigzag lines represent lightning bolts. The border of the rug usually has numerous symbols such as clouds, beetles, and feathers, but the main pattern of the rug shown above has a more Christian theme.

SERVICES IN TUBA CITY

Lodging

Diné Inn Motel Next to the Bashas' shopping center. (928) 283-6107.

Quality Inn A new eighty-room motel decorated in a Southwestern style. Rooms are moderately priced. It fills up fast in the summer. Reservations: (800) 644-8383; (928) 283-4545.

RV Park Register at the Quality Inn. Full hookups, shower, bathroom, pay phone, laundry room, cable.

Greyhills Inn On Warrior Drive off U.S. 160. Head northeast, take a left at the post office, then the first right, and the inn office is through the gate on the left. Greyhills Academy converted one dormitory into a thirty-two-room hostel for tourists. Most rooms have full or queen beds; some king beds available. Every room has a television. Dormitory-style bathrooms. Prices are in the budget range. You can make reservations by calling the Grey Hills High School switchboard, (928) 283-6271 or (800) 283-6271. The inn does not accept credit cards, but they will hold your room until 7 p.m.

Flea Market: Every Friday from about 9 a.m. to 3 p.m. behind the Chapter House on Main Street, you can get homemade mutton stew and frybread and good prices on jewelry, Navajo pottery, herbs, and unusual items.

Groceries: Bashas' is the major food store on the reservation. Prices are higher than off-reservation, but they have a good selection and an excellent produce section. Bashas' has stores in Tuba City, Chinle, Kayenta, and Window Rock. Open 8 a.m.–10 p.m. Monday through Saturday, and 8 a.m.–8 p.m. on Sunday. There is an ATM inside.

Banking Services: Wells Fargo Bank is about midway down the four-lane stretch of Main Street, next to Kentucky Fried Chicken. Monday–Thursday 9 a.m.–5 p.m.; Friday 9 a.m.–6 p.m., closed Saturday and Sunday. 24-hour ATM.

Tuba City Navajo Police: On the east side of Main Street next to the tribal courthouse. (928) 283-3111. Jim Chee, Tony Hillerman's fictitious police officer, transferred to this station from Shiprock.

END SCENIC DETOUR

160 miles (258 km) from Tuba City to Keams Canyon

NOTE: The Hopi Nation stays on mountain standard time throughout the year.

 THE HOPI NATION

The Hopi (pronounced HO-pee) have always lived in the Four Corners area of the Colorado Plateau. Even though the legal boundary of today's reservation has confined them to a relatively small land mass in comparison to the Navajos' reservation, evidence of their influence via trading and clan symbols is found at the ruins of Betatakin, Keet Seel, Mesa Verde, and as far east as Chaco Canyon.

The Hopis' aboriginal boundaries, or *tutsqua,* established by tradition and history, are Navajo Mountain to the north, down the Colorado River to Bill Williams Mountain to the west, over to the San Francisco Peaks or *Nuvatukya'ovi,* along the Mogollon Rim to the Zunis' Blue Lake for the southern boundary, and north to Canyon de Chelly and the Four Corners area for the eastern boundary.

The Hopis emerged from the underworld through a *sipapu,* an opening, in the Grand Canyon. They came into this, the Fourth World, with the help of a small bird known as the shrike, which brought them into the world of light. Here they made their vow of righteous living to *Sootukwnangwu,* the Supreme Creator. *Masauwu,* the guardian spirit over the land, told the Hopis that they were to serve as the earth's steward once their mandated four migrations to the north, south, east, and west in search of *tuuwanasave,* or "earth center," had come to an end. According to legend, the Hopis traveled to the Aztec temples in Mexico, on into South America, north to the Arctic Circle and to the east and west coasts of the United States. The center point of the cross formed from their four directional routes is the Hopi mesas. This was the chosen place because it was a harsh environment where adherence to the laws of the Supreme Creator must be followed exactly to ensure the survival of the clans.

It is believed that the Bear Clan, *Honwungwa,* was the first to arrive on the remote, barren Hopi mesas. As the many different clans began to arrive from their migrations, the Bear Clan asked what they could contribute to the benefit of all of the Hopi people. Each clan contributed a different skill or ceremony to ensure the survival and prosperity of all people on earth. One of the more important ceremonies contributed by the Bear Clan was the *Soyal,* an annual winter solstice ceremony. The Greasewood clan of Apache descent gather sacred wood for ceremonies as their special contribution.

To Page

To Kayenta

160

MOENKOPI WASH

Blue Canyon

Big Mountain

Tuba City

Moenkopi

Coal Mine Canyon

B L A C K   M E S A

Coal Mine Mesa

264

Dinnebito

THIRD MESA

SECOND MESA

Bacavi

Hotevilla

6 miles Kykotsmovi to Second Mesa

Old Oraibi

Kykotsmovi

Second Mesa Museum and Cultural Center

FIRST MESA

Walpi

Schimovi

N

Shungopavi

Shipalovi

W   **E**

Mishongovi

Hano

Second Mesa Trading Post

Polacca

S

15 miles Second Mesa to Polacca

11 miles Polacca to Keams Canyon

Hopi Buttes

87

Keams Canyon

ARIZONA HIGHWAY 264 East
Tuba City
to
Keams Canyon

89

Flagstaff

40

Winslow

To Holbrook

The Hopis have strictly adhered to a sophisticated ceremonial calendar. Specific holy men in each village continue to determine the timing of individual ceremonies by the position of the sun, making it difficult for outsiders to know exactly when a ceremony will take place.

Katsinas, or kachinas, as they are popularly called, are the very important spirit beings in Hopi cosmology who assure rain for the Hopis and all people on earth. The katsinas visit the Hopis and bring gifts. At the end of a dance, prayer feathers are given to the katsinas so that the prayers for rain and good things will be carried in all directions.

The Home Dance, or *Niman,* is the last katsina dance in the ceremonial calendar. This is when the katsinas leave the mesas to return to their home on the San Francisco Peaks. These dances are the way of communicating the Hopis' needs to the Supreme Creator.

Antelope Kiva, Walpi, First Mesa, ca. 1904–1906
Jo Mora Collection, Cline Library, Special Collections and Archive, NAU 281.
Jo Mora was an artist who lived with the Hopis from 1904 to 1907. He learned their language and was permitted to photograph the Hopi villages, people, and ceremonies.

Katsina dances are no longer always open to non-Hopis. For years, traders, and most recently tour companies, have brought tourists by the hundreds to view the ceremonies. But the villages and ancient rooftops were not designed to handle large crowds. More seriously, visitors have violated the Hopis' rules about not photographing or videotaping anything in the villages. This has resulted in the posting of "closed" signs at the road entrance during a dance. Do not enter a village if you see one of these signs.

Each village has a number of kivas, or underground chambers, entered through a hole in the roof. Specific societies use the kivas for meditation, prayer, and preparation for their own important ceremonies.

The Hopis knew through prophesy that they would be visited someday by a strange and powerful people who would be their white brother, *pahaana.* Hopi legend explains that all people, including white people, came from the underworld with the Hopis. Their white brother became separated during the migrations but promised to return as the savior.

The Spanish were the first to visit the Hopis around 1540, led by gold-hungry Coronado. During this time, many Spanish adventurers sought the Seven Golden Cities of Cíbola. The legend tells of a bishop who, during the Moors' invasion of Spain, escaped to the west on boats with more than 1,500 people. He allegedly established a community so lavish that its inhabitants used golden implements.

After finding the Zuni villages in New Mexico not to be the fabled seven golden cities he sought, Coronado sent Don Pedro de Tovar to investigate the Hopi villages. Indian informants had described a golden land where the Hopis lived. Coronado, not realizing that Indians had never seen gold, took their description literally. Perhaps what Coronado actually heard was a description of the yellow pottery made in the Jeddito area.

To recoup the expense of their expedition to this new country, the Spanish saw value in making the Hopi people slaves and converting them to Christianity. Franciscan monks descended upon the Hopi villages and began to build churches, often right over sacred springs and shrines. One was believed to have been built over a kiva. In addition to enslaving the Hopi people, the Spanish almost wiped them out with an epidemic of smallpox in 1634. Within a few years, seven thousand Hopis—three-quarters of the entire tribe—would be dead from this disease.

It wasn't long before the Hopis realized this was not the prophesied white savior. Tired of subjugation by the Spanish, and to protect their own beliefs and spiritual practices, all of the pueblo villages along the Rio Grande joined with the Zunis and Hopis in 1680 to secretly rise up and forcefully expel the Spanish from their land. Missionaries were killed and their churches destroyed. Totally beaten, the Spanish withdrew. Yet it was only a short twenty-one years after this Pueblo Revolt that, in 1701, the Spanish returned to Hopi land to establish another mission at Awat'ovi, intent on their goal to "convert the pagans."

Again, to the traditional majority, this encroachment on Hopi life and beliefs was intolerable. In 1703, the Hopi villages conspired to destroy the Franciscan monks and converted Hopi men living in Awat'ovi. The women and children were dispersed to other villages. (Today this village is in ruins.)

In 1810, Mexico won its independence from Spain, also ending Spanish domination of this area. This transfer of power placed the Hopis under Mexican rule, but Mexico was unable to protect the Hopis from constant damaging attacks by Navajo, Apache, and Ute raiders. With the signing of the Treaty of Guadalupe Hidalgo in 1840 between Mexico and the United States, the Hopis fell under the jurisdiction of the United States. In 1882, President Chester A. Arthur signed an executive order to create a 2.5-million-acre (10,156 sq km) Hopi reservation. But the new reservation boundaries took into consideration neither the Hopis' traditional use of the surrounding land nor the geography of the region.

Although the founders of the U.S. Constitution believed in the concept of religious freedom, they were thinking of Christian values, not centuries-old Native American religions and cultures. Government officials believed it was their responsibility to impart to the Indians the blessing of civilization. To do this, the Grant Peace Policy was passed in 1869 to allow the Office of Indian Affairs to facilitate placement of ministers among the Indians. Christian missionaries of all denominations began to arrive in Indian country, but the ones to have the most impact on the Hopi people were the Mennonites and The Church of Jesus Christ of Latter Day Saints, or the Mormons.

In 1830, *The Book of Mormon* was published. God had revealed to Joseph Smith, founder of the religion, that American Indians were the lost tribe of Israel, which traveled from Palestine only six hundred years prior to his revelation. For neglecting the true religion, Smith believed Indians, whom he called "Lamanites," were cursed with dark skin. If they could hear the word of God and convert to Mormonism, their dark skin would become "white and delightsome," and their past transgressions would be forgiven.

RULES ABOUT VISITING HOPI VILLAGES
1. Disruption of shrines or removal of articles is not allowed. All archaeological sites on the Hopi Reservation are protected by federal law and Hopi tribal ordinance.
2. Photographing, recording, and sketching villages and ceremonies are strictly prohibited.
3. Overnight camping is allowed for a maximum of two nights at designated camping areas only.
4. Alcoholic beverages and drugs are strictly prohibited.
5. Before spending any length of time in any village, permission should be obtained from the village leader.
6. Each village is autonomous and has the authority to establish its own governing policies supported by the Hopi Tribal Council. It is advisable to check with village community development offices before going into the village to visit or watch a ceremony.

ATTENDING A HOPI CEREMONY

All Hopi ceremonies are highly spiritual in content and should be viewed and respected as such. Dance participants are required to prepare extensively to accomplish the spiritual mission of the ceremony. Likewise, spectators are expected to provide their heartfelt prayers during the public viewing. In this way the collective positive energy will benefit all of the people on earth.

Dress is important, and visitors should pay attention to this detail because of their important role in the success of the ceremony. Men should wear long pants and shirts. Women should wear clothing that completely covers the body. Hats and umbrellas are discouraged. During the ceremony do not ask questions or discuss the events. Do not follow the katsinas or ceremonial participants out of the plaza. Choose a place to observe the ceremony and do not walk around the plaza or the village.

 MOENKOPI VILLAGE *(Munqapi)*

Head east on Highway 264 about one mile. When Mormon explorer Jacob Hamblin met the Hopis in 1858, there was no permanent village here. Hopis gradually built the village beginning around 1870. Hopi farmers from the village of Oraibi, more than thirty miles (48 km) away by trail, managed large cotton farms in the very fertile Moenkopi Wash, running several times a week from home to their fields.

In 1879, Hamblin met Tuuvi, the Oraibi chief of the Water and Corn Clans, farming at Moenkopi. They developed a close relationship, which eventually led to the establishment of the first Mormon colony at Moenave, eight miles farther west.

Tuuvi and his wife, Katsinmana, agreed to be Hamblin's guests in Utah for a year to learn about the Mormon way of farming and religion. The Mormons' high-speed loom greatly impressed Tuuvi.

Brigham Young's son, John, probably encouraged by Tuuvi's impression of the looms, built a woolen mill at Moenkopi. But the Hopi weavers, who had woven cotton on hand looms for generations, were not interested in a new vocation.

On the south side of Highway 264, overlooking Moenkopi, is an Arizona historical marker placed here in 1957 by the Arizona Economic Development Board. Although the face-piece is missing, it should say: "Near here in 1879 Mormon colonists built Arizona's first Woolen Mill. Hoping to utilize Hopi and Navajo wool and labor, the Mormons intended to build a new industry to supply the early settlers. The 192-spindle mill operated only a short time, its abandonment signaling failure of the missionary movement among the Hopi." The last statement may be true, but technically the Mormons were forced to abandoned the mill in 1903 because of the government's demand that they leave the newly expanded Navajo Reservation.

Hopi Weaver, ca. 1913–1934
Leo Crane Collection, Cline Library, Special Collections and Archives, NAU PH 658.220

One of Hamblin's original reasons for developing a relationship with the Hopis was to encourage them to move north of the Colorado River. Brigham Young thought that friendly Indians could serve as a buffer against more hostile groups like the Utes and the Navajos. Speculation is that Hamblin strongly encouraged the development of a permanent Hopi settlement in Moenkopi for the same reason: to provide protection to the Tuba City Mormon settlement.

Present-day Moenkopi actually consists of two villages. Upper Moenkopi is the more modern, established in the 1930s around the Bureau of Indian Affairs Day School. Lower Moenkopi is more traditional in its lifestyle, maintaining close religious ties to Old Oraibi.

Moenkopi Community Development Office: Call for permission to tour the village; (928) 283-6684. Office hours: 8 a.m.–5 p.m. Monday through Friday. Closed weekends.

 Mile 324.5 MOENKOPI WASH

Moenkopi Wash is one of five washes that drain Black Mesa. This major drainage, made primarily of Chinle Sandstone, forms the lower section of Blue Canyon. An older name for this wash, found on the Domínguez-Escalante map of 1776, is Cosonias. (*Cosonias* was the Hopi word for the

Havasupai Indians, who lived in the area prior to losing their land rights after the expansion of the Navajo Reservation in 1903.)

MM 336 COAL MINE CHAPTER AND SUBDIVISION (South)

This is one of 110 community units, called chapters, that govern local matters on the Navajo Reservation. Hours: 8 a.m.–5 p.m. Monday–Friday; (928) 283-3383. This newly created community is a result of the Navajo-Hopi land dispute, requiring the removal of Navajo families from Hopi land. (See pages 118–119 for an explanation of this ongoing controversy.)

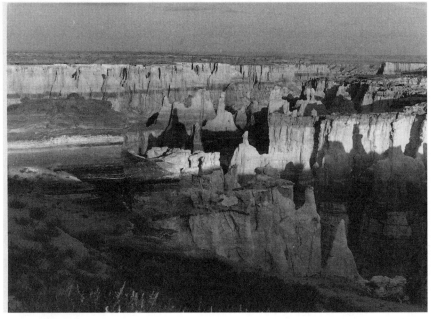

MM 336 COAL MINE CANYON (North)

Head north on the dirt road leading to the windmill. No services. This magnificent canyon is easily missed if you don't have the right map or are looking the wrong way as you drive by. It's known to the Navajo as *hááhonoojí,* meaning "jagged," which describes the erosion patterns in the canyon. Its top layer is Dakota Sandstone overlying Cowsprings Sandstone.

Coal Mine Canyon
Photograph by Christine Stephenson

Everyone in the local communities of Tuba City and the Hopi villages knows about the existence of the canyon ghost seen only during a full moon. In an article in *Outdoor Arizona,* the author tells the story of a ghost figure named *Quayowuuti,* or Eagle Woman, from Old Oraibi. She allegedly became mentally ill and wandered away from the village on the path to Moenkopi.

Along the way, she stopped to rest on the rim of the canyon and decided to end it all. Ever since, when the conditions are just right, her spirit will appear during the full moon.

Entrance to a coal mine at Coal Mine Canyon, ca. 1918–1920
Marie Olson Collection, Cline Library, Special Collections and Archives, NAU PH 16-17

The Mormons began to mine coal here in the late 1800s to heat their new homes in Tuba City. After the Bureau of Indian Affairs built the boarding school, the old coal mine was reopened around 1908 to fuel the steam generators to heat the entire complex. Because of the poor quality of the coal, however, it was never mined commercially, saving this beautiful canyon from the removal of its more than eight feet (.4 m) of coal. Coal Mine Canyon turns into Blue Canyon along the Moenkopi Wash heading east toward Red Lake on U.S. Highway 160.

Blue Canyon, 1927
Philip Johnston Collection, Cline Library, Special Collections and Archives, NAU, 413-53

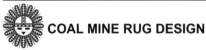 **COAL MINE RUG DESIGN**

In the 1970s, Dr. Ned Hatathli, once the manager of the Navajo Arts and Crafts Guild, and later the first president of Navajo Community College, encouraged weavers to add threads to outline the geometric designs in their rugs. Unfortunately, many important weavers of the Coal Mine Mesa area have relocated because they were on the wrong side of the 1979 boundary separating the Navajo and Hopi Reservations. (See MM 362.)

 348
MM 350 PANORAMIC VIEW

If you are heading east, look to your left (north). In your line of vision, from left to right are Preston Mesa, White Mesa, Wildcat Butte, and Navajo Mountain. See Chapter 10 for more information on these geologic features.

 MM 362 ROAD TO DINNEBITO (North)

In Navajo, *diné bitó* means "Navajo water." This community got its name because of the many springs that are fed from Third Mesa on the east and from the Moenkopi Plateau on the west, making this a prime agricultural and grazing area. The famous Navajo leader Narbona moved his family here from the Chuska Mountains sometime during the severe drought of 1820. He successfully farmed side by side with the Hopis for nine years. Two of his sons and one daughter married Hopis. When the drought lifted, he moved his family back to their ancestral home in the Chuska Mountains. (See page 226 for more information about Narbona.)

 BIG MOUNTAIN

About twenty miles (32 km) north of the Dinnebito Trading Post on an unimproved dirt road is the sacred and controversial Big Mountain. This area has long symbolized Navajo resistance to federally mandated relocation resulting from the Navajo-Hopi land dispute and the 1974 Navajo-Hopi Relocation Act.

In 1882, when President Chester A. Arthur set aside 2.5 million acres (10,156 sq km) of land for the Hopi Reservation, he used the words stipulating that the new reservation was for the Hopis "and such other Indians as the Secretary of Interior sees fit to settle thereon." Prior to that, and following their release from imprisonment in 1868, Navajos migrated into the area looking for good grazing land and were residing there when the land became part of the Hopi Reservation.

However, after a century, the Hopis were increasingly unhappy with what they saw as encroachment onto their land. In 1958, the federal government authorized a lawsuit between the tribes to determine which one actually held title to the land. The 1962 case of *Healing vs. Jones* created the Navajo-Hopi Joint Use Area, popularly known as the JUA. It gave the Hopis exclusive rights to the District Six grazing area surrounding their villages. But because the Hopis alleged that the Navajos still would not allow them to use the land, they took the situation to Congress for resolution.

In 1974, the Hopis succeeded in getting Congress to pass P.L. 93-531, the Navajo-Hopi Relocation Act. Ultimately, the law called for the division of the former JUA, leaving each tribe with 911,000 acres (3,701 sq km) of the land. It also called for the removal of families living on the other tribe's land, meaning the relocation of some 12,000 Navajos and 100 Hopis.

Since the beginning of this tribal land dispute (which most authorities now agree was created and exacerbated by the federal government), there has been Navajo resistance to the law and relocation. Today, about 250 Navajos continue to resist, and in 1989, these Navajos—independent of the Navajo Nation—filed a First Amendment religious freedom lawsuit, arguing that forced relocation impinged on their right to practice their traditional, land-based religion. The case, *Manybeads vs. United States,* 90-15003, was rejected by the Ninth U.S. Circuit Court of Appeals in 2000 and as a result of this ruling cannot proceed to the U.S. Supreme Court. Because the Hopi Tribe refused to participate and cannot be sued in federal court without its consent, the case is essentially over. Now the only alternative for the Big Mountain "resistors" is to sign lease agreements with the Hopi Tribe or face eviction.

THIRD MESA

Because early explorers entered the Hopi villages from the east, the mesa sitting on the southernmost tip of Black Mesa became First Mesa, with Second Mesa and Third Mesa following.

NOTE: For visitors traveling east, skip ahead to MM 371 and read about Old Oraibi first, then Mile 367.25 on Hotevilla, and then Bacavi to better understand the history behind the founding of these three villages.

 MM 367 BACAVI (North) *(Paaqavi)*

In Hopi, *Paaqavi* means "Place of the Jointed Reed." While the "hostile" leader Yukioma of Hotevilla was imprisoned at Fort Wingate, his people suffered terribly from lack of food. The first winter was particularly difficult. Hoping for reconciliation, a small group returned to Oraibi but were no longer welcome. In 1907, this displaced group started the community of Bacavi.

Even though the founders of this village were considered hostile to the U.S. government, they did consent to a BIA day school, built here in 1911, and allowed the Mennonite Church to build a mission in 1916. For a complete history of the founding of Bacavi, read *Bacavi: Journey to Reed Springs* by Peter Whiteley.

Bacavi Community Development Office: Call for permission to tour the village; (928) 734-2404. Office hours: 8 a.m.– 5 p.m., Monday–Friday.

Corn Planter from Bacavi Village, ca. 1914
Leo Crane Collection, Cline Library, Special Collections and Archives, NAU PH 658.39289
Leo Crane was the Indian agent at Keams Canyon beginning in 1911.

 Mile 367.25 HOTEVILLA (South) *(Hotvela)*

A common translation for Hotevilla is *hota,* "a back," and *veli,* "to peel," referring to villagers frequently scraping their backs upon entering or leaving the low cave where the spring was located. But according to a longtime resident, this is an old joke told by Second Mesa people about Hotevilla. The village name actually comes from *hotski,* meaning "cedar tree," and *atpela,* or "slope." This location had both cedar wood for fuel as well as a spring, making it a good site for Yukioma's displaced group.

Founded in 1906, Hotevilla became the refuge for Yukioma and his followers after his defeat in a pushing match at Old Oraibi with "friendlies." This was the name given to Hopis who accepted and worked with the Indian Service. Yukioma was the leader of a faction known as "hostiles" who wanted no services provided by the United States and resisted all intervention from the Indian Service and missionaries into the Hopi way of life. After the scuffle, Yukioma was arrested by the military and imprisoned at Fort Wingate. This led to a great deal of hardship for his people in their new home.

Hotevilla Community Development Office: Call for permission to tour the village; (928) 734-2420. Office hours: 8 a.m.–5 p.m. Monday through Friday. Closed weekends.

 MM 371 OLD ORAIBI (South) *(Orayvi)*

Orayvi means place of the Oray Rock, and to the people of Third Mesa this is *Tuwanasavi,* or "earth's center." Although contested by some villages, Oraibi is considered the oldest continuously inhabited village in the United States. The logs used to build many of the homes are from A.D. 1260 to 1344, according to tree-ring dating. It is thought that the logs came from the San Francisco Peaks, more than a hundred miles (160 km) away. You may walk through the ancient streets but cannot go past the old village where the ruins of a church stand.

Loololma was one of the strongest Hopis to challenge the U.S. government and missionary transgression in Oraibi. In 1880, he opposed Hopi children attending government schools, and wanted Hopis to live their lives as the Creator instructed them to live. Somehow, Thomas Keam, then the Indian agent, persuaded Loololma to visit Washington as his guest. When Loololma returned, his opinion had completely changed. When asked why, he said he saw that there were so many white people that it would be like "disturbing an ant hill," and he believed that the Hopis had no choice but to cooperate with the government.

Yukioma, ca. 1913
Leo Crane Collection, Cline Library, Special Collections and Archives, NAU PH 658.299

Lomahongyoma, another powerful member of Old Oraibi, disagreed with Loololma's conversion. This led to a severe split between the Bear and the Spider Clans in 1906. When Loololma died, Tawaquaptewa became chief and was like-minded in believing that it was possible to allow children to attend government schools while maintaining Hopi spiritual life. To end the increasing hostility between the "friendlies" (people cooperative with the government) and the "hostiles" (people opposed to the government), Tawaquaptewa ordered the hostiles to leave. He further demanded that the families from Shungopavi who had moved to Oraibi in support of the hostiles also leave.

Lomahongyoma had turned the responsibility of leading the hostiles over to Yukioma, who challenged Chief Tawaquaptewa to a contest. Yukioma drew a line in the sand, and the chief's men were to push him over it. If they could, Yukioma and his follow-ers agreed to leave the village. Placing their hands on each other's shoul-ders, with their individual faction members pushing from behind, Yukioma went on to lose the fight. As he had promised, he moved his group to the mesa near the spring known as Hotevilla.

Inscribed in sandstone below the village is a recording of the event. It reads:

> *Well it have to be this way not,*
> *pass me over this LINE*
> *it will be DONE.*
> *Spt. 8, 1906*

MM 372 PUMPKIN SEED POINT (North)

A great place to stop for a picnic and enjoy the tremendous view of the Hopi Buttes. (See page 130 for a discussion of the Hopi Buttes.)

MM 373 KYKOTSMOVI (New Oraibi) *(Kiqotsmovi)*

This is the location of the modern Hopi government. The modern-day poli-tics and bureaucracy that the Bureau of Indian Affairs brought to the "People of Peace" has been a constant source of irritation between villages and clans. Hopis do not differentiate between life and religion. Their sole purpose, and the source of their strength, is found in the adherence to centuries-old teachings and a plan for life. To this end, each village tradi-tionally has a *kikmongwi,* or "father of the people," who makes decisions for his village based on prayer and meditation.

Hoping to modernize the relationship tribes had with the federal govern-ment, Congress passed the Indian Reorganization Act in 1934. Two years later, the commissioner of Indian affairs, John Collier, decided that all tribes must have a tribal council. He believed this would help bring about changes in the administration and treatment of Indians under the BIA. Oliver LaFarge, an anthropologist and Pulitzer Prize–winning author of the novel *Laughing Boy,* was an advisor to Collier. He was responsible for writing the Hopi constitution and bylaws. The constitution stated that village chiefs were allowed to certify their village's representatives to the tribal council and that the spiritual leaders would be consulted on important matters. This pro-cess did not work as well as it sounded on paper. The Hopis abandoned the first tribal council in 1943.

In 1951, the Hopis began their fight for land with the federal government. To proceed with the case, the government would recognize only one repre-sentative of the Hopi people, and that would have to be the tribal council.

The Mennonite Church has had a strong presence in this community since Heinrich R. Voth built a chapel sometime around 1901 on a path to the "Kachina Resting Place Point." This, of course, upset many Hopis, but Voth claimed he had permission to build on the site from the *kikmongwi.* Interestingly, the church was struck by lightning, not once but twice.

The Mennonites were a German religious group that emigrated to Russia in 1786 to practice their religion freely. But in 1874 they left Russia for the United States and joined the established Mennonite congregation already living in Newton, Kansas. In 1892, Heinrich Voth and his wife traveled to Hopi land. Although he was very helpful to the Hopis during a severe measles epidemic and supportive of the hostiles' effort to maintain their tradition, the Hopis don't remember him warmly. Voth actively recorded and disseminated sacred and secret knowledge about ceremonies and displayed this information along with religious artifacts in museums. According to anthropologist Peter Whiteley, Voth went so far as to display an important religious altar in the Hopi House at the Grand Canyon.

Kykotsmovi Community Development Office: Call for permission to tour the village; (928) 734-2474. Office hours: 8 a.m.–5 p.m. Monday through Friday. Closed weekends.

The Kykotsmovi Village Store for many years was part of Babbitt Brothers Trading Co. Recently, the village chose not to renew the trading company's lease and decided to operate the store themselves. Open 7 a.m. to 7 p.m. (MST) Monday through Friday, and Sunday 8 a.m. to 7 p.m. year-round.

Mile 373.5 ORAIBI WASH PICNIC AREA (North)

SECOND MESA

At an elevation of six thousand feet (1,829 m), this mesa has two distinct sections. To the east are the villages of **Shipaulovi** and **Mishongnovi.** To the west is the village of **Shungopavi.** Artists living on this mesa are well-known for their coiled baskets, katsina dolls, and overlay jewelry.

MM 379 SILVERCRAFT COOPERATIVE GUILD (North)

Fred Kabotie—the famous artist from Shungopavi, known for painting the Hopi Room in the Grand Canyon's watchtower at Desert View and three murals at the Painted Desert Inn at the Petrified Forest and Painted Desert National Park—started the guild. More than three hundred Hopi artists display their handcrafted items here, and Hopi silversmiths work onsite.

To ensure that the jewelery is authentic, each piece bears both the Hopi Guild sun symbol and the individual silversmith's clan mark. Open 8 a.m.– 5 p.m. (MST) every day; (928) 734-2463.

 Mile 379.5 HOPI CULTURAL CENTER AND MUSEUM (North)

The cultural center is a nonprofit corporation with the goal of presenting accurate cultural and historical information to visitors traveling through Hopi country. It contains shops and one of the three restaurants on the reservation. Open from 8 a.m. to 5 p.m. Monday through Friday; Saturday 9 a.m.– 3 p.m. (MST). There is a small admission charge. (928) 734-6650.

To Hopis, no food is as important as corn, or *Qaa'o*. Not only is it a dietary staple, its role in Hopi spiritual life is incalculable. To the Hopis, corn is life. Every special event has corn associated with it. A perfect ear of white corn represents the spiritual mother of a newborn. At death, a cornmeal path leads the spirit of the deceased to its new home.

Hopi elder with grandchild, ca. 1930s
Fred Harvey Collection, Museum of Northern Arizona MS 301-5-118

WHAT IS PIIKI?

You will have the opportunity to buy piki, or *piiki,* bread throughout your travels on the Hopi reservation, usually for about $2 a roll. Try it. It's an ancient food that Hopi women have made for centuries. First, boiled water is mixed with blue corn flour and a small amount of juniper ash or saltbush ash (to enrich the color). A flat, seasoned stone is heated hot enough to burn the hand. Melon seeds are spread on the stone and their oil is allowed to bake in. Then batter is spread lightly on the stone with fingers, baking very quickly. Several tissue-thin sheets are made this way and then rolled and stacked.

Hopi Cultural Center Motel: The only motel on the Hopi reservation, this lodge has thirty-three rooms and fills up quickly in summer. It also has a campground. For reservations call (928) 734-2401. While here, try the blue corn pancakes and *noqkwivi,* traditional Hopi stew with lamb and corn. The restaurant also makes a very good Hopi taco, much the same as its Navajo counterpart. Open from 7 a.m. to 9 p.m. (MST).

Domínguez-Escalante Trail Marker: Located in the parking lot of the Second Mesa Cultural Center, this marker commemorates the trail that Sylvester Vélez de Escalante and Francisco Atanasio Domínguez took in 1776 in their attempt to find a route from Santa Fe, New Mexico, to Monterey, California. (See pages 68–69 for more on this famous expedition.)

 TSAKURSHOVI STORE

Located 1.5 miles (2.4 km) east of the Hopi Cultural Center on Highway 264, this small but interesting store belongs to Janice and Joseph Day. It could be one of the more educational stores you will visit on your travels. Because the Days supply Hopis with traditional items needed for their ceremonies, you will have an opportunity to see handmade rattles, turtle shells, fox furs, moccasins, herbs, sweet grass, and other paraphernalia needed by ceremonial participants. The concept of selling or trading completed items to dancers is not a new one. No one was able to make every required item or trap every animal skin needed for a particular ceremony. Specialists developed to supply different items, and this practice continues today.

 Mile 381.5 SHUNGOPAVI *(Songoopavi)*

In Hopi, *songoopavi* means "sand grass spring place." It was named for a nearby spring. By tradition, "Old Shungopavi" is the oldest village, established by the Bear Clan, the first clan to arrive on the Hopi mesas after the people's migrations. The older village is at the base of the mesa, where more than two thousand people lived until fear of retribution from the Pueblo Revolt of 1680 caused them to move the village to the mesa top.

Tourists may not attend ceremonies at this village unless they have an invitation or are guests of one of the residents.

Shungopavi Community Development Office: Call for permission to tour the village; (928) 734-2570. Office hours: 8 a.m.–5 p.m., Monday through Friday. Closed weekends.

SCENIC DETOUR

NOTE: To visit the Second Mesa Villages, turn north by the Texaco station across the street from the Second Mesa Day School.

 MISHONGNOVI (Musungnuvi)

The Crow Clan came to the Hopi mesas looking for refuge. Their contribution was to be guardian of the sacred Corn Rock for the people of Shungopavi.

Mishongnovi Community Development Office: Call for permission to tour the village; (928) 737-2520. Office hours: 8 a.m.–5 p.m., Monday through Friday. Closed weekends.

Mishongnovi is the home village of Tony Hillerman's fictitious character Officer Cowboy Dashee of the Hopi Tribal Police. He is a character in *Sacred Clowns, Dark Wind,* and *Talking God.*

SHIPAULOVI (Supawlavi)

Supawlavi means "place of the mosquitoes." This name stuck when villagers fled *Homol'ovi* to escape the mosquitoes. Homol'ovi refers to the area around Winslow on the Little Colorado River. (See pages 240–241 for information about Homolovi Ruins State Park.) As you enter the village, on the west side of the main road there is an old abandoned store before you go farther up the mesa. This is the original Secakuku Trading Post. The same family owns a modern trading post at the junction of Highways 264 and 87. Continuing on past the trading post will take you back to the Second Mesa Cultural Center.

END SCENIC DETOUR

Junction of Arizona Highway 264 and 87 to Keams Canyon

FIRST MESA

Artists on First Mesa are known for their pottery, katsina dolls, and weavings. If you wish to visit the First Mesa villages, you must stop at Ponsi Hall at the top of the mesa on the right, at the end of the road. Tours of Walpi are offered Monday through Friday, 9:30 a.m.–4 p.m., but depending on the number of guides available. The tours are free, but donations are welcomed. This is the only mesa that offers tours. (928) 737-2262.

MM 392 POLACCA

Tom Polacca, a Tewa and former resident of Hano, started this village in 1890. Encouraged by Polacca's move and looking for ways to disrupt the Hopis' ceremonial life, the Indian Service tried to lure people down off the mesa by building individual houses by the day school. They were completed in 1900, but no one wanted to move into the homes. By 1935, only 7 percent of the residents of First Mesa lived in Polacca. Today, the residents of Polacca have maintained their affiliation to political and ceremonial activities on First Mesa.

 MM 392 ROAD TO FIRST MESA VILLAGES (North)

 HANO *(Haano)*

This is the first village you drive through when climbing up the steep road to Walpi. Hano is a Tewa village, established by people who came from the Rio Grande area near Albuquerque after the Pueblo Revolt of 1680. As was customary, each arriving clan was asked by the Bear Clan what they could contribute to the good of the people. The Tewas of Hano contributed their ability to be guardians of First Mesa.

Nampeyo firing pots, ca. 1904–1906, with E. A. Burbank looking on
Jo Mora Collection, Cline Library, Special Collections and Archives, NAU PH 86.1.463
E. A. Burbank was an artist who painted the rug designs for Lorenzo Hubbell that hang in his home in Ganado (see pages 135–137).

Hano was the home of the famous potter Nampeyo, born in 1860. She developed her world-renowned pottery after two anthropologists, J. W.

Fewkes and F. W. Dodge from the Smithsonian Institution, excavated Sikyatki, a ruin on First Mesa. Nampeyo used the ancient pot sherds they brought to her as a guide for her geometric designs, maintaining the ancient techniques that developed into a pottery style known as Sikyatki Revival.

Nampeyo became so popular that Fred Harvey commissioned her to perform pottery exhibitions at the Grand Canyon. As her fame spread, she traveled on the newly completed Santa Fe Railroad to the Chicago Railway Exhibition, and even to the East Coast to display her skills. Over the years she became blind but taught her daughters how to copy her intricate earth tone designs. This skill has passed from one generation of the Nampeyo family to the next, making it possible for you to still buy a Nampeyo pot.

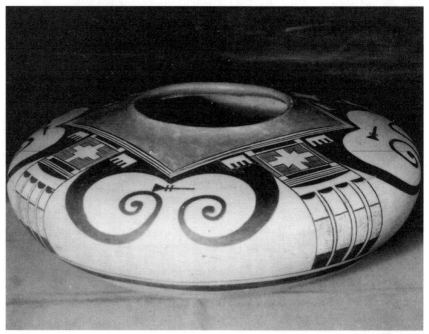

Nampeyo pot, purchased by the Babbitt family in the early 1920s
Museum of Northern Arizona Photo Archives, #10098

Hano is also famous for hand-coiled pottery. You may stop at homes with "Pottery For Sale" signs to buy these beautiful pieces directly from the potters.

Traditional Hopi pottery is not fired in a kiln but hand-fired over an open fire of sheep dung or coal, as was the custom at Awat'ovi in prehistoric times. You can tell the difference between open fire and kiln pottery. Kiln pottery has a more consistent coloring than the hand-fired pot.

SICHOMOVI *(Sitsomovi)*

The Hopi name means "place of the mounds where wild currants grow." Between Walpi and Hano, members of Walpi founded Sichomovi in 1750. The village has running water, electricity, and garbage pickup. At the end of the road, at Ponsi Hall, you can make arrangements for tours of Walpi. Your chances of being allowed to visit Walpi on a Saturday or Sunday are minimal in summer, the busiest time of the Hopi ceremonial calendar. Tourists may not attend these ceremonies without an invitation from one of the local villagers.

Ponsi Hall: Tours of Walpi Monday–Friday 9:30 a.m.–4 p.m., (928) 737-2262.

First Mesa Community Development Office: Call for permission to tour the village; (928) 737-2670. Office hours: 8 a.m.–5 p.m., Monday through Friday. Closed on weekends.

Walpi, ca. 1930s
Fred Harvey Collection, Museum of Northern Arizona Photo Archives, MS 301-3-160

 WALPI

Walpi means "the gap," referring to the opening in the mesa just below Hano. The village sits on the narrowest part of the mesa and is only 150 feet (46 m) across at its widest point. Just below this village on the northwest side of the mesa is the original village of Old Walpi, where the Hopis lived until they moved their village to the top of the mesa. They did this because they feared Spanish retribution after the 1680 Pueblo uprising. There is a ruin of a small Catholic mission, built during the Franciscan period, near the old village, but it is off-limits to tourists.

On your tour of Walpi, you may notice the **Hopi Buttes** far off to the south. They are located forty miles (64 km) away near Dilkon on the Navajo Reservation. In the 1900s, these buttes were known as the Moqui Buttes. The Hopis were forced to suffer with the name *moqui,* given to them by the Spanish and carried on by the Indian Service as their official tribal name. To the Hopi, it was an insult to be called moqui, meaning "dead" in their language. The name stuck until the tribe officially petitioned the government to change their name back to Hopi, meaning "peaceful people" or "people who live in the proper way."

 Mile 396.5 HOPI POLICE STATION AND JUNIOR-SENIOR HIGH SCHOOL (South)

Police: (928) 738-2234.

 COAL MINES

There are two abandoned coal mines along this road before you reach Keams Canyon. Hopis have mined coal from Black Mesa since A.D. 900. Well known for its vast deposits, the Jeddito Valley may have been the site of the first mine. It is estimated that the Hopis mined as much as 450 pounds (204 kg) of coal a day until the 1700s. When the Bureau of Indian Affairs began building boarding schools, the method of choice for heat was steam produced by coal-burning generators.

Mile 403.5 KEAMS CANYON

This remains a government town, named after Thomas Keam, a former trader and Indian agent. Before 1860 it was known as Peach Orchard Springs. The Hopis call this natural oasis *Pongsikya.*

The **Keams Canyon Indian Health Service Hospital** is located at the end of the canyon. Non-Indians may be seen here on an emergency basis only. Telephone: (928) 738-2211.

After the Navajos signed a treaty with the Spanish in 1819, they began to settle in Hopi territory. Prior to this, there had been a long history of conflicts between Hopi farmers and some Navajo clans, although the Navajos gave many Pueblo refugees safe haven from Spanish cruelty over the years.

Nonetheless, in 1863 when the United States decided that the Navajos were causing too much trouble for white settlers and Hopis, they sent in the Army. Col. Kit Carson, with the aid of one hundred Hopis, Utes, and white volunteers from New Mexico, waged a fierce and cruel campaign to force the Navajos to surrender and move from the area.

Carson assembled his legion in Peach Orchard Springs, or Volunteer Canyon, as he referred to it. Scored on the canyon wall behind the BIA Agency building is an inscription that reads: "1st Reg't N.M. Vol's., Aug 13, 1863, Col. C. Carson, Comm."

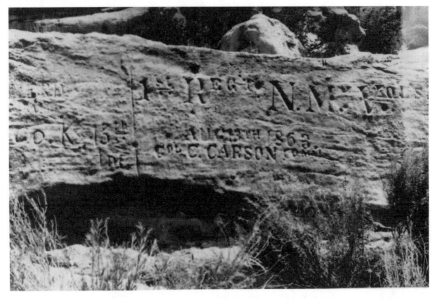

Kit Carson Inscription, 1863 Philip Johnston Collection, Cline Library, Special Collections and Archives, NAU PH 413-1225

Thomas Keam was born in England and came to this country around 1861. He rode with Gen. James Carleton and was one of the soldiers in charge of the Navajos' Long Walk to Bosque Redondo. While in Indian Territory, he learned to speak both Navajo and Hopi fluently and worked in Fort Defiance as an interpreter after his discharge from the army. It was here he met and married his Navajo wife, Grey Woman, in a traditional Navajo ceremony.

In 1872, Keam became temporary special agent to the Navajos and developed the first Navajo police force, with Chief Manuelito as its head. A year later, the permanent special agent arrived and Keam went back to England to visit his sick mother. Sometime during his year-long absence, Grey Woman, thinking that Keam was not coming back, married another man.

Thomas Keam, not dated
Portrait by Prince Artistic Portraits, Washington, D.C., Museum of Northern Arizona, Photo Archives, 68.1188

When he did return, he moved to Peach Orchard Springs and opened Keam's Tusayan Trading Post. In 1886, the government bought his property for $1,500 to build the new BIA boarding school. Keam moved his trading post to the mouth of the canyon, where the Keams Canyon Shopping Center stands today.

In 1899, Keam started to experience real trouble from the new BIA superintendent, Charles Burton. Burton demanded that the Hopi ceremonial dances stop, that Hopi children cut their long hair, and that all children attend boarding school, even if it required the use of force.

Keam publicly disagreed with Burton's beliefs and practices. This caused Burton to retaliate by charging Keam with defrauding the government in the sale of his property and for allowing gambling at his trading post. Burton also disliked Keam's marriage to a Navajo woman. Keam could not stand the allegations any longer and traveled to Washington to answer the charges, where he was found innocent. Now Burton's style of management was in the spotlight. Along with Keam, many Hopi people complained about Burton's cruel treatment, resulting in his removal from office.

Emotionally damaged by this episode, Keam decided his days as a trader were over. He sold his post to Lorenzo Hubbell in 1902 and went back to England, where he died two years later.

Hubbell's Trading Post, Keams Canyon, ca. 1920
Leo Crane Collection, Cline Library, Special Collections and Archives, NAU PH 658-98

70 miles (113 km) from Keams Canyon to Window Rock

Mile 407.5 JEDDITO SCHOOL (North)

A Bureau of Indian Affairs boarding school.

NOTE: If entering the Navajo Nation from April through October, change to daylight saving time.

Mile 427.5 STEAMBOAT CANYON (North)

About one mile (1.6 km) from this community on the north side of Highway 264 is a sandstone formation that looks like a steamboat, hence the name. This area was actually a very important watering place for the Navajos, who call it *Tóyéé* or "scarce water." The Hopis stopped at this spring for water on their journey to the Zuni Salt Lake near St. Johns, Arizona.

The Spanish came through here on their many incursions into Hopi land and called this area *La Mesa de las Vacas,* "the mesa of the cattle." On one of the canyon walls is the inscription:
"A 20 Abril, Año de 1666. P de Montoya."

Montoya might have been a guardian of the cattle for the Franciscans who established a mission at the Hopi village of Awat'ovi, not too far from Steamboat.

Another inscription found in this vicinity says:
"SHALL I NOT DRINK IT?"
St. John.
Colyer 1868
Centered beneath the inscription were carved two clasped hands with an arrow beside one hand and an American flag beside the other hand. It probably was carved by a soldier from Fort Wingate who was referring to the Treaty of 1868 signed that year between the United States and the Navajo people.

MM 438 THE CHUSKA MOUNTAINS (North)

Here you get a good view of the Chuska Mountains.

MM 441 GANADO

This settlement was originally named Pueblo Colorado for the wash of that name that runs by Hubbell's Trading Post. Lorenzo Hubbell changed the name to Ganado to honor his close friend and ally, Navajo leader Ganado Mucho. Hubbell also worried that people might confuse his town with Pueblo, Colorado, also a thriving community of the time.

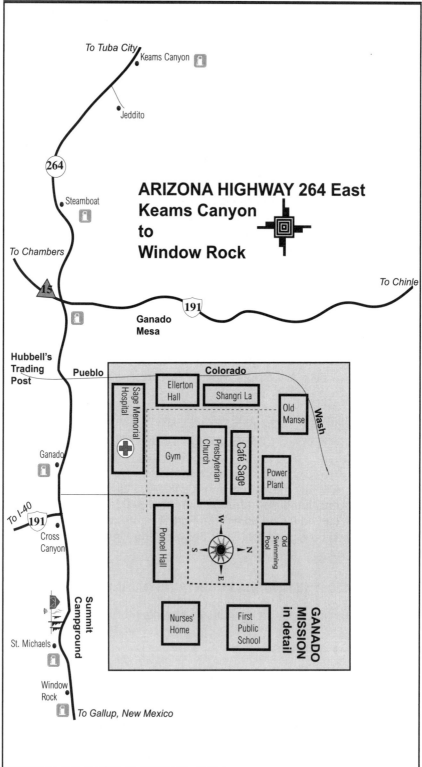

To Tuba City

Keams Canyon

Jeddito

264

Steamboat

To Chambers

15

191

To Chinle

Ganado
Mesa

Hubbell's
Trading
Post

Pueblo

Colorado

Sage Memorial Hospital

Ellerton Hall

Shangri La

Old Manse

Wash

Gym

Presbyterian Church

Café Sage

Power Plant

Ganado

To I-40

191

Cross
Canyon

Poncel Hall

W

N

S

E

Old Swimming Pool

Summit Campground

St. Michaels

Nurses' Home

First Public School

GANADO MISSION in detail

Window
Rock

To Gallup, New Mexico

**ARIZONA HIGHWAY 264 East
Keams Canyon
to
Window Rock**

Ganado Mucho was the western leader of the Navajos and the twelfth signer of the Treaty of 1868, which led to the release of the Navajos from Bosque Redondo. He was a short, stocky man of Pueblo-Navajo ancestry and was responsible for leading his people back to the Pueblo Colorado Wash area (around what is now called Ganado) to develop large farms, cattle, and sheep herds from the animals given to the Navajos by the military.

Warehouse at Hubbell Trading Post, ca. 1890
Photo by Ben Wittick, courtesy School of American Research Collections in the Museum of New Mexico, 16037

 HUBBELL TRADING POST (South)

Hubbell Trading Post is now a National Historic Site managed by the National Park Service. It's open seven days a week from 8 a.m. to 6 p.m. (DST) in summer and 8 a.m. to 5 p.m. (MST) in winter. It's closed on Thanksgiving, Christmas, and January 1. Guided tours of the Hubbell home are offered on a daily basis. Check at the visitors center for the daily schedule or call ahead, (928) 755-3475. This free tour is limited to fifteen people. You can borrow, or purchase for $1.00, a self-guided tour book for the exterior grounds, and there is a slide show about Lorenzo Hubbell available for viewing upon request at the visitors center. Navajo rug weavers and silversmiths demonstrate their arts daily in the visitors center.

Charles Crary built the original trading post in 1871 and sold it to Lorenzo Hubbell in 1876. Hubbell was to own many trading posts in his lifetime and became an important political figure in Arizona's history. He even ran for the U.S. Senate in 1914 but lost and was indebted to the first Navajo tribal chairman, Chee Dodge, for $30,000 in campaign expenses.

Hubbell began to make his fortune in 1875 when the price of wool was very high. He formed a partnership with C. N. Cotton of Gallup, and together they purchased and sold more than 40,000 pounds (18,144 kg) of wool.

Don Lorenzo Hubbell looking at a rug in front of his trading post, ca. 1890 Photo by Ben Wittick, courtesy School of American Research Collection, Museum of New Mexico, Santa Fe.

When the Navajo Reservation was enlarged by executive order in 1880, Hubbell's Trading Post was sitting inside the new reservation boundary. To keep the land his successful post was on, he went to the U.S. Congress. With the help of Cotton and the Arizona governor, he requested an exception of land from the Navajo Reservation, based on his prior claim as a settler. He was ultimately successful and received the claim to the land in 1908.

Hubbell was also friends with the eastern leader of the Navajos, Manuelito. A fierce warrior, Manuelito had won many wars against the Mexicans, and many believed him to have supernatural powers because of his great courage in battle. Highly intelligent, he was able to hold out longer than any other group against Kit Carson and surrendered only when his people were close to starvation.

After Manuelito was released from Fort Sumner, he was in charge of the first Navajo police department and was responsible for preventing renewed hostilities in the area.

In back of the Hubbell home is a hill named for the family. It now serves as the family graveyard, with Lorenzo Hubbell and his closest friend, Many-horse, Ganado Mucho's son, buried beside him.

The trading post still operates as it once did, with Navajos coming to trade for supplies. The only difference is that the post is run by the Southwestern Parks and Monuments Association as a nonprofit business.

GANADO RED RUG DESIGN

Hubbell was influential in helping Navajo weavers of the area develop the Ganado Red rug style. He promoted it through his successful mail-order catalog. This design always has a red background with a diamond or cross pattern in the middle. On the edges of the diamond are geometric designs and shapes such as zigzags and crosses. Hubbell encouraged the use of large, heavy Navajo rugs on the floor. You can see copies of Hubbell's original floor rugs during the tour of his home. The Fred Harvey Co. was one of the larger consumers of Ganado Reds, displaying them in their hotels and on trains, making them the most well-known of all of the Navajo rug designs.

Like J. B. Moore at the Crystal Trading Post, Hubbell hired artists traveling through Ganado to paint new rug patterns, which he framed and hung in his office. One of his favorite artists was E. A. Burbank from Illinois. Over

his lifetime, Hubbell collected more than three hundred of Burbank's oil paintings and sketches. (On page 127 there is a picture of Burbank watching Nampeyo fire a pot.)

Ganado Red, ca. 1900–1930
Photograph by Gene Balzer, Museum of Northern Arizona

◼ GANADO MISSION AND SAGE MEMORIAL HOSPITAL

Heading east on Highway 264, about one mile from Hubbell's Trading Post on the north side of the road, you'll find the largest Presbyterian mission to the Navajos, started in Ganado in 1903 with the help of Lorenzo Hubbell, a Roman Catholic. Hubbell saw the many advantages the Presbyterians could bring to the area and welcomed Charles Bierkemper, the first missionary, providing him a place to stay while his house was under construction.

The goal of the new minister was not just to preach the gospel but to provide formal education and health care services to the Navajo people. The first hospital, built in 1911, was a one-man operation. Dr. James Kennedy frequently made house calls on foot to visit the sick and to take them medicine.

In the 1960s, the Presbyterians began to move out of education and health care on the Navajo Reservation. They turned the school over to the College of Ganado, run by a Navajo board of directors, and the hospital was given to Project Hope, then called the Hope Foundation.

Project Hope ran the hospital until 1974, when the Navajo Nation Health Foundation, with an all-Navajo board, was organized to oversee the operation of the hospital and its community outreach programs.

HISTORIC DETOUR

Turn north (left) off Highway 264. At the stop sign is the newly remodeled Poncel Hall, named after Dr. Joseph Poncel, one of the past superintendents of the mission.

Poncel Hall housed the first Sage Memorial Hospital, named for Olivia Sage, who, along with the Navajo Tribe, contributed money to build the hospital in 1929. It was state-of-the-art when it opened, boasting an operating room and obstetrics unit.

Take a left at Poncel Hall. On your left is the current **Sage Memorial Hospital.** Because this is a private hospital, unlike Indian Health Service hospitals, anyone can be seen here. Emergency room: (928) 755-3411.

On your right is the **gym.** Take the next right. On your left is **Ellerton Hall,** built in 1929 to house the mission's administration offices and the Industrial Arts Program.

Next to Ellerton Hall is **Shangri-La,** named by Dr. Clarence Salisbury. He was a surgeon who came to Ganado on a one-month assignment during a diphtheria epidemic in 1927 and stayed twenty-one years. Salisbury had just left a seventeen-year mission to China and called his home Shangri-La to remind him of where he would like to be. He kept hoping for a transfer back to China, but it never came because he was indispensable in Ganado.

The classic book *Sagebrush Surgeon,* by Florence Means, is about the life of Clarence Salisbury in Ganado. When he arrived, modern medicine was foreign to the Navajo people. Hospitals were a place to die. Not surprisingly, when Salisbury's first surgical patient did die of an embolism, the Navajo community was outraged. Some considered killing him in retribution. After hearing of the death, many family members met at Hubbell's Trading Post down the road to discuss the danger this newcomer brought to their traditions. But it was a medicine man, Red Point, who persuaded the crowd to reconsider. He pointed out that even though the medicine man does everything in his power to help the patient, some do not recover. He told them that he was sure that this doctor also did everything to save his patient and did not want her to die.

Gradually the community began to trust Dr. Salisbury. In 1930, the first registered nurse training program in the state of Arizona opened its doors in Poncel Hall. At one time, many of the Navajo nurse administrators employed by the Indian Health Service and the Navajo Tribe graduated from this program.

Salisbury's wife, Cora, was responsible for planting most of the cottonwood, willow, spruce, and elm trees on the campus.

Directly across the street from Shangri La is the **Presbyterian Church.** It was constructed in 1941 using local sandstone quarried by masons from the Ganado area. Behind the church is a two-story adobe building constructed in 1920 as a dormitory and infirmary. It has been refurbished by the Navajo Nation Health Foundation to house **Café Sage,** a cafeteria-style restaurant that offers two or three entrees, an excellent soup and salad bar, and wonderful desserts. The prices are probably the lowest you will find on your travels. Open from 7 a.m. to 8 p.m.

Continue north, heading toward the Pueblo Colorado Wash. Straight ahead at the end of the road, over the wooden bridge, is the **Old Manse.** This was Mr. Bierkemper's home, built in 1903. It is the first and oldest building on the mission grounds.

Turn east on the dirt road directly behind Café Sage to continue around the campus. On your left is the **power plant** built around 1920. This building housed the coal power generator, replaced in 1960 by two surplus submarine turbines donated by the Navy.

An interesting story about the Ganado Mission has to do with the water supply. When you entered the mission grounds, you probably thought it a natural oasis like Tuba City. Not so, and according to geologists, the sandstone under the mission extends a thousand feet (305 m) down, making it next to impossible to drill a productive well. Needing a dependable source of water for the hospital and school, the superintendent contracted with a Bureau of Indian Affairs drilling crew to try drilling a much deeper well than the shallow one they had. After coming up dry three times, the Presbyterians held a prayer vigil. On the fourth attempt, the cable on the drill snapped at 450 feet (137 m), releasing 4,500 gallons (19,080 liters) of water an hour. It is known as the Presbyterian miracle.

Turn right at the intersection. On your left is the first **Public School Building** built in northern Apache County (built in 1929). Leaving the circle, you pass by the **Nurses Home,** behind Poncel Hall on the left, where students in Salisbury's nursing school lived while attending school. It now houses nurses and staff who work at Sage Memorial Hospital.

END HISTORIC DETOUR

Turn east on Arizona 264 to go to Window Rock. The road ascends through the Petrified Forest member of the Chinle Formation.

Mile 448.5 GANADO LAKE

The lake is north on I.R. 27 about one mile (1.6 km).

MM 455 CROSS CANYON

Arizona Highway 264 begins climbing the Defiance Plateau to the ponderosa pine forest at 7,719 feet (2,353 m). The canyon here, just past the junction with U.S. Highway 191, was named for a Navajo trail that crossed it.

MM 451 SAGE (North and south)

Sage grows in fields on both sides of the highway here.

MM 466 SUMMIT CAMPGROUND AND PICNIC AREA

A permit is required for camping; see page 32 for information. There is no water, but there are outhouses and picnic tables.

ST. MICHAELS MISSION (South)

This 440-acre (1.78 sq km) Franciscan mission was started in 1896 by Rev. Mother Katharine Drexel, founder of the Sisters of the Blessed Sacrament for Indians and Colored People. In 2000, Mother Drexel became the second native-born United States citizen to be declared a saint by Pope John Paul II.

Upon the death of her father—a wealthy investment broker—in 1885, Drexel became heir to a fortune. She purchased squatter's rights to a small piece of land to the north of the present mission. One year later she bought 160 acres (.65 sq km) of land from squatter Bill Meadows, where the Mission Museum and church stand today. The original Navajo Reservation boundary of 1886 was seven miles (11.3 km) north of the mission. (See page 11 for map.) Much of the land in St. Michaels was in a checkerboard pattern, with some land owned by the railroad and some designated as public lands. It was possible in 1896 for a settler to obtain title to railroad land through squatter's rights, requiring a person to live on the land one night each year.

In the late 1500s the Spanish Franciscans called this area *Cienega Amarilla* because of its masses of wild sunflowers. The Navajos called it *tso hootso*, meaning yellow meadow. After purchasing the land, Mother Katharine changed the name to St. Michaels after her childhood home in Pennsylvania.

Father Juvenal Schnorbus and Father Anslem Weber from the Franciscan Order of the Province of St. John the Baptist in Cincinnati, Ohio, were enticed by Mother Katharine to come to Arizona to run the mission. Many Navajos accepted the Ohio Franciscans for two reasons. First, the timing of the priests' encounter with the Navajos was just after their return from Bosque Redondo, and the Navajos needed the Franciscans' help to defend themselves against the bureaucracy of the Indian Service and hostile neighboring ranchers. Second, these Franciscans were willing to learn the Navajo language and incorporate Navajo traditions and ceremonials into their Catholic services. This distinquished them from the Spanish Franciscans of the 1500s, who were not successful in their dealings with the Navajos primarily because of their disregard for the highly developed Navajo belief system and language.

Luckily for the Ohio priests, they had help in learning the language from the first trader in the Cienega Amarilla area, Charles Day. He was very happy to see the mission established so his two sons, who spoke fluent Navajo, could learn reading, writing, and arithmetic. The Days agreed to serve as interpreters and help the priests learn Navajo in exchange for the education of their children. In 1902, the St. Michael's Indian Boarding School opened on the mission's grounds.

One of the more famous Franciscans to come to the region was Father Berard Haile. Credited with developing the Navajo written alphabet using the international phonetic alphabet, he published the first Navajo ethnographic dictionary in 1910. A prolific writer and anthropological researcher, he also helped with the reorganization of the Navajo Tribal Council under the Collier administration in the 1930s.

Father Anslem Weber voting in the first Arizona territorial election, 1912 St. Michaels Photo Collection of the Franciscan Friars at St. Michaels, Ariz., Museum of Northern Arizona Photo Archives, MS 119-104-81
From left to right, seated: Sam Day; the person behind Day is not known; Frank Walker, interpreter for the friars from 1900 to 1945; and Brother Simeon Schwemberger, who was responsible for taking many of the photographs in the Saint Michaels collection. Standing, from left to right: Father Anselm Weber and Daniel Holmes Mitchell.

The most important function the Franciscans performed for the Navajos was to negotiate with Washington for additional land for the growing population. Father Anslem learned how to survey from the team that came through St. Michaels to determine the boundaries of the new Arizona Territory. This skill was to become invaluable in the settlement of land disputes between Navajo clans and in Father Anslem's successful attempt to increase the size of the Navajo Reservation. He is said to have written over three thousand letters on behalf of the Navajos and made yearly visits to Washington to fight for the increased land base. Because of his efforts, over 1.4 million acres (5,687 sq km), to the east and south of the 1868 reservation boundary, were added to the Navajo Nation. He was also successful in obtaining more than 122,000 acres (497 sq km) for off-reservation Navajos. You can visit the **Saint Michaels Historical Museum** from Memorial Day (last Monday in May) to Labor Day (first Monday in September), Monday through

Friday from 9 a.m.to 5 p.m. (DST). No admission fee, but donations are welcomed. Mission telephone number: (928) 871-4171.

Tay Notah and John Foley delivering mail by burro
St. Michaels Photo Collection of the Franciscan Friars at St. Michaels, Arizona, Museum of Northern Arizona, Photo Archives, MS 119-167-2585

TOWN OF ST. MICHAELS, ARIZONA

On the north side of Arizona Highway 264, just past St. Michaels Mission, is the area considered the town of St. Michaels. It has its own post office and zip code.

WINDOW ROCK

Window Rock is named for the large window in the Cowsprings Sandstone behind the Navajo tribal government offices. John Collier, the federal commissioner of Indian affairs, centralized the headquarters for Navajo Indian affairs here in the 1930s. Collier understood the importance of including the Navajo people in the decisions made about their children's education and health care. He implemented changes such as starting day schools to replace the isolating and lonely boarding school system of education.

Window Rock is the fictional home of Lt. Joe Leaphorn, Tony Hillerman's first important character, who appears in *The Blessing Way, A Thief of Time, Dance Hall of the Dead, Listening Woman,* and *Skinwalker.* Hillerman has been named a "Special Friend of the Diné" by the Navajo Nation for his positive portrayal of the Navajo people.

MM 475 NAVAJO NATION FAIRGROUND (South)

The Navajo Nation Fair is held the first weekend after Labor Day each year and features an intertribal powwow, a Miss Navajo Nation contest, and a rodeo. For more information, call (928) 871-6478.

NAVAJO LIBRARY, MUSEUM, AND VISITORS CENTER

Opened in 1998, this 58,000-square-foot museum is one of the largest museums dedicated to Native American history in the country. It has a library, a children's museum, and Miss Navajo Nation's office. In the future, it will house thousands of valuable and sacred artifacts waiting for repatriation from museums all over the country. The facility is open Tuesday through Friday 8 a.m. to 8 p.m., and Monday and Saturday 8 a.m. to 5 p.m. For more information, call (928) 871-7941.

TSO BONITO PARK

Follow the pink bear signs to find the park, directly behind the new museum and library. The Navajo Nation Zoological and Botanical Park opened in 1962 to care for a bear abandoned by its owners while it was on display at the tribal museum. The mission of the zoo is to exhibit plants and animals important in the Navajo culture. But traditional thought does not condone keeping wild animals on display in cages or allow the zoo to purchase animals. All of the animals in this zoo were brought here because they were hurt or found abandoned and would not survive if left in the wild. A common reason birds of prey are brought to the zoo is because they were captured, had their feathers pulled out, and were then abandoned. Many people think feathers grow back, but they don't. And because the bird can't fly, it eventually will starve to death unless rescued.

The zoo has grown to include cougars, Mexican wolves, coyotes, deer, elk, bobcats, Navajo churro sheep, rabbits, and a pony. Birds of prey, wild turkeys, and roadrunners are also on display, along with an assortment of snakes, lizards, and turtles. Open from 8 a.m. to 5 p.m. Monday through Friday. Donations are accepted.

THE HAYSTACKS

Behind the Navajo Museum are formations that look like haystacks and are known as *Tségháhoodzáni,* or "wind going through the rocks," made of Entrada and Cowsprings Sandstone. Near here is *Tseyaato,* or "spring under the rock," which served as a watering stop for eight thousand Navajos on the Long Walk to Fort Sumner.

"A View in the Haystacks," Window Rock, Arizona, ca. 1890
Photograph by Ben Wittick, courtesy School of American Research Collection of the Museum of New Mexico, 15551

SERVICES IN ST. MICHAELS/WINDOW ROCK

Navajoland Days Inn: Just opened in 1998, this motel sits almost directly across from St. Michaels Historical Museum. It has an indoor pool, sauna, and cable television. Rooms cost around $75 for a double in winter but much more in summer. National reservations (800) DAYSINN; local (928) 871-5690.

Navajo Nation Inn: Moderately priced, this motel is decorated in a Southwestern style. The curtains and bedspreads have Navajo pastoral scenes. This is the only motel in Window Rock. A drive to Gallup, about thirty miles (48 km) away, is the only other option if the Days Inn in St. Michaels is full. Because this is the capital of the Navajo Nation, it is often difficult to reserve a room here. Reservations: (928) 871-4108 or (800) 662-6189.

Navajo Nation Inn Dining Room: This is the place to have lunch if you want to see members of the Navajo Tribal Council and the president having lunch. Open from 6 a.m.–9 p.m.

KTNN Radio: If you haven't had the chance to hear spoken Navajo, tune in to KTNN at AM 660. It is a very powerful radio station owned by the Navajo Tribe. Primarily a country western station, it also plays traditional Native American chants, and some of its advertising and interviews are conducted in the Navajo language.

Navajo Police Station: (928) 871-6113 or 911.

U.S. HIGHWAY 160
North
Tuba City
to
Kayenta

Kayenta

Peabody
Coal Company

Skeleton Mesa

Organ Rock Monocline

Longhouse Valley

Tsegi Canyon

BLACK MESA

Navajo National Monument

Black Mesa and Lake Powell Railroad

Shonto

Kletha Valley

Navajo Mountain

Inscription House

WHITE MESA

98

To Page/Lake Powell

Elephant Feet

160

Red Lake

K AIBETO

PLATEAU

Wildcat Peak

Uranium
Mill
Site

To Hopi Mesas
Window Rock

PRESTON MESA

Pasture Canyon

264

Tuba City

To Page/Lake Powell

89

89

To Flagstaff

78 miles (126 km) from Tuba City to Kayenta

GREY HILLS ACADEMY HIGH SCHOOL

Just east of the pedestrian overpass, turn right, and the school is on the right. This three hundred-student high school is one of the best examples on the Navajo Reservation of self-determination in education at work. Grey Hills transferred from the Bureau of Indian Affairs to an all-Navajo school board in 1989 and is now a university-system laboratory school.

Students accepted to the academy from other parts of the reservation and the country stay in former BIA dormitories. A portion of the dormitory is now a motel and youth hostel, where students learn hotel management skills. The school also operates the only high school radio station in Arizona— KGHR (91.5 FM), which broadcasts an eclectic mix of classical, country western, rock, and Native American music, plus National Public Radio's (NPR) "Morning Edition" and "All Things Considered." If you're listening to NPR on KNAU (88.7 FM) from Flagstaff on your way to the Grand Canyon and lose the signal along Highway 64 (because of the Gray Mountain), tune to 91.5 and pick up the signal clearly all the way to the canyon.

MM 323 PASTURE CANYON (North)

The cliffs surrounding this canyon are made of Kayenta Sandstone from the early Jurassic Period, laid down more than 190 million years ago.

Hopi families say their ancestors lived in this area when the first Mormon settlers began arriving in 1875. However, the Navajo story about the Mormon settlement of Tuba City is quite different than that told by the Hopis, who say no Navajos were then in the area.

Navajos say the Mormons told them they were just passing through on their way to settle along the Little Colorado. But because they had run out of food, they asked to camp in Tuba City for the winter. When spring came, the Mormons asked if they could stay for one planting season to grow enough crops to carry them through to their new home. The Navajo families agreed. But by the end of the planting season, permanent shelters had been built and more and more settlers were moving into the area. Finally, the Mormons were so well established they obtained a court document in Flagstaff claiming the land and all of the water in Moenkopi Creek as their own.

This caused resentment among the Navajos who had shared their land and food with the Mormons when they were in need. The situation became worse when fences kept Navajo sheep and cattle out of Pasture Canyon. The fence builder was a disagreeable Mormon leader named Lot Smith, who owned a large dairy herd he grazed in the canyon. During a long drought in 1892, he allegedly refused to allow any of the neighboring Navajos to use the watering hole. One day, two children accidently herded their flock of sheep into Pasture Canyon. Outraged, Smith got his gun and began shooting wildly at the sheep and children. The Navajos claimed that Smith killed seven sheep and twenty-three died later from their wounds. The Mormon version is that Smith killed two sheep. To retaliate, a Navajo shot six of Smith's dairy cows. Joe Lee, the grandson of John D. Lee, was in Pasture Canyon on that fateful day and says that a sniper, whom no one could identify, shot Smith. Chach'osh Neez was blamed for mortally wounding Smith because he had made many threats against him in the past.

A military officer traveled to the scene from Fort Wingate, near Gallup, New Mexico, to investigate the shooting. Before Smith died, he admitted that he should have stopped shooting when the Navajo shot his cattle, but he didn't think they would shoot at him. Not wanting to go to Fort Defiance for a trial, Chach'osh Neez, protected by many family and friends, hid in Blue Canyon, sending messages back and forth to the military investigator. Finally in 1895, he gave himself up to stand trial in Flagstaff, where he was acquitted in the death of Lot Smith.

Pasture Canyon is today part of the Hopi Reservation as a result of a federal court ruling. The Mormon settlers developed the series of reservoirs within the canyon now used to irrigate Hopi cornfields. It is also home to various species of water birds such as the blue heron.

Mile 323.5 TUBA CITY RODEO AND FAIRGROUNDS (North)

Every year, the Western Navajo Fair is held here during the first weekend after Columbus Day in October.

Mile 327.5 SITE OF RARE METALS URANIUM MILL (South)

Five miles north of Tuba City you will notice trees growing on both sides of the road. Beneath their branches are the foundations of homes built here in the late 1950s to house workers of the uranium mill that processed three

hundred tons (272,727 kg) of vanadium and uranium ore every day. Ore, or "yellowcake," came by truck from mines in Cameron, Monument Valley, and the Orphan

Rare Metals Uranium Processing Plant, ca. 1950s
Museum of Northern Arizona, Photo Archives

Mine in the Grand Canyon. In 1968, the Rare Metals Corp. of America went bankrupt and abandoned the site, leaving thousands of tons of low-level radioactive waste in huge piles to blow away in the wind. In 1981, a local group in Tuba City pressured the U.S. Dept. of Energy (DOE) to clean up the site. The waste was gathered into a pile, shaped to shed water, and covered with rock. What remains today is a huge, gray-colored pile with the radioactive waste buried beneath it. The DOE is monitoring to ensure that an underground aquifer is not contaminated.

MM 328 PRESTON MESA (North)

Seen to the north of Tuba City in the distance is a large red mesa made of Navajo Sandstone. The mesa is named in honor of Sam Preston, the first store clerk who worked for Charles Algert at the Tuba Trading Post in the late 1870s and who later became partners with the Babbitt brothers. Preston's original reason for coming to Arizona was to work for the Union and Pacific Railroad.

MM 336 COWSPRINGS SANDSTONE (South)

These Cowsprings Sandstone formations to the south are part of the San Raphael Group formed during the Jurassic era, 135–180 million years ago.

Mile 338.5 WILDCAT PEAK (Northwest)

This peak was formed by a volcanic intrusion, with surrounding dikes.

MM 344 TONALEA GENERAL STORE AND COMMUNITY

This community is built around the BIA day school. The Babbitt Brothers Trading Co. moved its store from the historic Red Lake Trading Post down the road to this new facility just a few years ago.

MM 344 RED LAKE TRADING POST

Also known as Tonalea Trading Post, because Tonalea is a close approximation of the Navajo word for lake, *tónteel.* Although smaller now, there once was a large lake below the trading post.

George McAdams built the first trading post, really a four-room fort, on the shore of the lake around 1880. Sam Preston, an employee of the Babbitt Brothers Trading Co., built this two-story trading post in 1891, with living quarters upstairs.

McAdams' sister, Jane, married John Richardson. Their sons, S. I., C. D., and Hubert, owned and operated many trading posts throughout northern Arizona, including the Cameron Trading Post.

Red Lake Trading Post
Warren Family Collection, Cline Library, Special Collections and Archives, NAU 412-2-94

The Babbitt brothers started in the trading business here in 1891 out of necessity when the owner, Sam Dittenhoffer, heavily in debt to them for his store merchandise, was killed in a poker game. According to Joe Lee, who worked at the post for a few months after McAdams sold it in 1889, Dittenhoffer was having an affair with a Mrs. Matthews, a widow from Flagstaff. A few days after he brought her to Red Lake, a strange man showed up. He talked Dittenhoffer into playing poker and at the start of the first hand accused the trader of cheating. Angered, Dittenhoffer jumped to his feet. The stranger, actually a secret admirer of Mrs. Matthews, took this as an attempt to draw on him and shot him dead, but Dittenhoffer didn't have a gun. The stranger took off for Colorado but was apprehended and brought back to Arizona, where he was found guilty of second-degree murder.

An interesting feature of this post is that the upper story and warehouse are made of Arbuckle Brothers coffee boxes. According to Floyd Boyle, the trader at Red Lake in 1948, Arbuckle "Ariosa" coffee was the most popular coffee sold on the reservation. It came packed in sturdy wooden cases, each containing a hundred one-pound packages of coffee. The coupons on the back of the coffee bags were redeemable for catalog items, so the traders bought back Arbuckle coupons from their customers for a penny a piece and redeemed them for "luxury" items. According to Boyle, many of the traders furnished their kitchens and bought clothes and pots and pans through the Arbuckle catalog. One Indian Health Service dignitary visiting the reservation from Washington commented to the Boyles about how popular their silver pattern was on the reservation; he had seen it at every trading post he visited.

The Mormon explorers established a trail through Red Lake in 1869. (See page 180 for map.)

Arbuckle Coffee-Box Wall, Red Lake Trading Post, 1992
Photograph by Gene Balzer

MOVIE LOCATION

The Red Lake Trading Post became the set for the fictitious Burnt Water Trading Post in the movie *The Dark Wind,* based on the Tony Hillerman novel. Produced by Robert Redford, the movie was filmed in the Tuba City/ Red Lake area in 1992. It was during renovation of the post for the movie that the Arbuckle coffee-box wall was discovered.

Mile 344.2 MORMON MONUMENT (North)

On the north side of the road, midway up the sandstone bluff, is a stone monument placed by the Mormon Church in 1938. This spot marks the place where in 1860 Jacob Hamblin's party met up with an unfriendly band of Navajos. The Navajos said they would leave the Mormons alone if they would give them their Paiute scout as a captive. The Mormons refused but did give the Navajos ammunition and supplies. Not happy with the negotiations, the Navajos attacked the party the next morning, killing George A. Smith, Jr.

MM 345 ELEPHANT FEET (North)

Made of Cowsprings Sandstone, these giant formations look like a pair of elephant's legs and feet. They are the result of wind and water erosion.

MM 346 WHITE MESA (North)

This heart-shaped mesa consists primarily of Dakota Sandstone from the Cretaceous Period, formed more than 65 to 135 million years ago. The mesa is about 8.5 miles (13.7 km) wide and 16 miles (25.7 km) long, running north and south. There are many traditional Navajo sheep camps beneath White Mesa. To get to the mesa you would have to drive through and disturb many private camps; please do not trespass here.

MM 359 PYGMY FOREST

This forest consists of Utah juniper and piñon pine on both sides of U.S. Highway 160.

Mile 361.5 JUNCTION WITH ARIZONA HIGHWAY 98, THE SHONTO/PAGE TURNOFF

MM 373 ELECTRIC TRAIN (North)

If you're lucky, you'll spot the Black Mesa and Lake Powell train, an 88-mile-long (141.6 km) railroad with one destination and one freight: the Peabody Coal silo in the Klethla Valley, and coal. This electric train travels from the Navajo Generating Station, a coal-fired power plant on the shores of Lake Powell. It crosses the desert and runs several miles along U.S. Highway 160. It makes three trips a day, carrying 24,000 tons (21,772,800 kg) of coal per trip. The BM & LP train is one of the longest electric coal trains in the world.

This is also the infamous electric train that George Hayduke, a fictitious character in *The Monkey Wrench Gang,* written by environmentalist Edward Abbey, plots to blow up, along with the Glen Canyon Dam, to protest the destruction of the Colorado River and Plateau.

SCENIC DETOUR

MM 374 NAVAJO NATIONAL MONUMENT

Turn north off U.S. Highway 160 on to Arizona Highway 564, and drive 10 miles (16.1 km). Hours: May to early September, 8 a.m.–7 p.m. (DST); early September to mid-December and March through May, 8 a.m.–5 p.m. (DST & MST); mid-December to March, 8 a.m.–4:30 p.m. (MST). Admission is free; donations welcome. Operated by the National Park Service. Camping is also free, on a first-come, first-served basis in the **Sunset View Campground.** A maximum of seven nights is allowed in this very nice campground. Shade is provided by Utah juniper and piñon pine in each of the thirty camping sites. There are toilets and running water but no showers or RV hookups. An RV longer than twenty-five feet (7.6 m) is not recommended because of the narrow, winding road through the campground. There is one wheelchair-accessible campsite with toilet. (928) 672-2700.

The road entering the monument travels on top of the Organ Rock Monocline with Navajo Sandstone lining both sides of the road. This is one of the most beautiful of all of the managed ruins because of its location in Tsegi Canyon and the many springs that feed the area. Towering ponderosa pines grow on the canyon floor because the vertical height of seven hundred feet (213 m) diffuses the sunlight, producing moderate temperatures at the bottom of the canyon. Take the short but steep **Aspen Forest Trail** behind the visitors center to see the beauty of the canyon interior. A grove of quaking aspen grows in the bottom of the canyon along with ponderosa pine. It is not possible to see Betatakin Ruin from this trail.

SANDAL TRAIL

A one-mile (1.6 km) round-trip, paved trail leads from the visitors center to the overlook for *Bitát'ahkin* ("ledge house" in Navajo). Built in a large cave around A.D. 1250, it had 135 rooms and a kiva. Approximately 125 Anasazi people lived in Betatakin and farmed in this fertile valley until A.D. 1300. It is believed they left the area after a serious drought changed the farming conditions in the canyon.

During the peak tourist season (May 31–August 31), Navajo National Monument rangers lead groups of twenty-five hikers to visit Betatakin at 8:30 a.m. (DST) and again at 11 a.m. (DST) daily. This strenuous five-mile (8 km) round-trip hike takes five to six hours. Time is allowed for an interpretive discussion of the ruin and its environment, and to hike the 700-foot (213 m) ascent. To join the free tour, you must obtain a ticket at the visitors center on the morning of the hike. No reservations are accepted, and the tickets are given on a first-come, first-served basis. Because temperatures approach 100 degrees (38° C) in the summer, carry at least a gallon of water per person. (You can buy water bottles at the visitors center, but bring a daypack so you can have your hands free.) Solid footwear like hiking shoes or good sneakers is required because the trail is rocky.

Betatakin Pueblo, ca. 1930–1940
Philip Johnston Collection, Cline Library, Special Collections and Archives, NAU PH 413-77.
Philip Johnston was born in 1892, the son of a missionary to the Navajos. During World War II he started the famous Navajo Code Talkers.

KEET SEEL RUIN

Kits' iiilí means "broken pieces of pottery" in Navajo. Although the pueblos were built around A.D. 1250, the Anasazi were known to have used the cave as early as A.D. 900. Keet Seel is located in a large cave in Tsegi Canyon and is one of the best-preserved cliff dwellings in the monument.

The first custodian of Navajo National Monument was John Wetherill, a trader and explorer from Kayenta. He was responsible for overseeing the building of trails from Marsh Pass to Keet Seel and the stabilization of the ruin in 1933. (See pages 161–162 for more about Wetherill.) Wetherill brought many famous visitors to Keet Seel. One of them was Zane Grey, who used the scenic beauty of Keet Seel as the backdrop for his book *Riders of the Purple Sage.*

Backcountry permits are available for twenty people per day to hike the 8.5 miles (one-way) to one of the most impressive cliff dwellings in the Southwest. It is possible to camp overnight. Tours of the cliff dwelling are provided by a ranger. Call the monument for more details: (928) 672-2700.

How are these cliff ledges formed? Water spilling over the edge of the sandstone cliffs works its way into the many cracks and crevices, freezing in winter. Over millions of years, sections of sandstone break loose from the larger mass, leaving a beautiful ledge beneath the overhang.

Inscription House Ruin, ca. 1930–1940
Philip Johnston Collection, Cline Library, Special Collections and Archives, NAU PH 413-77

Inscription House is another pueblo in the monument, but it is no longer possible to visit because of its fragile condition. Also, local Navajo families who live close to the ruin do not want visitors.

The history of the people who "found" Inscription House is interesting. The ruin gets its name from an inscription that reads: "S_____Hapeiro Ano Dom 1661." Because there was no recorded history of the Spanish visiting this area, many people thought the inscription was written by pothunters playing a joke. But Navajos who lived in the area knew that many unauthorized Spanish gold explorers came through Tsegi Canyon looking for riches. A Museum of Northern Arizona team researched the ruins in 1953 and concluded the inscription could have read "1861" because of a nearby Mormon inscription dated 1861.

Elizabeth Compton Hegemann talks about the validity of the 1661 date in her book *Navajo Trading Days.* Hegemann was owner of the Shonto Trading Post from 1929 to 1939. She was good friends with John Wetherill, who, with Byron Cummings, first saw the ruins in 1909. Wetherill's ten-year-old daughter was on the expedition with her father and Cummings. As an adult, she told Hegemann that she and Cummings's son Malcolm had found the inscription while playing. Hegemann, an accomplished photographer, took a picture of the inscription. In her book, the picture clearly shows 1661.

END SCENIC DETOUR

🐑 MM 374 BLACK MESA SHOPPING CENTER AND RV PARK
(South)

Limited space, showers, dump station, and electricity; (928) 677-3212.

🐑 MM 374 BLACK MESA & PEABODY WESTERN COAL CO. (South)

If you are traveling east, you have seen Black Mesa along the south side of Highway 160 since leaving the Red Lake Trading Post. Black Mesa is the largest single landmass in northern Arizona, embracing almost 20 percent of the entire Navajo Nation. It rises to an elevation of 8,210 feet (2,502 m) and extends from Red Lake to Kayenta, around to Chinle. Its southern escarpment includes the three mesas of the Hopi Nation, reaching like fingers into the plain. Because of its large underground sandstone strata, it holds the primary water source for the Hopi villages and surrounding Navajo communities. Next to Navajo Mountain, this mesa is one of the more remote and isolated areas in the Southwest. Roads are primitive, and the people living on the mesa remain some of the more traditional on the reservation.

The Peabody Western Coal Co. operates two of the largest open-pit strip mines in the country on Black Mesa. Large deposits of coal are found here because 65 to 135 million years ago this area was a coastal swamp where massive amounts of vegetation accumulated to form coal now found in the Dakota, Torvea, and Wepo formations that predominate in this area.

Coal from the Kayenta Mine travels to the Navajo Generating Station near Page on the second-largest coal train in the world and the only railroad operating on the Navajo Reservation. Coal from the Black Mesa Mine goes to the Mohave Generating Station on the Nevada-Arizona border through the Black Mesa Pipeline. Each year, it uses one billion gallons of some of the country's most pristine water from deep subterranean wells to slurry the coal more than 273 miles (439 km) around the Grand Canyon. The journey takes three days.

The Navajos and Hopis receive royalties from Black Mesa coal. But many, particularly Hopis, are angry that mining takes place at all. They believe the coal slurry pipeline's use of water is depleting many of the natural springs that farmers have traditionally relied on. Peabody contends that the amount of water used every day for the slurry is not enough to affect the water table and that the springs are recharged from other sources. Plans are underway to identify other sources of water for the slurry. Two alternatives include using the C-Aquifer at Canyon Diablo, west of Flagstaff, or piping water from Lake Powell. But in the meantime, Peabody Coal filed a permit application with the U.S. Department of the Interior that calls for an expansion of its mining operation on the Hopi Reservation of up to 1.5 million tons and to increase its use of the Navajo Aquifer to 5,700 acre feet.

MM 374 LONG HOUSE VALLEY (North and South)

This valley extends north and south all the way from the turnoff to Navajo National Monument to Tsegi Canyon. It was named for a ruin found here.

Mile 381.5 TSEGI CANYON (North)

The Navajo word *Tséyi'* means canyon. The sheer walls are primarily made of Navajo and Wingate Sandstone and were sculpted by Laguna Creek to make this incredible gorge. The creek was given its name because of the lagoon-like conditions Captain John Walker found while on a survey of the area for the military in 1860. He reported many pools and rich marshy growth in the canyon. Freshwater shells are commonly found along Laguna Creek. It is no wonder that so many important Anasazi sites have been found here. In summer you can see numerous Navajo cornfields along the creek.

NAVAJO DRY FARMING

Most of the small cornfields you pass along the highway are "dry farms." Crops are nutered only by the falling rain, which is minimal in most parts of the Navajo Nation, especially in the spring when crops need it most. The majority of rain falls in summer from July through September. The Navajos, like the Hopis, have adapted their ancient farming methods to take advantage of every drop of available moisture. Most fields are planted at the mouth of a canyon to capture the winter snow melt or rain that may fall far away and run through the canyon. Using a planting stick made of greasewood, seeds are planted deep in the earth to take advantage of the moisture in the ground. The time to plant is critical. To determine the correct time, farmers watch for the disappearance of the constellation Pleiades. Easily seen in the winter sky, these stars gradually disappear as the weather gets warmer and spring approaches.

MM 382 MARSH PASS

Between Black Mesa and Tsegi Canyon is Marsh Pass, named for the swamp-like environment that existed during the building of Arizona Highway 160, formerly known as Navajo Route 1.

SERVICES IN MARSH PASS

Anasazi Motel at Tsegi Canyon: Basic accommodations but an incredible location. Two double beds, TV, shower, no phones in the rooms. Prices average $75–$100/night. (928) 697-3793
Restaurant: Open 5 a.m.–11 p.m. in the summer and 5 a.m.–10 p.m. in the winter.

Marsh Pass along old Navajo Route 1 and Organ Rock Monocline, 1920 Philip Johnston Collection, Cline Library, Special Collections and Archives, NAU PH 413-514

MM 385 ORGAN ROCK MONOCLINE

Also known as Skeleton Mesa, this monocline visible to the north formed about 75–80 million years ago. It is an excellent example of geologic uplift along vertical faults caused during a period of large-scale earth movements. A monocline is a one-sided fold where the sedimentary rocks on top are draped over the displaced rocks exposed through the fault. At the bottom of the fault is Chinle Sandstone with a solid wall of Wingate Sandstone above it.

MM 387 PIÑON-JUNIPER FOREST

If you are traveling east, you have climbed more than 1,000 feet (305 m) in elevation since leaving Tuba City, to 6,000 feet (1,830 m). Notice the change in vegetation from desert scrub to piñon-pine and Utah juniper forest.

MM 390 AGATHLA PEAK

Agathla Peak, to the north, is a volcanic monolith near the entrance to Monument Valley (further discussed on pages 162–163).

MM 393 BURGER KING (North)

Owned by Navajo businessman Richard Mike, this restaurant has an excellent photographic exhibit on the **Navajo Code Talkers.** Mike's father, King Mike, was a Navajo Code Talker in WW II. Because Navajo was not a written language and has many complexities and nuances, it was the only military code the Germans and Japanese were unable to break.

☙ MM 393 NAVAJO CULTURAL CENTER (North)

Just east of the Burger King on the north side of U.S. Highway 160 is a new store built by the Navajo Tribe. Designed in the shape of a hogan with its entrance to the east, the center provides an opportunity for Navajo vendors to demonstrate their crafts. You can watch artisans create rugs, jewelry, and sand paintings, and ceremonial dancers perform on a regularly scheduled basis. Visitors are also welcome to tour authenic dwellings, including a sweathouse.

☙ COMMUNITY OF KAYENTA

The Navajo name for Kayenta, *Tódínéeshzheé,* means "water spreading out like fingers," referring to a seasonal spring that flows from the hill behind the old Wetherill Trading Post. This town has grown to provide housing for workers at the Peabody Coal mines and to accommodate the thousands of visitors to Monument Valley who come every year from all over the world. In the 1950s and 60s, there was also a booming uranium mining business in Monument Valley.

This is an interesting Navajo community to visit because it is the only township government located on an Indian reservation in the United States. It is the first municipal-structured government that allows the community to impose a sales tax. Proceeds are used to better their community rather than waiting for the Navajo Nation or federal government to do things for them. It seems to be working, and many other communities on the reservation are watching closely to see if this form of government will work for them.

SERVICES IN KAYENTA

Hampton Inn: This is a three-story adobe-style hotel on U.S. Highway 160 with interior hallways, an elevator, and 73 rooms. **Reuben Heflin Restaurant** serves lunch and dinner. (928) 697-3170.
Holiday Inn: Located at the junction of U.S. Highways 160 and 163, this motel has 163 rooms and a full-service restaurant featuring both authentic Native American cuisine and traditional American food. Office open 24 hours: (928) 697-3221.
Best Western Wetherill Inn: Located on Main Street in Kayenta, this inn has 54 rooms and an indoor pool. Office hours 7 a.m.–10 p.m. in summer; 8 a.m.–9 p.m. in winter. (928) 697-3231; (800) 528-1234.
Navajo Area Indian Health Service Clinic: Emergencies only, unless you are a Native American with a census number. Located on Highway 163 just past Wetherill Inn on the west side of the road. (928) 697-3211 or 911.
Kayenta Navajo Police Station: (928) 697-8669.

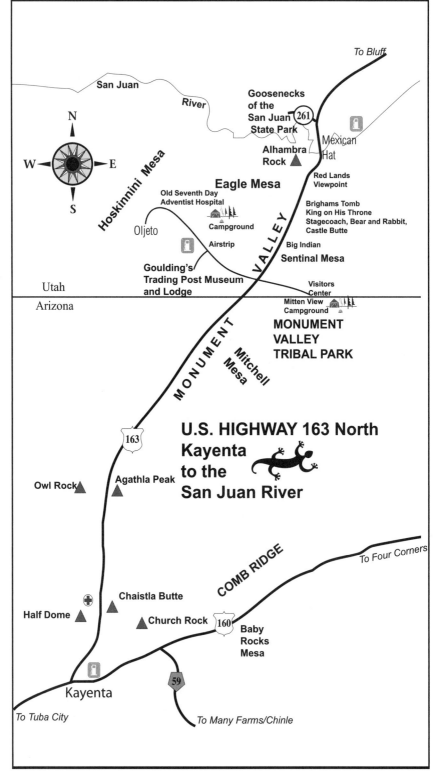

26 miles (42 km) from Kayenta to Monument Valley

🦎 MM 395 WETHERILL INN

John and Louisa Wetherill were famous traders in Kayenta, contemporaries in time and repute to the Richardsons of Cameron. John Wetherill was from Mancos, Colorado, and part of the large Wetherill family famous for their "discovery" of Mesa Verde. Louisa Wade's father was a hopeful miner who had traveled to Colorado to find his fortune. John married Louisa in 1896 and tried to make a life as a farmer in Mancos, but the first year was a complete failure. After their children Ben and Ida were born, the Wetherills moved to Oljeto, about 33 miles (53 km) from Kayenta and eight miles (13 km) past the present Goulding's Lodge in Monument Valley. Here they opened the first trading post in hostile country controlled by Hoskinnini. Even though Hoskinnini resented the intrusion, over the years he became a close personal friend of the Wetherills and, according to Louisa's autobiography, gave her the responsibility of dividing his wealth among his children when he died. In 1910, the Wetherills moved their trading post to Kayenta. John used to enjoy telling visitors that they were the "farthest point from a railroad in the United States."

John Wetherill was best known for his exploration of Mesa Verde, Keet Seel, Inscription House, and Betatakin ruins. He also served as a guide in 1909 for Byron Cummings, dean of arts and sciences at the University of Utah, in his quest for Rainbow Bridge. (See pages 63–64 for more on this expedition.)

The Navajos called Louisa Wetherill *'Anísts'óózi Ts'ósí,* or "Slim Woman." She spoke fluent Navajo and accompanied her husband on most of his expeditions, serving as interpreter. She was well-known for her depth of knowledge and respect for the Navajo lifeways.

Zane Grey, America's most prolific Western writer from 1908 to his death in 1939, spent a great deal of time in the Kayenta/Navajo Mountain area. He used Tsegi Canyon and Rainbow Bridge as the setting for *The Rainbow Trail,* a story about a tenderfoot named Shefford who goes west to find himself and his own true love.

Grey uses John Wetherill as the basis for his character Trader Withers, describing him as a man who was:
… muscular and weather-beaten, and appeared young in activity rather than face. A gun swung at his hip and a row of brass-tipped cartridges showed in his belt. Shefford looked into a face he thought he had seen before, until he realized the similarity was only the bronze and hard line and rugged cast common to desert men. The gray searching eyes went right through him.

He also used Louisa Wetherill as inspiration for Trader Withers's wife:

He [Withers] had lived at Kayenta for several years—hard and profitless years by reason of marauding outlaws. He could not have lived there at all but for the protection of the Indians. His father-in-law had been friendly with the Navajos and Paiutes for many years, and his wife had been brought up among them. She was held in peculiar reverence and affection by both tribes in that part of the country. Probably she knew more of the Indian's habits, religion, and life than any white person in the West.

Wetherill House in Kayenta, 1934, Louisa Wetherill on the right
Photo by Milton Snow, Museum of Northern Arizona, Photo Archives, #74.1198

MM 396 HALF DOME

To the east is an igneous intrusive rock formation. An intrusion is like a volcano that never broke the earth's surface. It solidifies in place because of the cooling effect of the rock layer into which it has intruded. Over eons, erosion wears off the top layers covering the intrusion, exposing the harder volcanic core.

MM 397 KAYENTA SANDSTONE

You can see this on both sides of the road.

MM 398 CHAISTLA BUTTE

To the east is another igneous intrusive rock formation.

MM 399 COMB RIDGE

See page 177 for a discussion of Comb Ridge, visible here to the east.

MM 402 AGATHLA PEAK

To the east is Agathla Peak, considered the center of the Navajo volcano field. An underground explosion formed this volcanic neck millions of years ago.

"Road to El Capitán"
Courtesy of the Atchison, Topeka & Santa Fe Railroad Collection, Kansas State Historical Society

According to Navajo legend, Agathla Peak is the center of the world. Because the sky was too low, the earth people were suffering from the intense heat of the sun. To help them, the Holy People placed this peak here to create a little more distance between the sky and the earth. It is also thought to be a transmitter to send prayers to the Holy People.

'Aghaałą means "much wool" in Navajo. This name comes from a Navajo story about an endless snake that became tired after traveling a great distance and made its home at the base of the peak. His wife, the owl, stayed with him and made her home close by (see Owl Rock). The snake lived very well here because of the plentiful supply of antelope. After eating his fill, the snake would throw the fur outside and thus the name "much wool."

Kit Carson renamed Agathla Peak El Capitán because of its commanding presence in the valley.

Mile 402.5 OWL ROCK

Seen from the right angle, this incredible monolith west of the highway looks just like an owl surveying the valley below. It is 6,547 feet (1,996 m) in elevation and is composed primarily of Wingate Sandstone.

🦎 MM 412 BEARS EARS

Directly north on the horizon are two identical buttes in the Manti-La Sal National Forest in Utah at an elevation of 9,058 feet (2,761 m). The bear plays an important part in Navajo legends and ceremonial healing. One of the stories about the bear teaches about the triumph of good over evil. Coyote desired a beautiful Navajo maiden, but she was repulsed by him because he was such an evil being. To put him off, she agreed to marry him if he could accomplish a series of seemingly impossible tasks. Through deceit and cunning, Coyote, the trickster, was able to perform every task she demanded. Forced to marry him because of her promise, the maiden began to take on the evil ways of her husband. She gained the ability to turn herself into a bear. When in a bear state she lost control of her human functions and her own identity. One day she killed two of her brothers, but the third brother escaped. Guided by the Wind, he found her human body parts (hidden while she was in a bear state), and threw them in different directions. Each part was turned into things of good. One part of her became the piñon pine nut, another became the acorn, and her head became the Bears Ears.

🦎 MM 412 MITCHELL MESA

In 1883, when Kit Carson was searching for Navajos to send to Fort Sumner in New Mexico, a small band led by Chief Hoskinnini was able to hide from Carson's troops. Chief Hoskinnini, "the angry one," was the ruler of Monument Valley from 1862 until 1912 and was particularly hostile toward white prospectors and settlers.

At the time Hoskinnini moved into Monument Valley, it was Ute territory, with Agathla Peak marking the boundary between Navajo and Ute country.

When word came that Carson and his troops were on the way, Hoskinnini and seventeen others ran for Navajo Mountain, where they lived beside a stream for six years, undiscovered except for one Ute who did not give away their hiding place.

One day, while Hoskinnini was riding on Navajo Mountain, he found silver. All of the male members of his group dug out all of the silver they could find and fashioned plain silver jewelry. When the band heard of the Navajos' release from Bosque Redondo, they moved back to Monument Valley a very rich group. Eventually, word began to leak to the outside world that Hoskinnini had found a rich silver mine, attracting many prospectors to remote Monument Valley. Hoskinnini and his band never revealed where they found the silver, but miners Merrick and Mitchell allegedly found the mine. Both volunteer soldiers with Kit Carson, they came to Monument Valley after the Navajo wars were over because of rumors of Hoskinnini's rich silver mine but didn't live long enough to enjoy their discovery.

It is thought that Mitchell and Merrick might have been successful in secretly removing one load of silver from the mine before their death. In her 1934 *Traders to the Navajo,* now a classic, Louisa Wade Wetherill claims that her father knew Mitchell and Merrick and saw the assay for their silver mine valued at $800 a ton (4,400 kg). Wade looked for the mine himself in 1882 but without success.

According to Hoskinnini's son, Hoskinnini-Begay, interviewed by reporter Charles Kelly in 1953, he had come upon Utes dividing up the miners'

possessions. The Utes told him they killed the miners when they refused to share their tobacco. Another version is that when the Paiutes found Mitchell's burro laden with silver, they became outraged at his abuse of Mother Earth and killed him. His partner Merrick escaped, but the Paiutes caught up with him at the base of the butte that bears his name. Merrick Butte can be seen between the Right and Left Mittens from the viewpoint at the visitors center. Chief Hoskinnini denied any knowledge of, or involvement in, the miners' deaths.

Hoskinnini and Ida Wetherill (detail), 1909
Stuart M. Young Collection, Cline Library, Special Collections and Archives, NAU 643-1-2

Another white man attempted to find the location of the silver mine by befriending Hoskinnini. Cass Hite, a Mormon settler who established a ferry across the Colorado River not too far from Monument Valley, just rode into Hoskinnini's camp one day, sat down, and asked for food. As it would be the height of bad manners to kill a guest in your camp, Hoskinnini had no choice but to feed this man who spoke very little Navajo. Hite gave Hoskinnini and his family presents and gradually developed a friendship with the group. After a respectable period of time he asked the family if they knew where he could find valuable minerals in the area. Hoskinnini was kind enough to tell Hite where to find gold in the Colorado River. In 1883, Hite built a trading post and a house near the river to begin panning for gold. This is where **Hite Marina** on Lake Powell stands today.

You are probably wondering what happened to the silver mine. According to Hoskinnini's son, the mine was completely exhausted and most of the silver is buried with his father, who died in 1912. The rest was divided among Hoskinnini's family. Hoskinnini-Begay's silver is buried with his eight wives.

Merrick Butte, not dated
Photo by T. Harmon Parkhurst, Courtesy Museum of New Mexico, #71068

SCENIC DETOUR

MM 416 *MONUMENT VALLEY NAVAJO TRIBAL PARK VISITORS CENTER*

Turn east and travel three miles (4.8 km) to the Monument Valley Tribal Park Visitors Center. Halfway, there will be a place to pay an entrance fee. National Park Service passes are not accepted at any tribal park. Park hours: April through September, 7 a.m.–7 p.m.; October through May, 8 a.m.–5 p.m.; closed Christmas, New Year's, and Thanksgiving Day. During the summer, the visitors center offers Indian dances on the patio from 8 to 9:30 p.m. Check at the desk to confirm the day and time for the performance. (435) 727-3353. From the visitors center, you can get a good view of the formations known as the Right and Left Mittens.

Right Mitten, Monument Valley, 1994
Photograph by Christine Stephenson

Once Paiute aboriginal land, the northwest section of the valley became part of the Navajo Reservation through the Treaty of 1868. The western and northern sections were added in 1884. In 1934, some of valley was converted to public domain, but the protest was heard in Washington and the land was reinstated to the Navajos by an act of Congress. The Navajo Tribe opened the park in 1960.

The Navajos view the whole of Monument Valley as a huge hogan. Its door, facing east, is near the visitors center. The fireplace, or the center of the hogan, is the butte behind Goulding's Trading Post.

You can hire a tour guide at the visitors center to take you through the valley or you can drive your own car. The road is unpaved and changes condition after each rainstorm. Sand traps and high road centers can cause problems for low-clearance vehicles. The self-guided tour is seventeen miles (27 km) along the valley floor. There are information signs that correspond to a map you can purchase in the visitors center for $1.

Tour Operators
The superintendent of the park controls all of the tour guide fees. Occasionally some prices will be lower but are not allowed to go any higher than the prices advertised. Most of the tour companies are Navajo-owned.
Bennett Tours
Monument Valley, Utah, (435) 727-3283; (800) 862-8270
Crawley's Tour
Kayenta, Arizona, (928) 697-3463

Three Sisters, Monument Valley, not dated
Atchison-Topeka-Santa Fe Collection, Kansas State Historical Society, Topeka, Kansas,
2/514.11

Daniel's Guided Tours
Monument Valley, Utah, (800) 596-8427; (435) 727-3227
Far Out Expeditions
Bluff, Utah, (435) 697-2294
Gouldings Tours
Monument Valley, Utah, (435) 727-3231
Jackson Tour
Monument Valley, Utah, (435) 727-3234 message
Keyah Hozhoni Monument Valley Tours
Kayenta, Arizona, (928) 309-7440
Roland's Navajoland Tours
Kayenta, Arizona, (800) 368-2785 or (928) 697-3524
Simpson's Tours
Monument Valley, Utah, (435) 727-3255

Sisco's Custom Monument Valley Tours
Kayenta, Arizona, (928) 697-3586
Totem Pole Guided Tours
Monument Valley, Utah, (435) 727-3313
Tsebiinizghai Tours
Monument Valley, Utah, (800) 874-0902; (435) 727-3225
Bigman's Horseback Tours
Monument Valley, Utah, (928) 674-1522
Ed Black Monument Valley Horseback Trailrides
Mexican Hat, Utah, (800) 551-4039 or (435) 727-3227
Homeland Horse and Van Tours
Monument Valley, Utah, (435) 727-3227; (800) 596-8427
Monument Valley Horseback Tours
Monument Valley, Utah, (928) 691-6161
Navajo Country Trailrides
Monument Valley, Utah, (435) 727-3210
Sacred Monument Trailrides
Monument Valley, Utah, (928) 691-6199

Mitten View Campground: Register at the visitors center. The campground is across the street. There are ninety-nine sites, thirty-seven tent spaces, thirty-six RV sites, nine pull-throughs, and nine day-use picnic areas. The campground operates on a first-come, first-served basis. The campground has men's and women's bathrooms and coin-operated showers, but no phones or hookups for RVs. There is a filling/dump station. A metal awning at each campsite provides the only shade. Summer temperatures at Monument Valley are usually over 100 degrees F (38° C). (435) 727-7870.

GOULDING'S TRADING POST MUSEUM

After leaving the visitors center, continue across Highway 163 and follow the signs. The museum is open from late March through October from 7 a.m. to 9 p.m. (DST); closed in winter. No admission fee but donations are welcomed. The lodge and restaurant are open year-round.

The Navajos called Harry Goulding *Dibé Nééz,* or "Tall Sheep," because of his height and interest in sheep. Harry first saw Monument Valley in the early 1920s when he came here as a representative of the Lybrook Ranch in Farmington, New Mexico, to buy Navajo Churro sheep. By the 1920s, these sheep, imported by the Spanish in the 1500s, were almost extinct. The breed has silky, long wool and four horns that grow from the tops of their foreheads and curl down into their faces. Crossbred with Merino sheep, the Churro was quickly losing the qualities that made it so valuable. Today the Merino sheep is the most common type you will see along the highway, but the Churro is gaining in popularity. (You can see a flock of Churro sheep at the Tso Bonito Zoo in Window Rock.)

As soon as Goulding saw Monument Valley, he knew this was to be his destiny. So when the opportunity arose to purchase 640 acres (2.6 sq km) of land beneath Big Rock Door Mesa for $320, he jumped at the chance.

Goulding's Trading Post under "Old Baldy," not dated
Courtesy Museum of New Mexico, #71078

The Paiute Indians had been given a small reservation here, but because of the poor farming conditions they were moved to a more fertile area in Utah, and the land became state property available for sale. Goulding officially bought the property in 1937 against protest by the Indian Service. The land had technically been added to the Navajo Reservation in 1933, but the sale was allowed because the State of Utah had maintained ownership of all school property and had the right to sell it.

During the Depression in the 1930s there was not much money coming onto the reservation. To make matters worse the BIA, under John Collier's administration, decided that Navajo sheepherders must reduce their herds because of severe overgrazing. Forced to sell their sheep at ridiculously low prices or slaughter them, many families became destitute. Even though Collier made positive changes in the education and health care systems on the Navajo Reservation, he is not remembered kindly by the Navajo people for his callous disregard for the importance of sheep. Samual Moon, in his book *Tall Sheep,* quotes Maurice Knee, Harry Goulding's brother-in-law, as saying that if a Navajo family had a dog they didn't like, they would name it "John Collie."

When Harry heard a rumor in 1937 that United Artists was looking for a place to shoot a movie in the Southwest, he packed his bags and traveled to Hollywood, hoping to attract the movie makers to the valley. With just a few pictures of Monument Valley and a lot of patience and persistence, Harry convinced John Ford to shoot his next Western on location in the valley. The first film, made in 1938, was *Stagecoach,* with John Wayne in the lead role. Other Ford movies followed, including *She Wore a Yellow Ribbon, My Darling Clementine,* and *Fort Apache.*

The success of John Ford's movies paved the way for many other movie companies to make their films or commercials here. Today, no self-respecting car company would make a commercial unless its backdrop is Monument Valley. One movie made here has a touch of irony to it. The movie was *Kit Carson*, the same person who had chased Hoskinnini's clan into the valley. Now Hoskinnini's descendants, just eighty years later, would work in a movie that glorified Carson's actions.

When the Gouldings retired, they sold their property to Knox College in Illinois in exchange for royalties and scholarships for Navajo students. In 1981, Knox College sold Goulding's to the LaFont family, which also owns the Canyon de Chelly Motel in Chinle and the Wetherill Inn in Kayenta.

SERVICES AT GOULDING'S

Lodge: A 62-room motel with each room facing Monument Valley. It also has an indoor swimming pool. Reservations: Goulding's Lodge, Box 360001, Monument Valley, Utah 84536, (435) 727-3231; (435) 727-3344.
Stagecoach Restaurant: Navajo-American, open 6:30 a.m.–9 p.m. (DST). (435) 727-3231, ext. 404. Limited hours in winter, but breakfast, lunch and dinner are served.
Evening Entertainment: *Earth Spirit: A Celebration of Monument Valley* is a slide presentation of Monument Valley by photographer Ric Ergenbright. Tickets are complimentary with purchase of a Gouldings Monument Valley Tour.

MONUMENT VALLEY AIRSTRIP

North of the turnoff to Goulding's Trading Post is the airstrip. Harry Goulding had to do some major land negotiations to get this built. He wanted it to transport critically ill patients to and from the hospital as well as to accommodate Hollywood's need to fly in actors, equipment, and crews for a day or two of shooting. Harry first asked the governor of Utah to finance the airstrip. Then, because the land he wanted was on the Navajo Reservation, he had to get congressional approval to exchange a piece of his own land for the airstrip land.

🦎 MONUMENT VALLEY HEALTH CENTER/OLD SEVENTH-DAY ADVENTIST HOSPITAL

Before 1950, no health care was available in Monument Valley. The Gould-ings frequently drove their neighbors to Tuba City, Arizona, about 120 miles one-way over unimproved roads. The last time they did this in 1949, the small child did not survive the trip. Harry Goulding gave the Seventh-Day Adventists a ninety-nine-year lease if the church, which operated medical missions around the world at the time, would open a clinic to serve the people of Monument Valley.

The first building constructed on the hospital grounds was made from ma-terials from the movie set of *She Wore a Yellow Ribbon.* No longer a Seventh-Day Adventist hospital, it is now a privately owned health clinic, open 8:30 a.m.–5:00 p.m. Monday–Thursday and 8:30 a.m.–noon Friday. Walk-ins welcome; health insurance accepted. (435) 727-3241.

🦎 GOULDING'S MONUMENT VALLEY CAMPGROUND

Open year-round. Located in Rock Door Canyon, this 66-site campground offers a grocery store, gift shop, laundry facilities, and barbecues, plus an indoor pool. Full hookups: water, sewer, electricity. (435) 727-3231 or 3235.

END SCENIC DETOUR

Return to U.S. Highway 163 and turn north to see the Goosenecks of the San Juan River. It's twenty-five miles (40 km) to Mexican Hat, Utah.

🦎 MM 4 SENTINEL MESA

You can see a piece of the Left Mitten in front of Sentinel Mesa.

🦎 MM 5 BIG INDIAN

To the east is the formation known as Big Indian.

🦎 MM 6 BRIGHAM'S TOMB, KING ON HIS THRONE, STAGECOACH, BEAR AND RABBIT, CASTLE BUTTE

If you look closely at all of these land forms to the east, you'll see that their names were well chosen.

🦎 MM 9 REDLANDS VIEWPOINT

This pulloff offers a different view of the formations to the south.

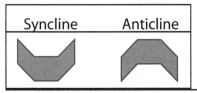

🦎 MM 10 SLEEPING UTE MOUNTAIN, CORTEZ, COLORADO

See page 184 for a description of this mountain, visible off to the east.

🦎 MM 18 ALHAMBRA ROCK

To the west is another igneous rock formation. Like Agathla Peak, in Navajo cosmology, it too supports the sky.

🦎 MM 21 MEXICAN HAT SYNCLINE

As you cross the bridge over the San Juan River, the syncline is directly in front of you. This is just one part of the combinations of synclines and anticlines that make up the Monument Upwarp. A syncline is a trough of stratified rock. An anticline is folded rock layers sloping downward from a common crest.

Syncline	Anticline

MM 21 SAN JUAN RIVER AND BRIDGE

The construction of this bridge in 1909 ended a long history of dangerous crossings by Paiutes, Navajos, and pioneers.

First Bridge Across the San Juan River, ca. 1930–1940
Philip Johnston Collection, Cline Library, Special Collections and Archives, NAU 413-525-526

This is the northern boundary of the Navajo Nation. The headwaters originate above Pagosa Springs and Wolf Creek Pass in Colorado and flow into Lake Powell. Before construction of the Glen Canyon Dam, the San Juan River flowed directly into the Colorado River.

MEXICAN HAT

Named "Black Hat" in Navajo, this town gets its name from a rock formation about 1.5 miles (2.4 km) northeast of the bridge that looks like an upside down Mexican sombrero. This is the takeout point for many San Juan River trips that start at Sand Island Recreation Area near Bluff, Utah, and travel about twenty-six miles (42 km) to Mexican Hat. Because of the popularity of this river, you must obtain a permit based on a lottery system to float the San Juan privately, but many commercial companies offer trips as well.

San Juan River Tour Companies
Adrift Adventures (800) 874-4483
Arizona Raft Adventures, Inc. (800) 786-7238 or (928) 526-8200
Four Corners School of Outdoor Education (435) 587-2159;
(800) 525-4456
O.A.R.S. (800) 346-6277 or (209) 736-4677
Sunrise Expeditions (800) 748-3730 or (207) 942-9300

Wild Adventures (800) 259 RAFT or (800) RIO-MOAB
Wild River Expeditions (800) 422-7654

MM 22 OIL DERRICKS

While prospecting along the San Juan River, E. L. Goodridge noticed oil seeping out of the rocks about where the bridge over the San Juan stands today. Others probably noticed this black stuff, but no one seemed to realize its value except Goodridge. He built a drilling rig about one hundred feet (30 m) from the natural oil seep and, at 225 feet (69 m), hit a "gusher" on March 4, 1908. This started an oil boom, and the bridge was built over the San Juan to accommodate the glut of oil tycoons wanting to haul equipment from Bluff to the oil fields.

The geology of Mexican Hat, at that time known as Goodridge, did not hold large reservoirs of oil because the river had already sapped most of it out of the rock over millions of years. It wasn't until 1956, when Texaco drilled a well at Aneth, Utah, on the Navajo Reservation, that the truly important oil field was discovered. The Aneth Oil Field is expected to produce more than 500 million barrels of oil over its lifetime.

SERVICES IN MEXICAN HAT

Lodging
Burch's Motel and Trading Company (435) 683-2221
Canyonlands Motel (435) 683-2230
Mexican Hat Lodge (435) 683-2222
The San Juan Inn (800) 447-2022
Valley of the Gods Bed and Breakfast (970) 749-1164
RV Parks
Burch's Motel and Trading Company RV Park (435) 683-2221
Full hookups; only three spaces available.
Valle Trailer Park (800) 683-2226
31 RV sites, full hookups, shower, restrooms, and dump station.

GOOSENECKS OF THE SAN JUAN RIVER
Just a few miles north of Mexican Hat, take Utah Highway 261 to the crookedest river in the world. This amazing geologic wonder formed about the same time as the volcanic plugs such as Shiprock and Agathla Peak, when the uplift created the San Juan Canyon. Once a wide, wandering river, as the shores rose around it, the San Juan River began cutting deeper and deeper. Once entrenched in harder and harder rock, the river had no choice but to follow the meandering path it had previously cut. The San Juan River travels 135 miles (218 km) through its

many twists and turns from the point where it enters the canyon to the point where it empties into Lake Powell, a distance of just sixty-three miles (102 km) as the crow flies.

Goosenecks of the San Juan River, ca. 1930–1940s
Philip Johnston Collection, Cline Library, Special Collections and Archives, NAU PH 413-534

78 miles (126 km) from Kayenta to Four Corners National Monument

 MM 400 CHURCH ROCK AND COMB RIDGE

Heading east on U.S. Highway 160 from Kayenta, you will see an excellent example of an igneous intrusive rock formation to the north. Like Agathla Peak, it formed when the sedimentary material surrounding the hardened volcanic plug eroded away, leaving the remains of a vent or cylinder eerily exposed in the general shape of a church and steeple.

Behind Church Rock is Comb Ridge, one of the larger monoclines in the world. This seventy-mile (112 km) ridge of Navajo Sandstone extends from Kayenta to Blanding, Utah.

Comb Ridge shows the characteristic pink, light orange, and gray colors that make up much of the beauty of the Southwest. Navajo Sandstone is simply compressed ancient sand dunes. If you look closely, you can see the way the wind was blowing from the directions of the lines on its surface. This makes it a favorite for photographers.

Many Navajos think of Comb Ridge as the backbone of the earth. They also see it as one long arrowhead, set on edge, one of four that protects the boundaries of the Navajo Nation.

MM 407 BABY ROCKS MESA

This assortment of spires and knobs to the south resulted from the erosion of the Entrada Sandstone formed during the Jurassic Era. Navajos use this mesa to teach their children values. One story tells of a big sister who refused to give blue corn bread to her baby sister. To put an end to the big sister's fighting and selfishness, the Holy People punished her by turning her to stone here, where she lives as one of the Baby Rocks.

This was once a Navajo farming community, but after a 1912 flood cut Laguna Creek too low to allow irrigation to reach Baby Rocks, the people moved fifteen miles (24 km) downstream to Dennehotso.

The trading post and gas station were built by Clark Hadley, a Navajo businessman, in the 1960s. His family has lived at Baby Rocks for generations. Since Hadley's death in 1985, the businesses have been closed, but his family plans to reopen the trading post.

Baby Rocks Mesa is the favorite place of Tony Hillerman's fictional Navajo police officer Jim Chee to wait for speeders along U.S. Highway 160. Who knows? Maybe the real Navajo police like this area also.

U.S. HIGHWAY 160
North
Kayenta
to
Four Corners

To Monticello, Utah

San Juan River

Bluff, Ut.

Cortez, Co.

160
491

Sleeping
Ute
Mountain

163

Mexican Hat

San Juan River

191

COMB RIDGE

COLORADO

Monument
Valley

Hunts Mesa

Four
Corners
Nat'l.
Mon.

UTAH

160

COMB RIDGE

Red
Mesa

Shiprock, NM

Agathla Peak

Tes Nez iah

160

Teec
Nos
Pos

64

Dennehotso

Mexican
Water

ARIZONA

NEW
MEXICO

Church
Rock

Baby
Rocks
Mesa

Rock Point

Carrizo
Mountains

Kayenta

191

491

Chilchinbito

N

59

W   E

Lukachukai
Mountains

BLACK MESA

S

Round Rock

Chuska
Mountains

Rough Rock

191

12

To Window Rock

Many Farms

To Chinle/
Canyon de Chelly

To Gallup, New Mexico

MM 408 HUNT'S MESA (North, behind Comb Ridge)

Locals consider this the back door to Monument Valley. Following a rugged, twisting four-wheel-drive trail, you arrive on top of Hunt's Mesa where you can look down upon the world-famous buttes and spires. Not recommended without a guide and proper back-road equipment. (See tour guides, pages 168–169.)

 ## MM 412 RED POINT MESA

You can see this mesa to the south.

 ## MM 418 DENNEHOTSO

This town's name comes from a Navajo word meaning "people's farms." The leader of the Baby Rocks group, named Old Crank, built an earthen dam in 1912 to promote farming along Laguna Creek. A concrete dam replaced it in the 1940s to irrigate nearly 800 acres (3.2 sq km). This area was also the site of a uranium mine.

MM 422 CARRIZO MOUNTAINS

See MM 465 for an explanation of these mountains, visible to the southeast.

MM 428 DENNEHOTSO CANYON

This canyon to the south was cut by the Chinle Wash.

MM 429 TES NEZ IAH

In Navajo, this name means "tall cottonwood grove."

 ## MM 436 MEXICAN WATER

Just past the junction with U.S. Highway 191 is the town of Mexican Water, or *Naakaii to' hadayiiznili*, which means "Mexicans dug shallow wells." In 1939, a steel bridge was built over Walker Creek, ending the use of the original **1879 Mormon Road,** which ran from Cedar City, Utah, crossed the Colorado River at Lees Ferry, and ran through Willow Springs, Moenkopi, Red Lake, Kayenta, and Mexican Water. It crossed the San Juan River at Bluff, Utah; the Colorado River at Moab; and circled back around to Cedar City.

Mexican Water Restaurant: Open 7 a.m.–10 p.m. According to locals they make a good Navajo taco.

WHAT IS A NAVAJO TACO?

The Navajo taco, voted the State Dish of Arizona in a 1995 poll conducted by the *Arizona Republic,* is an amalgamation of beans, chopped lettuce, sliced tomato, shredded cheddar, and an optional green chile sitting atop a piece of crispy frybread and eaten open-faced. Frybread cooked on the Navajo Reservation simply must be made with Blue Bird Flour from the Cortez Milling Co. to be considered authentically Navajo. The precise reason is ineffable, but it's believed its higher gluten

Photograph by Christine Stevenson

content holds the dough together better than other flours when flipped between palms to achieve the round, tortilla shape for cooking. Then the dough is fried in Crisco or lard in a heavy iron skillet. Now thought of as a "traditional food," frybread actually came from the Bosque Redondo era, when some eight thousand Navajos spent four years imprisoned and were given little more than white flour and lard to eat.

JUNCTION OF U.S. HIGHWAY 191 NORTH TO BLUFF, UTAH

MM 450 RED MESA

This incredibly red mesa to the north gets its color from mud sediment found in the Carmel Formation, part of the San Raphael Group formed during the Jurassic Era, 135 to 180 million years ago. It is mostly red, brown, and gray mudstone and sandstone.

MM 464 TEEC NOS POS

T'iis nazbas means "cottonwoods in a circle" in Navajo. The original Teec Nos Pos Trading Post was built in 1905 by the Foutz family. They are related by marriage to the Tanner family, the first Mormon settlers of Tuba City in the 1800s. When the original trading post burned in the 1950s, the decision was made to rebuild closer to the rumored new Navajo Route 1

Teec Nos Pos Trading Post, 1949
Photo by Milton Snow, Courtesy Museum of New Mexico #46042

(U.S. Highway 160). According to Kathy Foutz, who currently works at the post, Grandpa was just a little off in his calculations. The trading post lies about a quarter mile (.4 km) west of the turnoff to Four Corners on the north side of the road. Open 7:30 a.m.–6:30 p.m. DST.

Teec Nos Pos was the childhood home of Peter MacDonald, former chairman of the Navajo Nation. His maternal great-grandparents were prisoners at Bosque Redondo. Their son, Deshna Chischillige, became the second chairman of the Navajo Tribe in 1928, the same year Peter MacDonald was born. MacDonald was given the name Peter Donald by a BIA school official who couldn't pronounce his Navajo name, a common practice in most boarding schools at the time. When his classmates heard the name they changed it to MacDonald after the song *Old MacDonald.*

Once considered the most powerful American Indian in the country, MacDonald was sentenced to a fourteen-year prison term for corruption, accepting bribes, and conspiracy in relation to a 1989 riot in the Navajo capital of Window Rock that led to the deaths of two of his supporters. The riot resulted from the frustration his supporters felt over his suspension from office by the Navajo Tribal Council after he was implicated in fraudulent schemes by a U.S. Senate panel looking into fraud in Indian Country. Despite convictions in tribal and federal courts, MacDonald has always maintained he was duped and had done nothing wrong from a Navajo traditional context. Though he was discredited in the eyes of some, his supporters remain ardently loyal to him. He is a very popular figure on the Navajo Reservation, with large groups of supporters calling themselves *Diné Bóhoniih,* which means "the people are our boss." Many of his supporters believe that MacDonald was the victim of a federal and tribal vendetta, stripped of power illegally and treated unfairly. In April 1995, a newly elected Navajo Nation Council granted MacDonald a complete pardon and requested President Clinton to pardon him for his federal crimes.

Despite his legal problems, MacDonald accomplished much for the Navajo people during his nearly twenty-five-year reign as chairman. His rise to power came through his appointment as director of the Office of Navajo Economic Opportunity in 1964 by former Navajo chairman Raymond Nakai. In that position, MacDonald obtained the tribe's first federal grant under the newly legislated Economic Development Act of the Johnson administration.Through MacDonald's grant, a preschool program, small business development center, and neighborhood youth corps were established.

TEEC NOS POS RUG DESIGN

Usually a very large rug, the Teec Nos Pos design has an intricate center and wide borders, which many find similar to Persian rugs. Because of their intricacies and size, they can be very expensive.

Teec Nos Pos Rug, ca. 1970
Photograph by Gene Balzer, Museum of Northern Arizona

MM 465 CARRIZO MOUNTAINS

Since Red Mesa, you have been able to see these mountains to the south, rising gradually to their highest peak at an elevation of 9,420 feet (2,873 m). The Navajos call this mountain *Dzil Nahoozitii,* which means "the mountain that gropes around" or "circular mountain." Uranium is plentiful here because of the extensive Morrison Formation. Long coveted for its reported mineral wealth, the mountain has been the target of miners' attempted explorations since the late 1800s. In 1890, Indian agent C. E. Vendever heard a rumor that fifty prospectors illegally entered the reservation and were mining on the mountain. Vendever sent for troops from Fort Wingate, and along with Chee Dodge and famous photographer Ben Wittick, accompanied the troops to the mining site, where they found fifteen prospectors besieged by a mob of angry people defending their sacred land. Everything ended peacefully, with the prospectors escorted off the reservation by the soldiers.

When uranium miners asked Tall Bitter Water, a resident of the Carrizos, for permission to explore for oil and uranium in this mineral-rich area, he explained the significance of these mountains for the Navajo people. He said that the mountain has arms and legs. He was referring to the belief that the Chuska, Lukachukai, and Carrizo ranges make up a male figure. The Carrizos are the figure's legs and must not be tampered with. Bitter Water continued to explain that this mountain takes care of the Navajo people and helps people get well. It cannot do that if its legs are cut off.

Carrizo Mountains, 1890
Photograph by Ben Wittick, courtesy School of American Research Collections in the Museum of New Mexico, #15568

SLEEPING UTE MOUNTAIN

In the distance to the north (iin Colorado) is a landmark in traditional Ute territory known as *Dzil Naajinii,* or "black mountain sloping down" to Navajos. It's possible to see a human figure when you look at the mountain from the east. The story is told that a Ute chief is buried here. His head lies toward the north with his face to the sky. His arms cross over his chest and his feet point to the south.

FOUR CORNERS NATIONAL MONUMENT

The monument lies 5.8 miles north of the junction with U.S. Highway 64. There is a small entrance fee; National Park Service passes are not valid here. This is a Navajo tribal park, and camping is not allowed. If you stand in the center of the circle you will be able to tell your friends that you were in all four states at the exact same moment. In 1875, the first surveying marker was placed dividing the territories—later to become the states of Arizona, New Mexico, Colorado, and Utah. But it was not until 1962 that a paved road made the monument accessible and a plaque commemorating this surveyor's dream was dedicated. Each of the four states has its seal on the monument. The inscription reads, "*Here Meet, in Freedom, Under God, Four States.*" You will find jewelry and food vendors here.

Church Rock

To Four Corners

Mexican Water

160

To Kayenta

Chinle

Rock Point

191

Los Gigantes

Little Round Rock

191

Round Rock

Round Rock

Lukachukai Mountains

Chilchinbito

59

Wash

Chuska Mountains

Rough Rock

191

Lukachukai

12

B L A C K   M E S A

Many Farms

Tsaile

67

N

W   E

S

Chinle

Canyon de Chelly

7

To Tuba City

Ganado Mesa

DEFIANCE PLATEAU

Fort Defiance

Keams Canyon

Steamboat

264

Ganado

264

Window Rock

Junction of U.S. Highways 160/191 to Interstate 40

Hubbell's Trading Post

Klagetoh

191

Wide Ruins

P a i n t e d   D e s e r t

To Gallup, New Mexico

Chambers

To Holbrook

40

Navajo

MM 495 ROCK POINT

Established in 1926, this community fifteen miles south of U.S. Highway 160 is the starting point of "Red Rock Country." This scenic area stretches all the way from here to Red Rock on the east side of the Chuska Mountains. Most of the rock in this area is Wingate Sandstone, formed during the Triassic Era. The bottom layer, or Salt Wash Formation, holds large deposits of uranium, mined in the Lukachukai Mountains in the 1950s.

Throughout Red Rock Country lie countless prehistoric and historic ruins, natural bridges, coves, caves, and other interesting phenomena. In 1965, Stephen Jett of Ohio State University studied potential tourist attractions for inclusion in the Navajo Tribal Park system. He found Red Rock country to be "one of the most outstanding areas in the region, both from a scenic and an archaeological point of view...."

MM 486 LITTLE ROUND ROCK MESA AND ROUND ROCK MESA

Look for a window in Round Rock Mesa, visible from the road to the west.

Mile 482.5 LOS GIGANTES

East, behind the mesa, is a formation whose name means "the giants." This is the setting for Tony Hillerman's first Navajo detective novel, which won honorable mention from the Mystery Writers of America for Best First Novel.

Hillerman originally intended to call the book *The Enemy Way* because the plot centers around this ceremony, but his publisher at Harper & Row decided to change the title to *The Blessing Way.* The story is about an urban Indian who doesn't know his culture. An organized crime syndicate uses him to find a White Sands military rocket lost in the rugged Lukachukai Mountains so they can sell its secrets to the enemy. Navajo Police Lt. Joe Leaphorn deduces that the "relocation Indian" is the cause of a murder associated with the search for the missile, and related "Navajo Wolf" scares to keep people away from his find. Leaphorn figures this out because of the illogical reasoning used by this man without a culture.

THE BLESSINGWAY CEREMONY

The Blessingway is the cornerstone of the Navajo ceremonial healing system. This ceremony helps patients restore a sense of harmony with their surroundings and brings happiness back into their lives. The songs and prayers chanted during this lengthy "sing" describe the Navajo creation story. It tells about the emergence of the Holy People from the underworld, the birth of Changing Woman, the building of the first hogan, and the creation of the four sacred mountains. Patients feel like they are one with the story and important participants in the creation of the earth.

Native diagnosticians will prescribe this ceremony for people experiencing stress, anxiety, boredom, lack of confidence, or fear. Many Navajos have a Blessingway annually to ensure happiness and harmony throughout the year.

MM 485 LUKACHUKAI MOUNTAINS

To the east are the Lukachukai Mountains, a small range that runs from Round Rock to Lukachukai, where the Chuska Mountains begin.

MM 485 ROUND ROCK TRADING POST

This trading post once belonged to **Chee Dodge** and his partner Stephen Aldrich in 1881. Chee Dodge was the first chairman of the Navajo Tribe. He was appointed by a Bureau of Indian Affairs agent in 1884 because of his leadership and speaking skills. Dodge was born in 1860 in Fort Defiance; his father was a Mexican interpreter and his mother was a member of the Coyote Pass Clan. When Kit Carson carried out his scorched earth plan to subjugate the Navajos, Dodge's family fled for the safety of the Grand Canyon. On the way, his mother stopped at Walpi to ask for food but died at the hands of angry villagers tired of Navajo raiders. His family continued on to the Grand Canyon but eventually came back to Fort Defiance to surrender to Kit Carson when they heard that other Navajos had surrendered at Canyon de Chelly.

At the age of four, Dodge made the long walk to Bosque Redondo with his aunt. There he learned to speak English fluently. He became the "boy interpreter" and upon his release from Fort Sumner, returned to Fort Defiance to serve as an interpreter and Army scout. Dodge later became a very successful rancher who owned vast amounts of grazing land. He loaned Lorenzo Hubbell money and on two occasions loaned money to St. Michaels Mission. Dodge helped the Franciscans establish their mission school as an alternative to the repressive government boarding schools.

This trading post was the site of the famous Black Horse Rebellion of 1892. Black Horse and other Navajos held Indian agent David Shipley hostage to put an end to the deceitful methods he used to lure children to school, which included kidnapping and physical abuse. The people of Round Rock could stand no more and took the law into their own hands to protect their children.

A Navajo policeman barely rescued David Shipley, named *Tł'izinishchxon* (Smelly Goat) by the community, from being beaten to death. When a battalion of soldiers finally arrived at Round Rock, Black Horse and his followers were arrested and taken to Fort Wingate. There they testified to officials about Shipley's cruel treatment of their children, resulting in his removal from office.

JUNCTION OF U.S. HIGHWAY 191 AND NAVAJO ROUTE 12
Turn south on U.S. 191 to Chinle.

🐢 MM 470 CHINLE WASH

Cottonwood thrives in areas where water is plentiful, such as wash beds and around springs. They belong to the poplar family and have cotton-like hairs that grow around the seed. The Hopi use the cottonwood root to make katsina dolls and *paho* (prayer feather) sticks.

🐢 MM 462 MANY FARMS

Its Navajo name is *Dá´ák'ehaláni*, meaning large cultivated fields.

Tseyí Shopping Center (West): Working with the Center for Diné Studies at Chinle Public School, this Bashas' store labels more than two hundred food products in the Navajo language. This is not always a simple task. For some foods, like watermelon, translators had a hard time deciding if it should be called *Ch'eehjiyaan,* "to eat in vain," *or T'eehjiyaan,* "raw food." The goal of the project is to promote the use of the Navajo language.

🐢 MM 445 CHINLE COMPREHENSIVE HEALTH CARE FACILITY
(West)

This hospital truly incorporates Navajo tradition into its health-care system. Largely due to the influence of Ursula Knoki-Wilson, a certified nurse-midwife, the obstetrical unit takes advantage of many of the age-old Navajo beliefs and customs to make patients feel safe and comfortable during the labor and delivery experience. Cedar is burned as incense to provide a sense of calmness and to bless the room and the family. A Navajo sash belt hangs in each labor room for the pushing phase of delivery.

Once the baby is born, some traditional Navajo families take the placenta and umbilical cord back to their camp. It's buried on the south side of the hogan if the baby is a girl, so that she will be a good weaver, or buried in the corral if the baby is a boy, so he will take good care of the livestock.

Traditional healers use the hogan built inside the hospital to conduct ceremonies for their patients. Because it's necessary to have a connection with Mother Earth, the hogan fireplace reaches down through the foundation to connect it directly to the earth beneath the building.

As a visitor to the Navajo Nation, you can be seen at the hospital for an emergency only, such as an auto accident with injuries. For all other health conditions, you must visit a private physician or health facility.

Emergency room: (928) 674-7001.

🪲 MM 432 BEAUTIFUL VALLEY (East)

This is the same Chinle Formation found at the Petrified Forest and the Painted Desert.

🪲 GANADO MESA

The mesa to the east is capped by the Bidahochi Formation, which consists of sediment from ancient lake deposits.

JUNCTION OF U.S. HIGHWAY 191 AND ARIZONA HIGHWAY 264
Turn east to continue on U.S. Highway 191 to U.S. Interstate 40.

🪲 MM 441 GANADO

See pages 133–140 for a full description of Ganado.

JUNCTION OF ARIZONA HIGHWAY 264 AND U.S. HIGHWAY 191 SOUTH TO U.S. I-40

🪲 MM 397 KLAGETOH

In 1935, Leonard Walker, a well-known trader who would own many posts throughout the reservation, was a teenager working for the owner of the Klagetoh post. It was a quiet morning with people sitting around the warm fire burning in the pot-bellied stove when a woman dressed like a hard-working cowboy walked in with two Colt .45s strapped to her hips. She demanded to see the owner, but Walker said he was the only one available to help her. Angered by this, she proceeded to tell him the reason for her visit. She said she had heard from her customers that he was selling flour for $1.15 a sack when the going rate was $1.25. She then pulled out her guns and began shooting at the exposed nails in the wall. When she finished, a shaken Walker told her what she had heard was wrong. He, too, was selling flour for $1.25. Upon hearing this, she turned and headed for the door, only stopping to say, "Keep it that way." The woman was Winnie Balcomb, Walker's competitor at Wide Ruins Trading Post, a post Walker later would own.

KLAGETOH RUG DESIGN

Klagetoh is famous for a rug style very similar to the Ganado Red. Weavers of both rugs use red, black, and grey in their design, but the Klagetoh usually has a grey background instead of red. The weaver of the rug shown on page 191 has chosen to use grey around the center and in the zigzag design. Natural dyes are used in most Klagetoh rugs.

Klagetoh Rug, 1968, Photograph by Gene Balzer,Museum of Northern Arizona

WIDE RUINS RUG DESIGN

The Wide Ruins design developed during the classic period of Navajo weaving, dating back to between 1850 and 1883. Wide bands enclose complex geometric designs on a rug without a border. A Wide Ruin rug is finely woven, and usually only natural plant dyes are used.

Encouraged by the Lippincotts, traders at Wide Ruin Trading Post during the 1930s, weavers started to experiment with the development of subtle shades such as pastels of pinks, yellows, beige, tans, and browns made from vegetal dyes. Natural dyes are made from tree bark, flower petals, bulb skins, wild carrots, pine needles, leaves, lichen, corn, berries, cactus fruit, and walnut shells. Urine and juniper ash set the dye. In 1940, Nonabah Bryan wrote a book describing eighty-four different shades of vegetal dye. Today the number has increased to more than one hundred shades.

Wide Ruins Rug, 1972 Photograph by Gene Balzer, Museum of Northern Arizona

MM 392 WIDE RUINS

The name comes from the translation of *Kinteel,* or "wide house," the Navajo name for the ancient ruin found in this area.

Wide Ruins Trading Post, ca. 1930
Leo Crane Collection, Cline Library, Special Collections and Archives, NAU PH 658-967
Leo Crane was the Indian agent in Keams Canyon starting in 1911. All of his pictures were taken between 1913 and 1934.

**46 miles (74 km) from the junction with U.S. Highway 160
to Many Farms**

*NOTE: Navajo Route 59 does not have mile markers,
so set your trip odometer to zero when you turn off Highway 160.*

MILE 1 CARRIZO MOUNTAINS

See pages 183–184 for information on these mountains to the east.

MILE 15 CHILCHINBITO

In Navajo, *Chiiłchin Biíto* means "water in the sumac." Navajo artists use sumac, which grows around a spring here, to create baskets.

BLACK MESA

This mesa to the west extends all the way to Many Farms.

MILE 31 ROUGH ROCK COMMUNITY SCHOOL

Bob Roessel, a widely known educator who has had a significant impact on the improvement of education for Navajo children, once said, *"Education as the Indian knows it on the reservation can be characterized as the 'either-or' type. One is either an Indian or a white man, and the way we traditionally have weighted things, the good way always is the non-Indian way and the bad way always is the Indian way. We have told the child that he is superstitious and primitive… We try to impose our values on him and tell him he should eat green, leafy vegetables and sleep on a bed and brush his teeth. In short, we try to make a white man out of an Indian. The child listens and looks at himself and sees that he doesn't measure up. In his own eyes he is a failure. Education can be a shattering experience when one is taught nothing but negative things about himself…"*

Funded in 1965 by the Office of Economic Opportunity, Rough Rock Demonstration School attempted to teach Indian children about their own history, language, and heroes so that students would come away with a sense of who they are as individuals and collectively as Indian people. They did this by involving an active and interested community in the teaching of their children. Elders taught language and legends that children should have learned at home from their grandparents but may have missed because they were away at boarding school.

To Monument Valley

To Four Corners

191

COMB RIDGE

Owl Rock ▲   Agathla Peak ▲
163

Church
Rock ▲

Kayenta

To Tuba City

Baby
Rocks
Mesa

160   ● Dennehotso

● Mexican Water

Chinle

Rock Point ●

191

N
W   E
S

59

Chilchinbito ●

B
L
A
C
K

M
E
S
A

Wash

Los Gigantes
Butte ▲

Little
Round
Rock ▲

Round Rock ▲

● Round
Rock

● Rough Rock

191

Lukachukai Mtns.

12

● Many Farms

NAVAJO ROUTE 59
South
Chilchinbito
to
Many Farms

191

To Chinle/Canyon de Chelly

To Fort
Defiance

The school was originally built in 1930 by the Bureau of Indian Affairs, but an all-Navajo school board took control in the 1960s under the Indian Self-Determination Act. Rough Rock was the prototype upon which community members lobbied Congress to charter the first Indian-run community college, Navajo Community College, now Diné College.

Today the school's purpose is to "educate, enlighten, motivate, challenge, and assist in the proper cultural rearing of our Navajo children so they can be self-respecting, respectful of others, speak and practice their language and culture, and be totally functional in the Anglo society."

Navajo Police Sgt. Jim Chee, Tony Hillerman's second major fictional character, was first introduced in *People of Darkness.* He grew up at Rough Rock and was a member of the imaginary Slow Talking Clan. His uncle, Hosteen Frank Sam Nakai, who was a well-known "singer," or medicine man, was the mentor who taught Jim Chee his knowledge about traditional healing. Chee was learning the Nightway Chant and the Enemy Way ceremony.

THE ENEMY WAY
Also known as the Squaw Dance, this is an important ceremony for people who have been living off the reservation among "enemies." Many veterans have this ceremony when they return from a war zone. In summertime, it's common to see signs along reservation highways announcing a Squaw Dance. Please do not attend unless invited by a Navajo family.

MM 37 TSAILE BUTTE AND THE CHUSKA MOUNTAINS

These landmarks are visible to the east.

MANY FARMS (At the junction of N.R. 59 and U.S. 191)

Dá´ák'ehalání, the Navajo name for Many Farms, means large cultivated fields, a good name for the more than seven hundred small farms run by Navajo families since 1937. A very large lake two miles east of Many Farms on U.S. Highway 191 has largemouth bass, channel catfish, and black bullhead.

Many Farms Health Center: Open 8 a.m. to 5 p.m.; (928) 781-6246.

Many Farms Inn: At the intersection of Navajo Route 59 and U.S. Highway 191, head north one mile on 191. Turn left at the Many Farms High School sign, and follow the signs for another mile to the entrance of the inn. This inn was made possible through a School-to-Work federal grant project to give high school students a chance to learn about the hospitality industry. The school converted a vacant dormitory, and because it was a dormitory, bathrooms are shared. Each room has two single beds. Rates are $30 per room, single or double occupancy. There is a television lounge, pay phone, coffee, and vending machines. Because lodging is hard to find in the summer, a room at the inn will probably make some travelers very happy. (928) 781-6362.

Yé'li bicheii RUG DESIGN

Many weavers around Many Farms make the *Yé'ii bicheii* design. The *Yé'ii bicheii* is an important night ceremonial in which humans dress like *yé'iis,* or Navajo gods, for the purpose of healing. The dancers' proportions are life-like and the weaver places them in her rug according to the requirements of the ceremony.

Yé'ii bicheii **Rug, ca. 1910–1930**
Photo by Gene Balzer, Museum of Northern Arizona

30 miles (48 km) from Chinle to Spider Rock

𝍂 CHINLE

The Navajo name for this community is *Ch'inlih,* meaning "water flowing." Prior to 1941, many magazine writers referred to the town as Chin Lee. Father Leopold Osterman established the first Franciscan mission here in 1904. You can see the original Catholic church, dedicated in 1912, as you drive to Canyon de Chelly on Navajo Route 7. It's about one mile (1.6 km) on the south side of the road, behind the new hogan-style Catholic church.

In 1906, Doyalthi'ih, "the silent one," kidnapped Indian agent Reuben Perry for forcing Navajo children to go to boarding school in Fort Defiance about ninety miles (145 km) away. Convicted of kidnapping, Doyalthi'ih served one year in Alcatraz in San Francisco and then Fort Huachuca in southern Arizona. A BIA boarding school was built here in 1910.

𝍂 GARCIA'S TRADING POST (North)

Now the **Holiday Inn,** the former trading post is about three miles east of the junction of U.S. Highway 191 and Navajo Route 7. The first trader in this area was Naakaii Yazzi, a Navajo of Mexican descent who ran his store from a tent in 1882. In 1886, a small one-room building with a floor made of Arbuckle Coffee boxes was built on this site and is now under the kitchen area of the new Holiday Inn.

Lorenzo Hubbell and his partner C. N. Cotton traded in Chinle in 1886 out of an old rock hogan on the grounds of what would become Garcia's Trading Post. But due to a nationwide depression that caused a downturn in livestock and wool prices, Hubbell and Cotton let their trading license in Chinle expire. After the depression ended, Hubbell returned in 1900 and built a two-story trading post down the road that included rooms for the many visitors to Canyon de Chelly that he believed would soon be coming.

With the arrival of the Atchison, Topeka & Santa Fe Railroad in Gallup, Hubbell's prophesy was to come true. To help tourists see the canyon, Hubbell started a stage coach line in 1915 that picked passengers up in Gallup, took them by his post in Ganado, and then brought them to Canyon de Chelly.

Camillo Garcia, known to the Navajos he traded with as the "Mexican who blinked all of the time," took over the post in the 1920s and enlarged the compound to include eight buildings. Garcia ran the post successfully until the 1960s, when he and his son were killed in a plane crash at the Chinle airport. The Holiday Inn took over the site in 1992 and built this hundred-room motel with a restaurant and swimming pool.

To Mexican Water

CHUSKA MOUNTAINS

12

Tsaile

Massacre Cave Overlook

Diné College

To Kayenta

59

191

Many Farms

Mummy Cave Overlook

Antelope House Overlook

64

Canyon del Muerto

N

W E

S

To Window Rock

Ledge House Overlook

CANYON DE CHELLY
NATIONAL MONUMENT

Chinle

Monument Headquarters

Tsegi Overlook

Junction Overlook

Black Rock Canyon

Black Rock

Cottonwood Campground

White House Overlook

Canyon de Chelly

7

Sliding Rock Overlook

Spider Rock Overlook

Thunderbird Lodge

191

Monument Canyon

Beautiful Valley

NAVAJO ROUTES 7 & 64
North and South Rim
of
Canyon de Chelly

To Ganado

CANYON DE CHELLY NATIONAL MONUMENT

Perhaps the most obvious question about this canyon is why is it named de Chelly (pronounced de-SHAY)? The generally accepted answer is that de Chelly is the Spanish mispronunciation of the Navajo word *Tséyi'*, meaning "rock canyon."

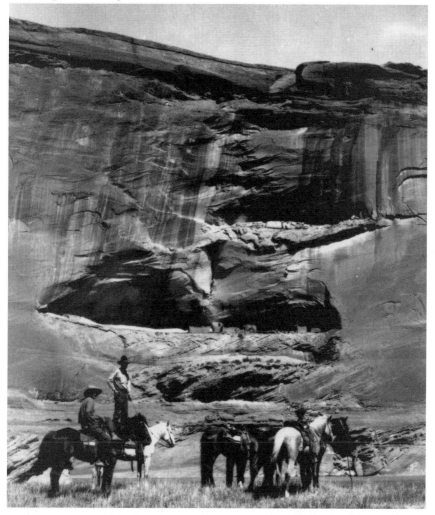

Cowboys in Canyon de Chelly, ca. 1930s
Fred Harvey Collection, Museum of Northern Arizona Photo Archives 301-3-114

People have lived in Canyon de Chelly since 2000 B.C. The canyon's famous cliff dwellings were built by the Anasazi. The Navajos are believed to have migrated here in the seventeenth century. They developed large peach orchards and farms, which remain to this day. According to Richard Van Valkenburgh, an Indian Service anthropologist in the 1930s, it was the

Hopi and Jemez Indians who gave the Navajos peach trees. Forced to flee to Canyon de Chelly after the Pueblo uprising against the Spanish in 1680, these refugees slowly became part of the Navajo tribe through intermarriage and are known as the *Ma'ideshgezhnih* Clan.

At the height of Kit Carson's slash-and-burn campaign, Canyon de Chelly and the Chinle area were his primary targets because of the many farms on the canyon floor. Carson signed the peace treaty with the Navajos in 1864 on the knoll where the Canyon de Chelly Monument Headquarters sits today.

Canyon de Chelly became a national monument in 1931, but unlike all other U.S. national monuments, the Navajo Tribe holds claim to the land. The park is administered by the National Park Service, whose visitors center provides valuable information about the ethnohistory and geology of the canyon.

The Southwest Parks and Monuments Association operates a nonprofit bookstore in the visitors center specializing in books and maps about the local area and the Navajo and Hopi nations.

Canyon de Chelley Tour Guides

You will probably want to hire a Navajo guide to take you on a tour of the canyon. Except for **White House Ruin Trail,** you may not enter the canyon without an authorized guide.

Members of the Tsegi Guide Association offer interpretative hikes, horseback trips, and jeep tours. You can also hire someone to take you for a tour through the canyon, using your own four-wheel-drive vehicle. Make arrangements and obtain a permit at the visitors center.

De Chelly Tours	(928) 674-5433
Tseyi Jeep Tours	(928) 674-3262
Footpath Journey	(928) 724-3366
Antelope House Tours	(928) 674-5231
Justin Tso Horse Rental	(928) 674-5678
Twin Trail Tours	(928) 674-8425
Totsonii Ranch	(928) 755-6209

Cottonwood Campground: Free year-round camping on a first-come, first-served basis. Five-day limit per visit or fourteen days per year. From April through October, facilities include restrooms, picnic tables, and water. From November through March, there are portable toilets and picnic tables only. There are no shower facilities. RVs are allowed but are restricted to thirty-five feet (11 m). A dump station is available.

Sam E. Day's Trading Post, Chinle, Arizona, 1902
Photograph by Ben Wittick, courtesy School of American Research Collections in the Museum of New Mexico 15988

THUNDERBIRD LODGE

In 1902, Sam Day built a trading post that would eventually grow into the beautiful Thunderbird Lodge of today. Originally from Canton, Ohio, Day came to Arizona in 1883 as a homesteader at Cienega Amarilla (St. Michaels) and worked with a survey party to determine the boundaries of the Navajo Reservation. He sold his land at St. Michaels and built a log trading post, facing east, that became the social center of the Chinle area.

Because of competition from Lorenzo Hubbell, Day sold his trading post in 1905 to Charles Wiedemeyer from Fort Defiance. Day continued to own trading posts in Cienega Amarilla and Navajo, Arizona, and served as a member of the Arizona legislature. His favorite causes were the prohibition of alcohol on the Navajo Reservation and ending gambling.

In 1912 his son Charles married Kate Roanhorse, the daughter of Chief Manuelito, and continued his work on the preservation and documentation of Navajo life ways.

In 1919, "Cozy" McSparron, a legend in trading circles because of his good humor and creative storytelling, bought the trading post and turned it into a dude ranch called the Thunderbird Ranch. He developed the Thunderbird logo for promotional brochures, and the Fred Harvey Co. included the Thunderbird Ranch in its itinerary for the Harveycar Motor Cruises. Wanting more of a Wild West atmosphere at his ranch, Cozy offered gambling and boxing matches on Saturday nights.

In 1931, Herbert Hoover declared Canyon de Chelly a national monument, and Cozy became its temporary custodian for two years until a permanent custodian was named. Cozy and his wife, Inja, were host to many movie stars filming in the area from 1930 to 1950, including Claudette Colbert, Guy Madison, and Rory Calhoun.

When Cozy's health failed, he sold the Thunderbird Ranch to the Nelsons, who were former employees of the Babbitt brothers in Flagstaff. One of the Nelsons suffered a heart attack, and the ranch was again up for sale.

The LaFonts took over in 1960 and built the first motel units to accommodate the increasing number of visitors to the monument. Odessa LaFont further developed the image of the Thunderbird Ranch as an oasis in the desert by expanding many of the plants, lawns, and trees that Cozy had started. Not long after they purchased the trading post and ranch, the LaFonts asked for permission from the Navajo Tribe to close the trading post. They did this because most of the local people came to eat in the new cafeteria rather than trade. The tribe approved the closure, and today you can dine in this popular cafeteria located in the original 1902 trading post built by Sam Day.

In 1984, the LaFonts sold the ranch to Mary Jones, who proceeded to develop the lodge and, in 1986, added the new pueblo-style motel rooms in the back of the original trading post and motel.

The Thunderbird Lodge offers half- or full-day jeep tours of Canyon de Chelly. Half-day tours will take you to the lower halves of both Canyon de Chelly and Canyon del Muerto. The full-day tour takes you on a sixty-mile roundtrip tour of Canyon del Muerto to Mummy Cave and Canyon de Chelly to Spider Rock. The jeeps are open, so bring a hat and sunscreen.

Half-day tours: Departs at 9 a.m., 1 p.m., or 2 p.m.

Full-day tour: Departs at 9 a.m., returns at 5 p.m. For reservations call: (800) 679-2473 or (928) 674-5841.

CHINLE RUG DESIGN

One of the more common rug designs throughout the Navajo Nation

because of its relatively easy pattern is the Chinle design. It is simply a banded rug without borders. Developed during the Revival Period of weaving, from 1920 to 1940, the Chinle Rug has solid lines of color alternating with more complex bands that contain geometric designs.

Chinle Rug, ca. 1947
Photograph by Gene Balzer, Museum of Northern Arizona

In 1923, Cozy McSparron, in collaboration with Mary Wheelwright of the **Wheelwright Museum,** encouraged the reintroduction of natural vegetal dyes instead of the commercial dyes that were introduced in 1870.

Some weavers felt limited by the colors available in natural dyes, so a dye expert from the DuPont Chemical Co. came to Chinle to research the kind of natural coloring and variety the weavers were seeking. That same year, DuPont introduced the new dyes to the reservation, but the weavers had to mix the dangerous acid components themselves. In 1932, the Diamond Dye Co. came out with a dye called "Old Navajo" that did not require mixing but still offered the variety and subtle color shading so admired by the weavers. Because of this influence, the Chinle rug style may have either vegetal or commercial dyes or both in its coloring.

MILE 0 SOUTH RIM OF CANYON DE CHELLY

There are no mile markers on the South Rim, so set your odometer to zero at the visitors center.

Blade Face from Tsegi Overlook, no date
Courtesy Museum of New Mexico, #68800

MILE 2.5 (4 km) TSEGI OVERLOOK

Tséyı means "canyon" in Navajo. From this overlook you can see the traditional homes and farms where Navajos live in the summer. They move to their winter camps on the rim when the weather turns colder.

Across the highway from this overlook are sand dunes just like the ones that formed the de Chelly Sandstone more than 200 million years ago. The de Chelly sandstone makes up the majority of the vertical cliffs that line the Rio de Chelly. If you look closely, you can see lines in the rock indicating that the wind that shaped the sandstone came from the north.

MILE 3.9 (6.2 km) JUNCTION OVERLOOK

This overlook is named for a ruin that sits at the junction of Canyon del Muerto and Canyon de Chelly. James Stevenson of the Smithsonian Institute gave Canyon del Muerto its name, meaning the "Canyon of the Dead," because his expedition found prehistoric Indian burials here. **First Ruin** is across the canyon on your left, so-named because it was the first ruin to be explored and chronicled by archaeologist Cosmos Mindeleff in 1882.

MILE 5.7 (9.2 km) TURNOFF TO WHITE HOUSE OVERLOOK AND TRAIL

This is the only ruin in the park that you may hike to without a Navajo guide and is well worth the time and effort. It is about 1.25 miles (2 km) one-way to the ruin, with a drop in elevation of about 500 feet (152 m). The well-marked trail starts at the south end of the parking lot. Because of the high temperatures in summer, carry at least a quart (1 L) of water with you on this hike. This trail is not wheelchair-accessible. You can buy a White House Trail guide at the visitors center for 50 cents, which explains the history of the ruin, as well as the geology and plant life found along the trail.

WHAT IS DESERT VARNISH?
On the canyon wall above White House Ruin is a good example of desert varnish. The blue-black color is caused by the leaching over centuries of iron and manganese oxide from the sandstone. If there happens to be a crack where water collects, lichen forms, turning the rock orange and green.

MILE 12.9 (21 km) SLIDING ROCK OVERLOOK

On your way to the overlook you will walk across sandstone that has eroded into shallow basins. These basins are an important source of fresh water for humans and animals after a rain storm. The larger ones can hold water for several weeks.

Across the canyon on a narrow ledge is **Sliding Rock Ruin,** named appropriately because the ancient people who lived here had to build retaining walls to keep their homes from sliding into the canyon.

MILE 21.8 (35 km) SPIDER ROCK OVERLOOK

The paved trail to the overlook is two hundred yards (183 m). Spider Rock, or *Tse' Na'ashjé'ii,* is the center point of the junction of Canyon de Chelly and Monument Canyon and stands eight hundred feet (244 m) from the base of the canyon floor.

Spider Rock, Canyon de Chelly, no date
The Kansas State Historical Society, 4/D-16.12

SERVICES IN CHINLE

Canyon de Chelly Motel is on the right as you turn onto Navajo Route 7 from U.S. Highway 191. This hotel has an indoor pool and restaurant. (800) 327-0354 or (928) 674-5875.
Holiday Inn: (800)-HOLIDAY or (520) 674-5000.
Thunderbird Lodge: (800) 679-2473; (928) 674-5841.

Navajo Police: (928) 674-2111.

26 miles (42 km) from Chinle to Tsaile

From the north rim of Canyon de Chelly, there are no mile markers, so set your trip odometer to zero at the visitors center and refer to the map on page 198.

MILE 5.4 (8.7 km) LEDGE RUIN

It's .8 mile (1.3 km) to the viewpoint. Ledge Ruin is visible across the canyon in an alcove about one hundred feet (30 m) above the canyon floor. The pottery found in the ruin dates from between A.D. 1050 and 1275.

MILE 8.2 (13.2 km) ANTELOPE HOUSE TURNOFF

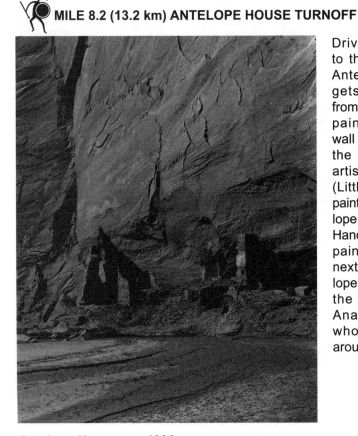

Drive two miles to the viewpoint. Antelope House gets its name from the antelope painted on the wall to the left of the ruin. Navajo artist Dibé Yazhı (Little Sheep) painted the antelope around 1830. Hands and figures painted in white next to the antelope are probably the work of the Anasazi people who lived here around A.D. 693.

Antelope House, ca. 1890s Photo by Ben Wittick
Courtesy School of American Research Collections, Museum of New Mexico, 149225

The **Tomb of the Weaver,** about fifty feet (15 m) above the canyon floor across from Antelope House, is a carefully constructed crypt so finely made that even in this windblown country, no dust or sand had worked its way into the burial house. Inside was the well-preserved body of an old man, believed to be a weaver because of a spindle whorl found sitting atop skeins of cotton yarn. A blanket of golden eagle feathers wrapped the body, and a bow and arrow, cornmeal, corn, piñon nuts, beans, and salt were lying on top of the blanket. Under the feather shroud was a cotton blanket so white that when archaeologists unearthed the crypt in 1920, the blanket looked like it had just been woven.

 NAVAJO FORTRESS VIEWPOINT

The "fortress" is the sandstone butte directly across the canyon from Antelope House Viewpoint. Navajo Fortress was one of the many hiding places for Navajos hunted by the Spanish and later by Kit Carson's troops. On the east side of the butte, which you can't see from the overlook, is a trail leading to the top of the Fortress. Log poles were used to climb to the nearly inaccessible top and are still visible on a jeep tour through the canyon. Once the Navajos climbed on top of the butte, they pulled the poles up after them. Rock walls were used as shields to hide behind while throwing rocks on their tormentors below. At night, Navajo men would sneak down to get water and food for the people, but vigilant Kit Carson waited at the bottom until the starving Navajos surrendered to him in 1864.

Mummy Cave Ruins, ca. 1890s
Photo by Ben Wittick, Courtesy School of American Research Collections in the Museum of New Mexico, 149217

🏃 MILE 17.5 (28 km) MUMMY CAVE TURN-OFF

Drive 1.6 miles (2.6 km) to the overlook. Col. James Stevenson, who named Canyon del Muerto, found two mummies at this site in 1880 and called the ruins Mummy Cave. This is one of the longest continuously inhabited ruins in Canyon de Chelly, believed to have been occupied from A.D. 300 to 1300. Set in two caves, the architecture is like that found at Mesa Verde in southwestern Colorado. Both ruins have similar masonry and both have a three-room tower. The ceiling timbers in the tower were cut in A.D. 1284. In 1938, this 711-year-old tower was in danger of collapsing but was saved with financial assistance from the Bureau of American Ethnology and the Southwestern Monuments Association. Earl Morris, well-known for his renovation of the Temple of Warriors at Chichén Itzá, was able to stabilize the ancient structure.

🏃 MILE 21 (33.8 km) MASSACRE CAVE OVERLOOK

The Spanish were not welcome in the Navajo homeland, and raids against them by Navajo warriors were common. To put an end to these attacks, Lt. Antonio de Narbona was sent to Canyon de Chelly in 1805. A bloody battle ensued, according to his reports sent back to the Spanish governor in Santa Fe. Narbona reported killing ninety men and twenty-five women and children, and capturing another thirty-six women and children. The Navajo version of what happened was quite different. Hosteen Tsosi, a lifelong resident of Canyon de Chelly, told anthropologist Richard Van Valkenburgh in 1940 that the ninety men allegedly killed by Narbona were away in the Lukachukai Mountains hunting deer. Defenseless and fearing for their lives, the women, children, and elders hid in a nearly inaccessible cave across from the north rim when they saw the Spanish coming.

Narbona didn't know where the group was hiding as he rode above them on the canyon rim. But a woman in the cave, a former Spanish slave, could not resist taunting the Spanish soldiers. Once sharp shooters identified the location of the woman's voice, musket balls were ricocheted off the cave's ceiling, killing most of the helpless people huddled there. There was no escape to the canyon floor because the Spanish had worked their way below the only exit from the cave.

Hosteen Tsosi's grandmother survived the attack by hiding under a big rock. When the Spanish made their way up to the cave to finish off survivors with their bayonets, they did not find the little girl. Two days later, the Navajo men returned from their hunting trip. Realizing what had happened, the hunting party took off after the Spaniards to avenge their loved ones' deaths. They caught up with them around Wide Ruins but were no match against the Spanish muskets and inflicted little damage on the troops.

MILE 25 (40.2 km) DINÉ COLLEGE

This was the first tribally controlled community college in the United States, founded in 1968 by an act of Congress. Today there are twenty-nine tribal colleges. The college philosophy is *Sá ah Naasghái Bik'eh Hózhóón*. It summarizes the Navajo philosophy of life that places all human beings in harmony with the earth and the universe. The entire campus is laid out like a giant hogan, designed to promote the philosophy of *hozhóó* (harmony). As in a hogan, the buildings used for sleeping, eating, living, and spiritual well-being are in traditionally prescribed locations on the campus. Medicine men blessed the campus with white corn meal and yellow corn pollen during the groundbreaking ceremony, representing the four footprints of the Navajo people. The logo of the college is an arrowhead within a *yé'ii* rainbow. The arrowhead stands for protection from danger, and the rainbow represents harmony with all creation. Diné has campuses in Shiprock, Tuba City, Chinle, Crownpoint, and Ganado. It offers two-year associate degrees and also prepares students for transfer to a university. A major focus of the college is Diné studies and teaching and preserving the Navajo language.

Ned Hatathli Museum and Gallery: Open 8 a.m.-12 noon and 1 p.m.-5 p.m. Monday through Friday; closed weekends and holidays. On the third and fourth floors of the six-story glass hogan is a wonderful museum that explains the history of the Navajo people with displays of cultural artifacts and local artists' work.

On the second floor is a beautiful sanctuary in the shape of a hogan. Its dirt floor is actually connected to the earth by a chimney that extends through all six floors to the sky. The walls of the anteroom leading to the hogan depict the history of the Navajo people. They were handpainted by Paul Willeto, longtime art instructor at the college.

The gallery on the third floor offers an array of local handcrafted silver jewelry, rugs, purses, pillows, concho belts, and books. All proceeds from the sale of items in the gallery support the work of the college.

R. C. GORMAN LIBRARY COLLECTION
World-renowned Navajo artist R. C. Gorman donated his personal library collection to Diné College in 2003 in honor of his late parents. Included in the collection are believed to be the earliest Navajo Christian hymns, translated by Gorman's grandmother into Navajo. Also entrusted to the college is his father's Congressional Medal of Honor. Carl Gorman was recognized for his service during World War II as one of the Navajo Code Talkers.

SERVICES AT DINÉ COLLEGE

Dormitory: Rooms with two single beds and a shared bathroom are available to tourists. It's a good idea to bring your own towels and soap. You can make reservations by calling the residence director at (928) 724-6782 from 8 a.m. to 5 p.m., Monday through Friday. It may be difficult to get a room during the academic semesters, which run from around the middle of August to the middle of December, and from the middle of January to the beginning of May every year. Summer school begins in early June and lasts through August. Dormitory vacancies are most likely during the summer.

Cafeteria: Meals are available only when school is in session. The cafeteria is open only 7–8 a.m., 11:30 a.m.–1 p.m. and 5–6 p.m. A snack bar is open all day during the school year.

Bookstore: Excellent collection of Native American books and T-shirts. Open 8 a.m.–noon and 1–5 p.m. Monday through Friday.

 TSAILE LAKE

Halfway around the college's circular drive are three very large gas tanks. From there, head south on the dirt road to the lake. Fishing is allowed here with a tribal fishing license, available at the gas station on the corner of Navajo Routes 12 and 64. If you continue to the end of the dirt road, stop where a wash obviously crosses the road. To the west of the wash, at the edge of the canyon, is a seasonal waterfall that runs after heavy rains or during the spring snowmelt. This is the start of Canyon del Muerto.

Towering over Tsaile Lake is beautiful **Tsaile Butte** or *Tsézhin Dits'in*.

56 miles (90.1 km) from Lukachukai to Window Rock

 LUKACHUKAI

Lók'a'ch'égai is the Navajo word for "slender reeds." It is descriptive of the cove at the base of the pass over the Lukachukai Mountains, located at the end of town. Many people use this dirt road to cross the mountains but it is not recommended, especially in winter. The Lukachukai Creek runs through town and divides the Lukachukais from the Chuska Mountains.

George Barker started the first trading post here in 1892. The friars from St. Michaels built a church in 1912 and added a dispensary in the 1950s. This offered the only health care in the area for many years.

Lukachukai Catholic Church, not dated
St. Michaels Photo Collection of the Franciscan Friars at St. Michaels, Arizona.
Museum of Northern Arizona Photo Archives, MS 119-181-3511

 NIZHONI FIVE FINGERS, INC.

Located in this area is a small business owned by Annie Tsosie Kahn, a member of the Water Clan. Annie has offered workshops for many years for Navajos and non-Navajos interested in learning more about the lifestyles and beliefs of the Diné. She offers women a traditional sweatlodge and the chance for both men and women to experience the beauty of the Lukachukai region and Navajo life. For more information, write to Annie Kahn, P.O. Box 1347, Lukachukai, Arizona 86507.

COMMUNITY OF TSAILE (West)
Tséehyílį (pronounced SAY-lee) means "flows into the rocks" and refers to Tsaile Creek, which flows into Canyon del Muerto.

MM 69 TSAILE BUTTE

To the east, this sacred place known as *Tsezhin Dits'in* is frequently visited by medicine men to collect herbs needed for ceremonies. It is an igneous volcanic formation.

CHUSKA MOUNTAINS

This mountain range to the east extends from Lukachukai all the way to Window Rock. In Navajo, *ch'ooshgaii* means "white spruce or fir." In Navajo tradition, the spruce is a sacred tree that attracts rain.

The Chuska Mountains are one part of a system of mountain ranges, or cordillera, that forms a sacred male figure called *Yoo tzill,* or "Goods of Value Range." The head of the male figure is the Chuska Mountains. The Lukachukais form the body and the Carrizo Mountains make up the legs.

In some historic accounts of the area there are frequent references to the Tunecha Mountains. This is because in 1851 the U.S. military cartographers separated the Chuska Mountains into two sections. They called the northern section the Sierra de Tunecha and the southern section Sierra de Chusca. The U.S. Geological Survey added the Lukachukai Mountains as the third section in 1892. Today the entire range is known as the Chuska Mountains.

MM 65 BLACK PINNACLE

The Navajos know this volcanic ridge to the east as "where the bear lives." The Indian Service built a fire lookout here in 1937 to protect the pine forests surrounding the volcano.

MM 60 WHEATFIELDS LAKE

Col. John Washington traveled through here in 1849 and reported numerous Navajo wheat fields, thus its name. Wheatfields Creek feeds the lake with runoff from the Chuska Mountains. It has the best fishing for rainbow and brook trout on the Navajo Nation. You can purchase a tribal fishing license at the Wheatfields store, or in Tsaile or Navajo. Camping is free for two weeks. There is no running water; outhouses only.

MM 60 WHITECONE

An important place for gathering healing herbs, this mountain to the east is called *Sei' heets'ozii,* or "slender female sand." It's a good name for a mountain made of friable Chuska Sandstone.

MM 51 SONSELA BUTTES

These buttes, seen from both sides of the road, have rather unusual vertical basaltic lava at their top with the rest of the butte consisting of Chuska and Entrada Sandstone.

MM 44 JUNCTION OF INDIAN ROUTE 12 AND ROUTE 32 TO SHIPROCK

MM 44–45 GREEN KNOBS

A most amazing but subtle color change occurs around this volcanic plug. You're traveling along at 55 mph (89km/hr) enjoying the beautiful red rock sandstone when suddenly the area turns green, then back to red again. The reason is that peridotite, a volcanic rock made up of green ferromagnesium minerals and olivine, covers this area. This material forms the semiprecious stone peridot. Green Knobs is a highly sacred place to the Navajo people. Please do not walk on or take any of these fragile rocks.

MM 43 NAVAJO LAKE

This wetland is home to many aquatic birds.

MM 41.5 BOWL CANYON RECREATIONAL AREA TURN-OFF

Head east for about nine miles (14.5 km) on a dirt road to get to this campground. At the entrance to the area is **Cleopatra's Needle.** As you travel into the bowl made from a dry lake bed, you'll see **Venus Needle. Camp Assayi** for children is located in the recreation area. The cabins and running water are for Navajos only. You may camp anywhere in this 645,000-acre (2,600 sq km) designated area, but RVs are not recommended because of the rough road.

MM 45 NAVAJO, NEW MEXICO

Highway 12 dips into New Mexico for a short distance, then returns to Arizona before entering Fort Defiance. Located fifteen miles (24 km) from here is Tanner Springs, known as "sitting willows" to Navajos. Part of Chee Dodge's expansive ranch was here and included a two-story house where he held many parties and entertained guests from throughout the country. (See page 188 for more on Chee Dodge.)

Dodge's most famous offspring, **Annie Wauneka,** grew up here. Today she's a beloved legend and role model to the Navajo people. She had a major impact on the tribe's public health policies in her effort to eradicate tuberculosis. In 1929, Annie became the first woman elected to the Navajo Tribal Council. In her role as chairperson of the council's health committee, she took the lead in learning about the horrendous health conditions of the Navajo people and deadly diseases.

TB was especially tricky to educate the people about because of its transmission through the air. Navajos were long-accustomed to sharing the same dwelling, eating from the same bowl, drinking from the same cup, even spitting on the hogan's dirt floor, all very easy ways to spread TB from one person to another. In addition, Wauneka had to persuade medicine men that she was not out to discredit their methods of spiritual curing. She participated in innumerable ceremonies with families during her years of traveling the reservation, going from hogan to hogan. Many times she had to hide the fact that she was not eating or drinking from the same vessel used by others in ceremonies or meals so as to not offend her hosts or the medicine man. She persevered and taught families about the cause of TB and why it was important to follow the "white man's" treatment for the disease.

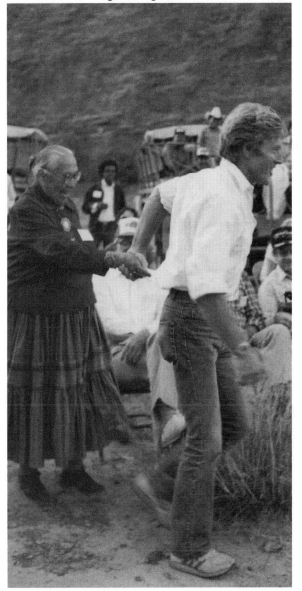

Annie Wauneka with Robert Redford at a Diné College Function
Photograph by Ed McCombs

Annie had the difficult task of persuading many Navajos to leave the reservation to spend months at a time in a sanitarium. She explained that TB affects people all over the world and that the power of the medicine man alone was not going to be able to cure this disease. She taught the concept of germs and that TB was spread by tiny unseen creatures that lived in saliva and spread from one person to another through coughing.

Wauneka's efforts at health education did much to slow the epidemic spread of the disease. For this, President Lyndon Johnson honored her with the Presidential Medal of Freedom in 1964.

Navajo is also the site of the tribal sawmill, which generated jobs and revenue from the processing of the tribe's 600,000 acres (2,437 sq km) of ponderosa pine on the Defiance Plateau. Managed by the Navajo Forest Products Industry, the mill closed in 1994 because of a $7 million debt.

THE BEAST

East, behind the Pine Forest building, is a volcanic plug that's also called Frog Rock on the U.S. Geological Survey's topographic map.

FORT DEFIANCE

Take a right at the stoplight if you are traveling south from Tsaile. If you are traveling from Window Rock, continue straight through the stoplight. Go all the way to the end of the road to the Indian Health Service hospital. The fort was located at the end of the canyon, but no ruins remain.

Officers Quarters, Fort Defiance, Arizona, not dated
Museum of Northern Arizona Photo Archives

Col. Edwin Sumner, known as Bull Head Sumner after a musket ball bounced off his head without causing any damage, was in charge of building Fort Defiance in 1851. He chose this site, at the junction of Bonito and Black Creeks, for its defensive position in a box canyon. Bonito Canyon surrounds the fort with sheer red cliffs on the east, north, and west. The top of the cliffs mark the boundary of the Defiance Plateau. Actually, this site was not a very secure position, because the Navajos could spy on the soldiers' activities from the top of the plateau.

The First Dragoons, the fighting regiment assigned here, named it Fort Defiance because they had come to defy the Navajos. The word "dragoon" means to harass, or to force into submission by violent measures.

The original fort is no longer standing, because it deteriorated so badly during the Civil War when troops went back east to fight. Because of the absence of the army, Navajo raids on white settlers and miners increased and became an obstruction to settlement of the West. To protect the settlers, the military reopened the fort in Bonito Canyon and renamed it Fort Canby for the commander of the New Mexico forces in 1860. Fort Canby was the first stop on the 300-mile (484 km) journey to Fort Sumner for 2,500 Navajos Kit Carson had managed to starve out of hiding in Canyon de Chelly. The Long Walk ended on the Pecos River in New Mexico in a place called "the round grove," or Bosque Redondo. President Lincoln set this land aside for the Navajos and any other "unruly Indians." The other unruly Indians at the time were Apaches and Mescaleros. All of these people tried to survive on the same small desolate reservation. After four long, miserable years, and the complete failure to turn Navajos into farmers, the survivors were allowed to return to their homeland. (See pages 10–11 for more on Bosque Redondo.)

Fort Defiance was one of the boundaries of the new reservation created for the Navajos and would become the first Indian agency for the Bureau of Indian Affairs. (See page 11 for a map of the original reservation boundaries.)

The first licensed reservation trading post opened in Fort Defiance in 1868 to accommodate the needs of the Navajos returning from Bosque Redondo. Licensing of all traders on the reservation was a requirement of the Indian Service and is now required by the Navajo Tribe.

FORT DEFIANCE INDIAN HEALTH SERVICE HOSPITAL

The area in front of the hospital, planted in cottonwoods, was the parade ground used by the military at Fort Defiance. The Episcopalians at the Good Shepherd Mission down the road were actually the first to provide health care to the people in this area. The Indian Service built a 110-bed hospital and tuberculosis sanitarium here in 1938.
Emergency room number: (928) 729-3209.

BIA BOARDING SCHOOL

Located across from the Indian Health Service hospital, the buildings now house BIA administrative offices, but they were once part of the first government boarding school built on the Navajo Reservation. It was established in 1881, thirteen years after the signing of the peace treaty that promised an education for every child from age six to sixteen.

Even though the signers of the treaty saw the benefit of educating their children, they did not know it would mean sending them to boarding school. As one mother said, "It is like giving up our hearts." In 1887, Congress passed a law to force Navajo parents to send their children to school. This led to even more problems and hard feelings between parents and Bureau of Indian Affairs officials. Mission schools became popular at this time because parents were able to choose where their children would go to school rather than being forced by government authorities.

OUR LADY OF THE BLESSED SACRAMENT CATHOLIC CHURCH

On the left just past the post office is the church built in 1915 with native sandstone by the Franciscan friars at St. Michaels.

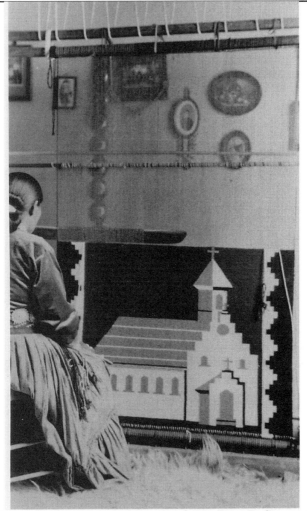

Anna Curley weaving a pictorial rug of the Fort Defiance Catholic Church, not dated Museum of Northern Arizona Photo Archives, Photo Collection of the Franciscan Friars at St. Michaels, Arizona, MS 119-181-3497

 GOOD SHEPHERD MISSION

As you head back out onto the four-lane road, the mission is on the left about halfway to the stoplight, before you get to the high school. The Episcopalians came to Fort Defiance in 1892, five years after the U.S. government required all children to attend school. They had actually "drawn" the Sioux Reservation under the Grant Peace Policy of 1869. It was the Presbyterians who were responsible for educating the Navajos, but all of their attempts to establish a school and mission at Fort Defiance had failed.

Women played an important role in the development of the **Good Shepherd Mission.** The "woman who laughs," Eliza Thackara, superintendent of the mission, opened the first hospital in Fort Defiance in 1897 on a forty-eight-acre (0.19 sq km) plot deeded to the Episcopalians. As you drive through the mission gates, the old hospital is the first building on the right. It is now the administrative building.

In the early 1900s, trachoma—caused by a highly contagious rickettsia microorganism that frequently resulted in blindness at an early age—was one of the most debilitating diseases treated at the new hospital. The only treatment at the time was the painful scrubbing of the everted eyelid with "blue stone" three times a day. Because the treatment forced patients to stay at the hospital for a long time, some children lost contact with their parents, and the mission eventually became an orphanage.

To generate more donations for her growing hospital, Miss Thackara wrote a frantic letter to her benefactors in New York, telling them that the Roman Catholic Church was "about to establish a large school at a mission nine miles (14 km) from us at St. Michaels ... they always have money." Rev. Mother Katharine Drexel (now Saint Katharine Drexel) opened the St. Michaels Boarding School in 1902. (See pages 141–143 for more about St. Michaels Mission.)

The **Chapel of the Good Shepherd,** the first building to the left as you drive through the entrance, honors the charitable work of one of the mission's more generous contributors, Cornelia Jay of New York. It was built in 1954 by architect John Gaw Meem, who was renowned for his Southwestern style of architecture. Some of his most famous buildings are the La Fonda Hotel in Santa Fe, and Scholes Hall and Zimmerman Library on the campus of the University of New Mexico in Albuquerque.

MM 27 BLACK ROCK

This volcanic intrusive rock to the west formed from molten lava. It's a natural landmark along the old military road that ran more than 200 miles (323 km) to Albuquerque. The road was heavily used from 1851 to 1864, and the military grazed their horses here because of its abundant water supply. The Navajos call Black Rock "Big Snake House." It plays an important role in the Wind Way ceremony.

THE WIND WAY CEREMONY

Navajos attribute much power to the wind. Because it is everywhere, taking different forms and colors, it may be a source of illness for some people. To overcome its effects, a Wind Way ceremony may be prescribed as the necessary treatment. Through this ceremony the patient regains harmony with the supernatural power of the wind and is protected in his or her future travels.

BEALE WAGON ROAD

In 1857, Lt. Edward Fitzgerald Beale surveyed the trail that would eventually become part of Route 66, the famous highway connecting the east and west coasts. His assignment was to find a direct route from Fort Defiance to the Colorado River on the California border. To expedite his mission, Beale used camels to carry his heavy load of supplies.

It was Jefferson Davis, then secretary of war, who first suggested the use of camels. Beale, who had traveled in the Southwestern deserts with Kit Carson, agreed with Davis because of the need to carry water and feed for their riding and pack animals. With the help of Davis, Beale persuaded Congress to appropriate $30,000 for the purchase of twenty-three Arabian camels from Egypt and Arabia. He purchased forty-four more in Asia Minor and shipped them all to a valley outside of San Antonio, Texas. Here they rested before making the long trip to Fort Defiance.

The trip from San Antonio to Fort Defiance took sixty-six days. The camels did extremely well. Able to carry almost a thousand pounds (2,200 kg), the camels handled the rocky terrain with ease, because they pick up their spongy feet for each step rather than shuffling them like mules do. They could eat anything and especially liked creosote bushes.

Given all of these wonderful characteristics, why didn't the camel catch on as a pack animal in the desert Southwest? Primarily because mule drivers felt threatened by their abilities, and cowboys didn't want to treat them gently. In their traditional homeland, attendants pamper their camels and treat them like members of their family.

Because of their unpopularity with the wranglers, some camels "escaped" during Beale's expedition. Encountered in the wild many years later, they were surviving quite well. In 1901, a crew surveying the International Boundary Line between the U.S. and Mexico reported seeing very healthy camels in southern Arizona. None survive today.

Take a left at the light and follow the signs to Window Rock Tribal Park.

NAVAJO NATION TRIBAL COUNCIL CHAMBERS

Designated a National Historic Landmark in 2004, this beautiful 1923 building is constructed in the shape of a traditional Navajo hogan, with the door facing east to allow the Holy People to enter. Handpainted murals by Navajo artist Gerald Nailor depict Navajo history and cover the interior walls of the council chamber. A bell given to the Navajo Tribe by the Santa Fe Railroad sits next to the entrance. It commemorates all of the Navajos who helped build the railroad.

The Bureau of Indian Affairs created the Navajo Tribal Council—now the Navajo Nation Council—to facilitate the signing of oil leases with American companies wanting to tap the large oil reserves discovered near Farmington.

This is the largest Indian legislature in the country, composed of 88 delegates from the 110 chapters, or communities, of the reservation. Chapters operate like town councils, except meetings are conducted in the Navajo style. Anyone who wants to may speak on a subject, generally uninterrupted, until finished. Because of this, meetings can last long into the night.

A complete reform of the tribal government occurred in 1991 to create a three-branch tribal government with executive, legislative, and judicial branches. This action was due primarily to former tribal chairman Peter MacDonald's conviction in tribal and federal courts on corruption and conspiracy charges. A four-term chairman of the Navajo Tribe, he was sentenced to a fourteen-year prison sentence. (See page 182 for more on Peter MacDonald.)

The council holds regular sessions four times a year but calls many special sessions as well. Much of its deliberations are in Navajo. You are welcome to visit the council chambers during the day. All of the tribal council meetings are open to the public. For more information call the Office of the Speaker at (928) 871-7160.

WINDOW ROCK

The "window" in the Cowsprings Sandstone formed from water and wind erosion. Called *Tségháhoodzání,* or "perforated rock," this is one of the four places medicine men collect water for use in the Waterway ceremony.

In 1936, John Collier, then-commissioner of Indian Affairs, centralized in Window Rock all federal agencies governing the Navajo. Instead of Window Rock, some wanted to call the new capital *Ní'ałníígi,* meaning "earth's center." But medicine men objected because it is inappropriate to use a ceremonial name in everyday conversation. It was also a difficult word for the many non-Navajos working for the Indian Service to pronounce. So the name Window Rock was adopted.

Window Rock, ca. 1890
Photo by Ben Wittick, Courtesy School of American Research Collections in the Museum of New Mexico

NOTE: For services in Window Rock, see page 145.

To Kayenta

Mexican Water

To Four Corners

160

Northern Navajo Medical Center

64

San Juan River

Shiprock

191

N
W E
S

Los Gigantes

Shiprock

Round Rock

Lukachukai Mountains

Rol-Hay Rock

191

Beautiful Mountain

Barber Peak

To Many Farms

Lukachukai

C H U S K A

Sanostee

Tsaile

491

Ford Butte

64

Wheatfields Lake

Bennett Peak

Newcombo

Two Grey Hills

To Canyon de Chelly

Narbona Pass Campground

Sheep Springs

NAVAJO ROUTE 32 and NEW MEXICO 491 North Tse-Be-Toh to Shiprock

Crystal

32

M
O
U
N
T
A
I
N
S

Owl Springs Picnic Area

Tse-Be-Toh

Camp Asayi

Navajo

491

12

Fort Defiance

Window Rock

To Ganado

264

To Gallup

60 miles (97 km) from Tse-Be-Toh to Shiprock, New Mexico

TSE BE TOH

This Navajo Housing Authority project is at the Junction of Navajo Routes 12 and 32.

MM 18 CAMP ASSAYI AND BOWL CANYON

A few miles south on a rough dirt road (not recommended for RVs) there is camping but no services. The elevation here is 7,800 feet (2,377 m) with frequent monsoons in summer. The average temperature is 75 degrees (23.8° C) during the day. You must have a Navajo tribal fishing permit to fish in Lake Assayi.

MM 18 CRYSTAL TRADING POST

J. B. Moore was the trader at the Crystal Trading Post from 1890 to 1912. Like Lorenzo Hubbell, he wanted to improve the quality of Navajo rugs. One of the unusual features of rugs woven for Moore was that he had weavers bring in raw wool for him to send back east for machine processing. Clean wool was easier to weave and made exceptional rugs.

CRYSTAL RUG DESIGN

The Crystal design has two or three complex bands with arrows, stars, crosses, or triangles. It's traditionally woven using natural colors such as brown, grey, and rust, but modern weavers may use pink, light green, and yellow pastels.

Crystal Rug, ca. 1910–1925
Photograph by Gene Balzer, Museum of Northern Arizona

MM 14 BLUE SPRUCE, ASPEN, AND PONDEROSA PINE
   FOREST

Mile 12.5 NARBONA PASS (Elevation 8,150 feet or 2,484 m)

This was referred to as Washington Pass on most maps, until a group of Diné College students fought to rename the pass in honor of Navajo leader Narbona.

Following the signing of the treaty with Mexico in 1840 and the addition of land to the U.S. (which would later become New Mexico and Arizona), the U.S. military turned its attention to controlling Navajos. Lt. Col. John Macrae Washington rode into the Chuska Mountains to meet with Narbona and his son-in-law, Manuelito. He hoped to sign a treaty with the Navajos to end raids against the Mexicans as promised in the Treaty of Guadalupe Hidalgo. To make his point, Washington noticed that one of the horses in Narbona's party belonged to the Mexicans and ordered the horse and rider seized. When the rider took off running, Washington's troops fired, killing Narbona. Witnessing his father-in-law's death, Manuelito vowed never to negotiate with the military again.

The headwaters of the Rio de Chelly start in Narbona Pass at Coyote Wash and are known as "sparkling water" to the Navajos.

Mile 12.5 NARBONA CAMPGROUND

MM 10 OWL SPRINGS PICNIC AREA

At the junction of Navajo Route 32 with New Mexico Highway 491 to Shiprock, turn north at the community of **Sheep Springs.** This was a popular camping site for the military in 1847 because of the spring that flows here. Charles Newcomb established a trading post here in 1912.

MM 59 NEWCOMB

The town was originally named *Pesh-do-clish* but was renamed Newcomb after the family who purchased the trading post in 1914.

Franc Newcomb and her husband, Arthur, developed a close relationship with the famous Navajo medicine man, sandpainter, and weaver Hosteen Klah. Over the years, Franc attended many healing ceremonies conducted by Klah. She had a photographic memory capable of reproducing the intricacies and colors of each sandpainting Klah and other medicine men made for their patients. Once home she drew more than 450 designs on paper.

Newcomb's Trading Post, not dated
St. Michaels Photo Collection of the Franciscan Friars at St. Michaels, Arizona. MS 119-186-4010

As Klah got older, the apprentice he had trained to take over his ceremonies died. This left Klah with no one to learn his complex ceremonies. Because of his fear that all of his knowledge would be lost, Klah consented to the recording and interpretation of his ceremonies by Franc Newcomb and Mary Wheelwright, a wealthy anthropologist from Boston. In an unprecedented move, Klah also wove many of his sandpainting designs into rugs. To preserve these valuable cultural artifacts, Mary Wheelwright built the **Museum of Navajo Ceremonial Arts in Santa Fe** specifically to house Klah's sandpaintings and weavings. This sandpainting rug pictured is from the Nightway ceremony. (See page 231 for more on this ceremony.)

Klah Sandpainting Rug, ca. 1930–1936
Photographer Gene Balzer, Museum of Northern Arizona

In 1926, the Crown Prince of Sweden and his wife, Princess Louise, stopped at the Newcomb Trading Post for lunch on their way to Mesa Verde. The prince wanted to see the ruins where his father, the king of Sweden, had purchased prehistoric artifacts for the Royal Museum of Stockholm. With only two hours' prior notice, Mrs. Newcomb was expected to feed the entire royal entourage. The party was so large that Henry Ford sent six Lincolns from Detroit to Gallup, New Mexico, by rail to accommodate the prince's ground trip to Mesa Verde.

Traders were accustomed to feeding travelers who stopped by their trading post without notice, so the luncheon came off without a hitch. Upon meeting Klah, the prince asked Arthur Newcomb if Klah was the Navajo king because of his dignified manner.

TWO GREY HILLS RUG DESIGN
Down the road from Newcomb is the Two Grey Hills Trading Post, established in 1897, famous for the rug pattern of the same name. Originally

based on J. B. Moore's Crystal design, weavers soon discarded his use of red and other bright colors in favor of subtle, natural, undyed colors of white, grey, brown, and black. By 1925, Moore's design was completely abandoned. A design that focused on a center piece with surrounding smaller designs in each corner emerged to take its place. The Two Grey Hills is a finely woven rug with as many as 120 wefts to the inch compared to thirty to fifty wefts found in other high-quality rugs. All of the wool is handspun. To get different shades of a color, weavers card different colors of wool together.

Two Grey Hills, ca. 1920–1940
Photographer Gene Balzer, Museum of Northern Arizona

In the center of the two diamonds of this particular rug are swastikas, ancient symbols used by many Indian tribes. To the Hopi, it symbolizes the direction the clans traveled on their migrations. To the Navajos, it represents the four sacred directions.

The primary setting for Tony Hillerman's novel *The Ghostway* is the Two Grey Hills Trading Post. The surrounding Chuska Mountains are also featured as well as Shiprock, character Jim Chee's first assignment as a police officer.

MM 64 BENNETT PEAK

This peak to the west is known as Black Rock in Navajo. Narbona placed warriors on this peak to send smoke signals when U.S. troops were approaching in order to give him enough time to defend his people. He also used this pinnacle to warn of the arrival of Ute and Apache raiders.

MM 64 FORD BUTTE

Ford Butte, to the east, and Bennett Peak are both igneous formations with dikes similar to Shiprock.

MM 67 SANOSTEE

Six miles (9.7 km) off New Mexico Highway 491 to the west is the small community of Sanostee. This is the birthplace and traditional home of Narbona. Renowned for his strong leadership and strategic skills, he is said to have led more than a thousand men into battle.

MM 70 BEAUTIFUL MOUNTAIN (West)

Rising to 8,340 feet, this mountain was the site of the Beautiful Mountain Uprising of 1913. About thirty-five Navajos went into hiding here in protest of the government's stand against plural marriages, a traditional practice not commonly seen today.

MM 78 BARBER PEAK

To the east is a peak of volcanic intrusive rock associated with Shiprock, and to the west is Table Mesa.

Mile 85.5 SHIPROCK SCENIC PULLOUT

Tsé Bit´áí, or the Winged Rock, rises 1,700 feet (518 m) above the earth and has many volcanic dikes radiating from the center of the plug. The southern dike is ten feet (3 m) wide and two miles (3.2 km) in length. The geologic cause of this spectacular rock formation was an explosion of built-up gases below the surface of the earth. When Shiprock exploded more than five million years ago, swamps and vegetation of all types covered this area. At the time, the top of the volcano was level with the surrounding plateau. Gradually, as the seas receded and the region turned to desert, the plateau was worn away from wind and water erosion, leaving the impregnable volcanic core standing alone on the landscape. There are hundreds of volcanic plugs throughout the Colorado Plateau, including Agathla Peak and Church Rock in Kayenta.

To the Navajo people, Shiprock represents one of the battles to cleanse the world of the evil monsters that tried to kill the Earth Surface People. Changing Woman's twin sons, Monster Slayer and Child-Born-of-Water, fought the man-eating eagle here and won. At the top of the monolith are the sharp feathers pointing up to the sky. At the base are the wings of the bird that trail into the ground.

In the first edition of *Native Roads,* I said that the Sierra Club of California attempted to climb Shiprock in 1939, but Navajo medicine men objected, and that no further attempts to climb the volcanic plug had been made since. But I have received numerous letters from readers telling me that this is not true. According to Eric Bjornstad, author of *Desert Rock,* four members of the California Sierra Club did successfully climb "America's toughest climbing problem" in 1939. After twelve failures by Colorado climber Robert Ormes, the California team was successful because of the development and use of new technology—the expansion bolt. According to Bjornstad, in 1952 there were three more ascents on Shiprock and by 1963, eighty-six ascents had taken place, with the last group removing twenty-seven expansion bolts and fifteen pitons.

SHIPROCK COMMUNITY

Bureau of Indian Affairs superintendent William Shelton was in charge of this area in 1903. Shelton, called "Tall Boss" by the Navajo, initiated an agricultural program here using irrigation water from the San Juan River. The original buildings and homes in Shiprock were made of logs and adobe. Most were swept away in the flood of 1912. In the reconstruction that followed, the new bridge across the San Juan replaced the ferry that "Jimmy the Boatman" ran for many years.

In 1921, oil, gas, and helium were found close to Shiprock. This led to a period of increased oil exploration and discovery on Navajo land, making the tribe one of the richest in the country. In the 1950s and 60s, uranium was found in the Carrizo Mountains, turning Shiprock into a boomtown for about twenty years. The community had a hotel and a few more restaurants at that time.

Shiprock Fair, traders' booths, 1913
Cline Library, Special Collections and Archives, NAU.PH.2000.48.3

NORTHERN NAVAJO TRIBAL FAIR

Held in October, this fair features the *Yé'ii bicheii* ceremony, or Nightway Chant. This lengthy and expensive ceremony treats patients with chronic illnesses or people experiencing visual, hearing, or mental disturbances.

A "hand trembler," someone gifted with the ability to diagnose illness through touch, determines the need for the ceremony. If the diagnostician prescribes this ceremony, it is conducted only "after the thunder sleeps" in the winter.

This ceremony is a complex and laborious commitment from the family that agrees to hold it for their ill relative. The host must feed everyone who attends the nine-night ceremony, and the medicine man and his many helpers must be paid. The most popular part of the ceremony is when the *yé'iis*, or Holy People, dance in public on the seventh and ninth nights. The dancing lasts all night and is open to anyone. However, the healing ceremony and sandpainting in the hogan are for the patient's family and invited guests only.

The Northern Navajo Fair in Shiprock is usually held the first weekend in October. The "Two Yé'iis Coming" dance starts on Saturday afternoon with the *Yé'ii bicheii* dancing in the evening. The sacred masked dancers begin late on Saturday night and continue in the morning on Sunday. No photography is allowed at the *Yé'ii bicheii* ceremony. For more information contact Shiprock Navajo Fair, Inc., P.O. Box 1893, Shiprock, New Mexico, (505) 368-5108.

Nearby lodging

There are no motels in Shiprock; the closest ones are in Farmington, New Mexico, thirty miles (48 km) to the east.

Anasazi Inn	(505) 325-4564
Apple Tree Inn—National 9	(505) 326-1555; (800) 524-9999
Best Western Inn & Suites	(505) 327-5221
Budget Inn	(505) 326-5521
Casa Blanca B & B	(505) 327-6503; (800) 550-6503
Comfort Inn	(505) 325-2626; (800) 228-5150
Courtyard by Marriott	(505) 325-5111; (800) 321-2211
Days Inn	(505) 325-3700
Economy Inn	(505) 326-6614
Encore Motel	(505) 325-5008
Holiday Inn Express	(505) 325-9811; (800) Holiday
Journey Inn	(505) 325-3548
Knight's Inn	(505) 325-5061
Kokopelli's Cave	(505) 325-7855
La Quinta	(505) 327-4706; (800) 531-5900
Motel 6	(505) 326-4501
Ramada Inn	(505) 325-1191; (800) 228-2828
Sage Motel	(505) 325-7501
Silver River Adobe Inn	(505) 325-8219; (800) 382-9251
Super 8	(505) 325-1813; (800) 800-8000
Travel Inn	(505) 325-0233
Travelodge	(505) 327-0242
Villager Lodge	(505) 327-4433

SERVICES IN SHIPROCK

Northern Navajo Medical Center: This is a U.S. Indian Health Service facility. Non-Navajos are seen on an emergency basis only. (505) 368-4971.

Shiprock Navajo Police: On the north corner of the junction of New Mexico Highways 666 and 64, this was the first assignment for Tony Hillerman's fictional character Jim Chee before he was transferred to Tuba City. (505) 368-4383.

140 miles (225 km) from Chambers to Flagstaff

MM 333 CHAMBERS

Chambers prospered through the sale of bentonite clay deposits used in the manufacture of fine porcelain china.

MM 325 NAVAJO, ARIZONA

Not to be confused with the town of the same name in New Mexico, Navajo, Arizona—also known as Navajo Springs—was a popular watering stop for settlers and western explorers. It was here on December 29, 1863, that John Goodwin of Maine took the oath of office as the first governor of the new territory of Arizona.

MM 311 PETRIFIED NATIONAL FOREST AND PAINTED DESERT

There are two entrances to the forest. If you're pressed for time and want to see only the petrified wood, enter at the south entrance. At Holbrook, take U.S. Highway 180 south and follow the signs to the Painted Desert. The road from here to the north entrance is twenty-five miles (40 km) one-way. Both entrances charge $10 per car or $5 per person on bicycle or foot. The National Parks Pass is accepted. There are no camping facilities or motels.

Petrified Logs, ca. 1889
Detroit Publishing Company Collection
Cline Library, Special Collections and Archives, NAU PH 516.30

Walnut Canyon National Monument

Flagstaff

Raymond Buffalo Ranch

Winona

Canyon Diablo

Meteor Crater

Two Guns

40

Little

PAINTED DESERT

Colorado River

Winslow

Homo'lovi Ruins State Park

Cholla Lake

Joseph City

87

To Second Mesa

Hopi Buttes

Holbrook

180

PAINTED DESERT

Petrified Forest National Monument

Puerco River

U.S. I-40 West Chambers to Flagstaff

Navajo

Klagetoh

To Window Rock

191

Ganado

Chambers

Wide Ruins

To Gallup, New Mexico

There is a restaurant at the north end of the park next to the **Painted Desert Visitors Center.** The park is open 7 a.m. –7 p.m. in summer and 8 a.m.–5 p.m. (MST) the rest of the year. Closed December 25 and January 1.

The Chinle Formation is responsible for much of the beauty of northern Arizona. It is in this layer of geologic time that we see the beautiful red, brown, purple, gray, and green shales of the Painted Desert plus the phenomenon known as petrified wood. More than 220 million years ago, this area was the site of a large Triassic lake and floodplain heavily covered with vegetation. Most of the logs found in the park are *Araucarioxylon arizonicum,* distant relatives of trees found today only in wet areas of New Zealand, Australia, and South America.

Over time the Chinle Formation, rich with minerals, encased the fallen vegetation and trees. Eventually, where the conditions were just right, the organic matter in the wood was replaced with minerals, or "petrified." The Painted Desert visitors center shows a seventeen-minute movie every half-hour that explains how wood is petrified.

The Petrified National Forest contains the largest collection of entire petrified logs, but smaller pieces of wood decorate much of northern Arizona.

As more settlers moved into this area, petrified wood was used to make everything from coffee tables to lamps. Eastern towns ordered truckloads of the stones for various commercial uses, and the new Atlantic & Pacific Railroad cut right through the Petrified Forest, helping to speed up the export of these rare stones. One entrepreneur even built a mill in Jasper Forest to grind petrified wood into abrasives. This venture failed, however, because cheaper abrasives were on the market. Alarmed at the rapid destruction of this natural treasure, local citizens petitioned Congress for protection. In 1906, President Theodore Roosevelt set the area aside as a national monument with the Painted Desert section added in 1932.

SCENIC DETOUR

Begin at the north entrance, in the Painted Desert section of the park.

PAINTED DESERT INN MUSEUM
Originally built in the 1920s, the Painted Desert Inn was rebuilt by the Civilian Conservation Corps for the National Park Service in 1938. The Fred Harvey Co. became the concessionaire at the park and asked Mary Colter to design the interior of the inn. She combined the Spanish theme of the building with native Indian designs. Fred Kabotie, the artist who painted murals in Colter's Grand Canyon Watchtower at Desert View, painted the Buffalo Dance in the dining room of this hotel. No longer a hotel, the Painted Desert Inn has been preserved as a museum and is a National Historic Landmark. Behind the inn is a sweeping vista of the Painted Desert.

PUERCO INDIAN RUINS

After leaving the Painted Desert Inn, continue south six miles (9.5 km) to these ruins, dated to A.D. 1100. This was a desirable location for farming because of the nearby Puerco River, but in A.D. 1200, the site was abandoned because of a great drought. In A.D. 1300, it was reinhabited, but abandoned for the last time in A.D. 1400, possibly because of the damaging erosion of the Puerco River on the farming area, which made it too difficult to grow a sustaining crop.

NEWSPAPER ROCK

About one mile (1.6 km) south is an overlook where you can view hundreds of petroglyphs.

WHAT ARE PETROGLYPHS?

These pictures and symbols, pecked into the surface of rocks many centuries ago, are common in the Southwest, particularly on the Colorado Plateau. Some think they were used by prehistoric people as a way to communicate with supernatural powers that they believed controlled the universe and the tribe's success or failure. Many of the images, pecked into the soft sandstone, have to do with fertility, rain, or abundant hunting animals. Some of the supernatural beings depicted include *Ye'iis* (Navajo), *Katsinas* (spirit beings), migration and clan symbols, and myriad other images that probably played a part in ceremonial life. Pictographs are rock paintings that often depict the same images as petroglyphs. Naturally occurring colors such as hematite, an iron-laden mineral, for red; charcoal for black; and clay for white are used as paint. You will find most rock art near springs, places where people lived, or along commonly traveled routes.

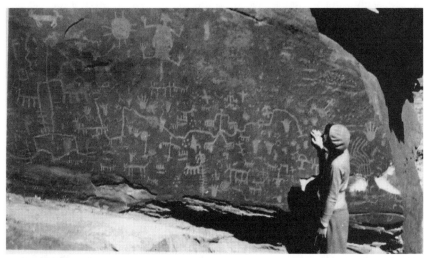

Newspaper Rock, Petrified Forest, not dated
Mary Jane Colter Rock Art Collection, Museum of Northern Arizona, MS 301-5-415

Leaving Newspaper Rock, turn south to travel though the **Tepees,** part of the Painted Desert badlands, and on to the Petrified Forest section of the park. Interesting stops are the **Jasper Forest,** where you can see petrified logs with root systems indicating that some of the trees grew in this area. **Crystal Forest** was given its name because of the many amethyst and quartz crystals found here by gem collectors before the area became a national park. The **Agate House** is an interesting stop because this A.D. 1050 pueblo is made entirely of petrified wood. The **Rainbow Forest Museum** at the south entrance to the park has interesting displays about petrified wood and the ethnohistory of the area.

END SCENIC DETOUR

 MM 285 HOLBROOK

Holbrook was born a classic Western town. It developed around Horsehead Crossing, where the skull of a horse on a post marked the safest crossing across the treacherous quicksand of the Little Colorado River.

Named for Henry R. Holbrook, chief engineer of the Atlantic & Pacific Railroad, Holbrook was little more than a sleepy little town before the railroad arrived in 1866. It soon turned into one of the wildest burgs in the Southwest, boasting the only churchless county seat in the U.S.

To help subsidize the expense of building a transcontinental railroad, the government gave the railroad company land grants extending twenty miles (32 km) on either side of the tracks that could be sold to generate capital.

The Boston financiers who were charged by President Chester A. Arthur to build the railroad from Albuquerque to California liked the rich grazing land the railroad passed through in northern Arizona. They saw an opportunity for a new business venture. Under the laws of the State of New York, the owners of the railroad created the Aztec Land & Cattle Co. They then bought one million acres of grazing land around Holbrook at 50 cents an acre. The Hash Knife outfit in Texas sold 33,000 head of cattle to the new cattle company and sent them by railroad to Holbrook.

Holbrook turned into a bustling, dangerous city overnight. Hundreds of cowboys, many with criminal records, headed for the town looking for work with the Aztec Cattle Co. When off the range, the cowboys spent most of their free time and their $25 monthly wages at the Bucket of Blood Saloon. The original but now-abandoned saloon still stands at 119 E. South Central in Holbrook. It is one of Holbrook's first stone buildings constructed after the fire of 1888, which destroyed the entire town.

Horsehead Crossing of the Little Colorado, Arizona, ca. 1882–1883
Photo by Ben Wittick, courtesy School of American Research Collections in the Museum of New Mexico, 15813

To give you an idea of what it was like to be thrown into jail during this time in history, stop by the Navajo County Courthouse. This 1898 jail came completely assembled by railroad from St. Louis to be placed in the courthouse, found on the northeast corner of Navajo Boulevard.

One of the first Harvey Houses opened in Holbrook in 1884 and was staffed by Harvey Girls, who gave prompt and efficient service during the thirty-minute stop for meals. To speed up the service, rail passengers ordered their dinner selection from the conductor, who signaled ahead how many of each menu items to prepare. The meals were hot and waiting for the passengers as soon as they arrived. The most popular item on the menu was steak, imported from Kansas City. But passengers also had the choice of oysters, turtle, quail, or antelope.

The restaurant sat right next to the train depot in five converted railroad cars painted bright red and decorated in an Indian motif. Unfortunately, as rail travel decreased over the years, the Harvey Houses in railroad towns like Holbrook and Winslow disappeared.

Lodging

Best Western Adobe Inn	(928) 524-3948; (800) 528-1234
Best Western Arizonian	(928) 524-2611; (800) 528-1234
Brad's Motel	(928) 524-6929
Budget Host Holbrook Inn	(928) 524-3809; (800) 283-4678
Budget Inn Motel	(928) 524-6263
Comfort Inn	(928) 524-6131; (800) 221-2222
Days Inn	(928) 524-6949; (800) 329-7466
EconoLodge	(928) 524-1448; (800) 424-4777
El Rancho Motel	(928) 524-3332
Heward House B & B	(928) 524-3411; (877) 740-0452
Holiday Inn Express	(928) 524-1466; (800) 465-4329
Moenkopi Motel	(928) 524-6848
Rainbow Inn	(928) 524-2654; (800) 551-1923
Ramada Limited	(928) 524-2566; (800) 272-6232
Super 8 Motel	(928) 524-2871; (800) 800-8000
Travel Lodge Inn	(928) 524-6815; (800) 578-7878
Western Holiday Motel	(928) 524-6216

Campgrounds

KOA (928) 524-6689
OK RV (928) 524-3226

MM 277 CHOLLA LAKE COUNTY PARK

This manmade lake has a campground patrolled by three rangers. Basic camping is $7 per night. Campsites with electricity and water are $10 per night. There are community bathrooms and showers but no dump site for RVs. Sites are given out on a first-come, first-served basis. The rangers lock the gates to the park at 9 p.m. (MST). If you want to get out earlier than 8 a.m., they will give you the combination. For more information call (928) 288-3717.

MM 274 JOSEPH CITY

This is the only one of four Mormon settlements to survive along the Little Colorado River during the late 1800s. First called Allen's Camp for the mission's leader, the community members decided to change the name to St. Joseph in honor of their prophet Joseph Smith.

The original group, sent here by Brigham Young, was to establish Mormon communities based on the social concept of a United Order. Successful in Brigham City, Utah, the United Order idea was based on the principle of cooperation rather than competition. Article 1 of the incorporation of Allen's Branch of the United Order of 1877 reads: "Resolve that we the under-signed of our own free will and choice form ourselves into a Company and combine all of our means and labor that we may more fully carry out our agricultural, manufacturing and all other industrial pursuits necessary for our mutual benefit."

This would prove to be a beneficial way for the people of Allen's Camp to survive in this harsh country. If they were to be successful farmers, irrigation from the Little Colorado was a necessity. Over a period of eighteen years, the settlers built twelve dams on the Little Colorado. It was a river like nothing they had ever seen before. It had a mind of its own, one year a raging torrent and the next year completely dry.

Their first attempt at dam building came in March 1876. It was a simple design relying on tons of rock brought to the river from a nearby quarry and dumped on the sandy river bottom. But in July, when the seasonal monsoons hit, the river rose in flood to erase any sign of their hard work. They tried other types of dams. One suggested by engineers from the nearby Atlantic & Pacific Railroad consisted of wooden piles driven deep into the river bed. Although this was a successful design for the railroad, it failed for the Mormons. But they persevered and finally, in 1894, they built a dam that held for twenty-nine years.

Life along the Little Colorado was hard. Just to have a cool, clean drink of water was a luxury reserved for trips to the mountains or Tuba City. St. Joseph's drinking water came from the Little Colorado River and was laden with salt, gypsum, and tons of sediment. They called it the river that was too thick to drink and too thin to plow. Yet for almost forty years this was the only source of potable water. Even when wells were dug, the resulting water was not much better than the river because of its high concentration of salt.

In 1923, the town's name of St. Joseph changed to Joseph City because the mail kept being confused with St. Joseph, Missouri. A half-mile (0.8 km) east of Joseph City is a marker placed by the Daughters of the Utah Pioneers commemorating the spot where the St. Joseph Fort stood.

 MM 257 HOMOLOVI RUINS STATE PARK

The visitors center is open 8 a.m.–5 p.m. every day except Christmas. The ruins are open from 8 a.m. to sunset. There is an entrance fee. This is an Arizona state park, so the National Parks Pass is not accepted. All park facilities have been designed for access by physically impaired visitors. If you have difficulty walking any distance, check at the visitors center for alternate access to Homolovi II. The center has information in Braille and has sign language interpreters available for their public workshops if you call in advance, (928) 289-4106.

In the Hopi language, *Homol'ovi* means "the place of little hills." This settlement is an ancestral home to some clans currently living in Hopi villages to the north. It's a different kind of interpretative site to visit because most of the three hundred ruins have not been excavated. This gives you an idea of the effort required to restore many of the ancient sites you may have already visited. At Homolovi II, thought to have more than a thousand rooms, you'll have the opportunity to look inside an ancient kiva.

Homolovi is one of the pueblos built by ancestors of the present-day Hopi along the ancient **Palatkwapi Trail.** In Hopi legend, it is believed that when the Hopis emerged from the underworld, some went to live at Palatkwapi, or "the place of the red rocks," in the Verde Valley. Here they became lazy and failed to continue their migrations, as Masauwu instructed, before permanently settling down in one place.

As their lifestyle deteriorated, a great flood came to punish the people. They had no choice but to abandon their paradise. The clans at Palatkwapi began to gradually move northward, building pueblos at various springs along the trading route, one of which was Homol'ovi. The Palatkwapi Trail begins at the village of Walpi, passes by springs located about every fifteen to thirty miles (24–48 km), crosses the Little Colorado at Sunset Crossing by Winslow (where there is solid rock and less danger of quicksand), skirts around the impassable Canyon Diablo, and drops down into Verde Valley to the mineral-rich, modern-day towns of Jerome and Prescott.

At the Homolovi visitors center take the short walk to the **Sunset Cemetery,** which overlooks the Little Colorado River. Mormon leader Lot Smith founded a community named Sunset near here in 1876. Because of floods and drought, the group could not survive and abandoned the town in 1887. Smith then moved to Tuba City, where he prospered raising dairy cattle but died in a shootout with a Navajo. His body was brought back to Sunset to be buried in this cemetery. (See pages 147–148 for more about Lot Smith.)

The Homolovi visitors center has exhibits, video programs, and a great bookstore specializing in the local native cultures, natural history, and Southwest archaeology. Throughout June and July you can watch archaeologists working Monday through Friday. The last weekend in July is the park's annual archaeology day, with tours of the summer's excavations. All of the ruins are reburied to protect them during the rainy season, which usually starts by early August.

Homolovi Campground: There are fifty-three sites with electricity, dump stations, and restrooms year-round. Water hookups and showers are available from mid-April through mid-October. Pull-through sites are available for large RVs, and some pads for tents are available.

MM 257 LITTLE COLORADO RIVER

The river's name in Hopi is *Paayu,* and it is a constant source of water throughout the year. Even when it looks dry, there is water just inches below the surface. During prehistoric times, the river flowed year-round, but since upstream damming, there is no surface flow during the dry season.

MM 257 WINSLOW

Before the coming of the railroad, Winslow was called Sunset Crossing and was the only safe way across the treacherous Little Colorado River. In 1866, the Navajos called Winslow "iron lying down" because of the iron rails stored here during construction of the railroad heading west.

The town is named for Gen. Edward Winslow, president of the St. Louis & San Francisco Railroad, which also owned most of the Atlantic & Pacific Railroad.

Famous Grand Canyon architect and designer Mary Colter built the La Posada Hotel and train depot in Winslow in 1929. Believing that a building should be an extension of its surroundings and blend with the history of the area, Colter designed La Posada in the grand hacienda style of the Southwest.

La Posada, The Last Great Railroad Hotel, A National Historic Landmark Photograph courtesy Alan Affeldt

La Posada was Colter's favorite project, and in its day it was the finest small hotel in the Southwest. There were seventy-five guest rooms, six dining rooms, grand public spaces, and acres of beautiful gardens full of the smell of orchards and flowers.

Colter filled the hacienda with furniture from around the world—centuries-old Spanish engravings, Mexican chandeliers, Navajo rugs, Italian benches, and beds made by her own craftsmen working onsite.

It cost the Santa Fe Railroad $1 million to build La Posada and another million to landscape and furnish, but the beautiful retreat survived only twenty-seven years. Doomed from the start, the hotel's grand opening came one year after the worst stock market crash in the history of Wall Street.

Luckily, the Santa Fe Railroad saw the value in keeping the building and turned it into their division headquarters, but they sold all of the expensive, handmade La Posada furniture and fixtures at auction. Finally, in 1993, the Santa Fe announced plans to move out of La Posada, and it looked like Mary Colter's love was doomed.

But local historians began a fight to save this treasure and got protection for the building through designation as a National Historic Landmark. Alan Affeldt, with city and state support, bought the old hotel in 1997, and today it is considered one of the top five historic hotels in Arizona. There are twenty guest rooms now available, and La Posada is open for tours every day. Amtrak stops daily at the depot, and PBS, the History Channel, and Garden TV have all produced specials on the restoration of La Posada.

One of the best features about this hotel is the **Turquoise Room Restaurant and Martini Bar.** Created by renowned chef John Sharpe, the restaurant recreates the elegant dining experience of the famous Turquoise Room dining car on the Santa Fe Railway's Super Chief. The menu includes entrees inspired by Fred Harvey such as elk medallions with cherry sauce or, for an appetizer, crisp piki bread with Hopi humus. Open Tuesday through Sunday; breakfast 7–10 a.m., lunch 11:30 a.m.–2 p.m., and dinner 5–9 p.m. For more information and a brochure, call (928) 289-2888.

Hubbell's Trading Post, Winslow, Arizona, not dated
Arizona Historical Society-Pioneer Museum

Lorenzo Hubbell owned a large wholesale trading post and warehouse on Hicks and First streets. This location provided access to the railroad to ship Hubbell merchandise throughout the Four Corners area and the country. A spur line came up beside the building. The building is now owned by the Arizona Historical Society, and the Affiliation of Native American Groups is working to renovate the building for office space to provide needed programs to Native Americans living in Winslow.

Winslow is also famous for a stretch of old **Route 66** found at Second and Third streets. Called the "Mother Road" by novelist John Steinbeck, Route 66 was, at one time, a destination in itself. Chartered in 1926 but not completed until 1938, it connected Chicago with Los Angeles and popularized the great American tradition of driving across country for summer vacation.

The ruins of **Brigham City,** one of the four Mormon United Order settlements of the Little Colorado River, are located just north of the interstate at North Park Drive. (See pages 239–240 for more on the United Order.) A local community group hopes to restore the fort and other historic buildings for visitors to enjoy.

A new feature in Winslow is the **Standin' on the Corner Park** in historic downtown Winslow. The park features a mural by John Pugh and a life-size bronze statue by Ron Adamson. Inspired by the song made famous in the 1970s by the Eagles, the park is located at the corner of Kinsley and Historic Route 66.

Lodging in Winslow

Amerisuites Hotel	(928) 774-8042
Bel Air Motel	(928) 289-4727
Best Western Adobe Inn	(928) 289-4638
Days Inn	(928) 289-1010
Desert Sun Motel	(928) 289-5130
Economy Inn	(928) 289-3328
Econolodge	(928) 289-4687
La Posada Hotel	(928) 289-4366
Motel 6	(928) 289-9581
Motel 10	(928) 289-3211
Super 8 Motel	(928) 289-4606
Travelodge of Winslow	(928) 289-4611
Westerner Motel	(928) 289-2825
Winslow Inn	(928) 289-9389

MM 233 METEOR CRATER

This is a privately owned commercial venture. It's a five-mile (8 km) drive one-way to the visitors center, where there is a snack shop, curio shop, and entrance to view the crater. Open Memorial Day to Labor Day 7 a.m. to 7 p.m. (MST), the rest of the year 8 a.m. to 5 p.m. A rim tour of the meteor is available starting at 9:15 a.m. hourly until 2 p.m.

RV Park: There are seventy-one pull-through spaces, full hookups, and private restrooms with showers. (800) 478-4002, (928) 289-4002.

Dr. D. M. Barringer was the first person in the late 1880s to think that the huge bowl, more than a mile (1.6 km) wide and eight hundred feet (243 m) deep, was a meteorite crater. Most experts in geology at the time believed the crater was the result of a steam explosion. Dr. Barringer, a mining engineer, disagreed with this explanation because the usual cause of steam explosions, volcanic activity, is completely absent in this area.

For twenty years, Dr. Barringer scoured the crater and surrounding area for evidence to support his theory. His problem was that he could not find any recognizable meteorite big enough to have caused this kind of depression. He theorized that the meteorite hit the earth at an angle and broke into small pieces from the force of the impact. To prove his theory, Barringer hired a driller and finally found extraterrestrial material at a depth of 1,346 feet (410 m).

Evidence of other small meteor craters in the world began to surface. One was discovered in Odessa, Texas, in 1923. Eight years later, thirteen craters were found in Australia, all with only small chunks of meteorite in the vicinity. This was the proof Dr. Barringer needed for his theory to gain worldwide support. Unfortunately, he died before his theory became universally accepted. To honor the man who spent more than thirty years of his life and a substantial portion of his own money to prove that this is a meteorite crater, the Meteoritical Society officially named it Barringer Meteorite Crater. A crater on the far side of the moon also honors Barringer.

No one knows exactly when it hit the Earth, but scientists think it occurred around 20,000 to 50,000 years ago. The meteorite hit the earth so hard that it displaced 300 million tons of rock in the center and pushed the edge of the crater 150 feet (45 m) high. Scattered over an area of 100,000 acres (405 sq km) are meteorite chunks of nickel and iron, some as heavy as 200 pounds (30.7 kg). One of these large pieces can be seen at Verkamps, a curio shop next to the Hopi House, on the south rim of the Grand Canyon.

MM 230 CANYON DIABLO

In 1540, when Coronado failed to find the Seven Golden Cities of Cíbola in the Zuni villages of New Mexico, he dispatched Lt. García López de Cárdenas to the west to look for the possibility of gold in the Hopi villages. The Hopis told Cárdenas about a magnificent river even farther west where he might find gold. The expedition pushed on, crossing the Little Colorado at Winslow. Encountering Canyon Diablo, Cardenas named the canyon after the devil because it was so difficult to cross.

In 1857, Lt. Edward Beale reported Canyon Diablo to be a major obstacle in his attempt to survey a road from Fort Defiance to the Colorado River. His party had to travel forty miles (64 km) out of its way to find a way across.

Herman Wolff built the first trading post in the area, about ten miles (16 km) from here, in 1870. Because of the nearly impassable canyon, Wolff had to bring freight from Albuquerque, more than 300 miles (482 km) away. In 1882, the Atlantic & Pacific Railroad built an iron bridge with a span of 928 feet (158 m) across Diablo Canyon. Standing 254 feet (77 m) above the canyon floor, the bridge ended the problem of hauling supplies by wagon over such a long distance.

After Wolff's death, S. I. Richardson and his uncle, George McAdams of Red Lake, bought the post. S. I. managed it alone for a couple of years. The Babbitt brothers later bought the post but sold it a short time later to an inexperienced Eastern archaeologist named Leander Smith.

One day, thinking Navajos would enjoy his joke, Smith displayed a human skull in the front window of his store. Smith had found the skull while excavating around his post and was obviously unaware of Navajo beliefs regarding death and human remains. To his surprise, customers shunned the post, and he was soon out of business. Because of this serious faux pax, the Wolff post never reopened and lies in ruin today.

Charles Algert set up his first trading post along the canyon in an abandoned boxcar to serve the needs of the railroad crews. Following the completion of the railroad, he shifted his attention to trading with Navajos and built a limestone trading post north of the tracks. He sold his post to Frederick Volz in 1897 and moved to Tuba City to open the Tuba Trading Post.

First Trading Post, Canyon Diablo, ca. 1870
Kansas State Historical Society, Topeka, Kansas ATSF.1/0074

Canon Diablo, A.T.

Wittick Photo

Canyon Diablo, Arizona, ca. 1883
Photograph by Ben Wittick
Courtesy School of American Research Collections, Museum of New Mexico, 51054

Aware of tourists' interest in the Hopi Snake Dance, Volz began to haul people by the hundreds from the train station at Canyon Diablo to the Hopi mesas. To accommodate the travelers on this dry, hot journey of more than sixty miles (100 km), Volz built another post called "the fields" along Oraibi Wash, halfway between Canyon Diablo and Oraibi.

In 1898, Volz bought some interesting iron pieces from two sheepherders and sent them to a metallurgist. The specimens turned out to be meteorites. The iron sold for 75 cents a pound (.45 kg), so Volz hired local laborers to collect meteorites around Meteor Crater and sold two railroad cars full.

MM 230 TWO GUNS

The ruins of the town of Two Guns are on private property and the owner does not want visitors because of liability issues. You can see the ruins from the south side of the highway.

It is hard to believe that anything of interest ever happened here. But because of major trails heading east to Albuquerque and west to Flagstaff, this was an important stopping-off place. Navajos used a trail through Two Guns that ran north and south to the Mogollon Rim, where they traded with Apaches.

As elsewhere in northern Arizona, the first non-Indian explorers were with Coronodo's expedition of 1540, searching for mineral wealth. It is believed that in 1769, Franciscan fathers actually found silver somewhere in central Arizona. Traveling from their mines and loaded down with silver, the padres came through Two Guns on their way back to Santa Fe. Indians attacked the expedition, and the friars were too encumbered by the silver packed on their mules and horses to escape. To lighten their load, the padres hid their silver bars in what they thought was an abandoned Indian village. Splitting up, half the party took off toward California and the other half tried to get through to Santa Fe.

In 1902, a treasure hunter found a map of the location of the alleged cache of silver in the archives of San Miguel Mission in Santa Fe. Hordes descended on the Two Guns area to find the lost treasure. But it was a local sheepherder who found one bar of silver weighing a hefty sixty-four pounds (29 kg). The rest of the silver from the Lost Mines of the Padres was never recovered.

In the effort to build a permanent route from the East to West Coasts, Capt. Lorenzo Sitgreaves brought an exploration team through here in 1851 to determine the navigability of the Little Colorado River. Two years later, Lt. Amiel Whipple came through looking for a railroad route along the 35th parallel. Four years later, Lt. Edward Beale brought his famous camel corps through Two Guns in his search for a route from Fort Defiance to the Colorado River. According to Gladwell Richardson's account, in 1858 Beale's party may have built some of the stone buildings now lying in ruin around Two Guns.

In 1882, the Atlantic & Pacific Railroad construction crew set up a temporary town at Two Guns to build a bridge across the canyon. The growing town turned into one of the more lawless and wild towns in the Southwest, not unlike Holbrook.

Many of those who worked on the railroad were outlaws who found Two Guns a perfect safe haven. Sheriffs sworn into office in the morning were dead in the evening. One street in town, aptly named Hell Street, boasted fourteen saloons, ten gambling houses, and four bordellos. The famous outlaw Billy the Kid passed through Two Guns around 1879 herding cattle stolen in New Mexico.

Death at an early age was very common. The only person buried in the cemetery south of town to die of natural causes was Herman Wolff, the original owner of the Wolff Trading Post. He died in 1899.

Train robbery at Two Guns was also common. One of the more famous robberies occurred on March 7, 1889, and involved four Hash Knife cowboys. They jumped on the Atlantic & Pacific No. 7 when it stopped at Canyon Diablo for water. They blew open the safe and took watches, jewelry, and money totaling more than $100,000. The four ran for Lees Ferry and crossed into Utah. But Sheriff William "Bucky" O'Neill (the same Bucky O'Neill who built the first cabin on the South Rim of the Grand Canyon; see page 43) caught them as they crossed the border.

Convicted of robbery, the four were sentenced to twenty-five years each in the territorial prison in Yuma, Arizona. According to Joe Lee, John D. Lee's grandson who was working at Red Lake Trading Post at the time, there was a fifth train robber named Sam Kurt, who took off for Black Mesa when the group split up after the robbery. He stopped by the trading post and showed Lee his sack of money and even gave him one of the stolen silver watches. Kurt was never caught and went on to Wyoming hoping to meet up with the rest of the gang.

MM 225 RAYMOND BUFFALO AND ANTELOPE RANGE

This range, purchased from Dr. R. O. Raymond by the Arizona Game and Fish, covers 15,000 acres (961 sq km) compared to the 60,000 acres (243 sq km) at the buffalo ranch in House Rock Valley. (See pages 83–84 for information about House Rock Valley.) The smaller area makes it a little easier to find the eighty-five bison living here. Call ahead to make an appointment: (928) 774-5045.

MM 211 WINONA

Once a tourist camp in 1920, Winona is now a picturesque little community next to the railroad and one of the stops on Route 66 memorialized in song.

SCENIC DETOUR

Mile 204.5 *WALNUT CANYON NATIONAL MONUMENT (South)*

Open 8 a.m.–5 p.m. (MST) every day except Thanksgiving and Christmas. The National Park Pass is accepted. No campground or services available in the park. Water and bathrooms are available at the visitors center. Unfortunately, most of the park is not wheelchair accessible.

This beautiful Kaibab Limestone canyon was formed more than 60 million years ago. The canyon housed the prehistoric Sinagua Indians, named by Harold S. Colton, founder of the Museum of Northern Arizona. Colton conducted an extensive archaeological survey of the more than 300 ruins found under ledges in the canyon. He took the name *Sinagua* from the Spanish name for the area, *Sierra Sin Agua,* or "mountains without water."

Like all native peoples of the Southwest, the Sinaguas understood how to survive on very little water. Using the dry-farming techniques still practiced by modern-day Navajos and Hopis, the Sinaguas built dams to catch run-off and farmed in washes to capture every available drop of moisture. They supplemented their diet with wild plants and nuts such as the plentiful piñon and Arizona black walnuts, for which this canyon is named.

Flute Player Petroglyph, ca. 1930s
Walnut Canyon National Monument, Fred Harvey Collection, Museum of Northern Arizona
Photo Archives

The Sinagua people moved into the Walnut Canyon area around A.D. 1120 and were part of a large community of Sinaguan people that extended from Wupatki National Monument to the Verde Valley, where Montezuma Castle and Tuzigoot are located.

It is amazing that there is anything left to see at Walnut Canyon. When the railroad reached Flagstaff at the end of the 1800s, pothunting was one of the recreational pursuits of many tourists and local settlers. It was not uncommon for people to brag about the artifacts they found in many of the cliff dwellings in Walnut Canyon. This grew to such an extreme that one group dynamited the ruin's walls to make their job less difficult. Prompted by concerned local citizens, Woodrow Wilson declared Walnut Canyon a national monument in 1915.

One of the truly important discoveries at Walnut Canyon was the burial site of a Sinaguan man. Archaeologist John McGregor found the tomb in the 1930s. Inside were hundreds of offerings, including handpainted pots, arrowheads, and twelve handcarved wands resembling hooves of animals and human hands.

Not sure of what he had found, McGregor asked the nearby Hopis if they had any clues to his puzzle. Some present-day Hopi clans claim Walnut Canyon as their ancestral home, and it is known that the people of Old Oraibi were building their village at the same time the Sinaguans lived comfortably in Walnut Canyon. It is because of their sophisticated oral history, carried down through generations, that the present-day Hopis were able to name and describe the purpose of each item found in the ancient grave.

Island Trail: Behind the visitors center is a paved trail that descends into the canyon to allow you to visit more than twenty-five ruins. The trail drops 185 feet (56 meters) and can be strenuous for someone not accustomed to the 7,000-foot (2,134 m) elevation. There is also a rim walk.

SERVICES IN FLAGSTAFF

Contact the Flagstaff Chamber of Commerce at (928) 774-9541 for information on the many places to stay, dine, and explore.

Flagstaff, Arizona, July 1883
Photo by Ben Wittick, courtesy School of American Research, Collections in the Museum of New Mexico, 15796

WORDS OF CAUTION AND EXPLANATION

Extensive research and actual traveling experience have gone into the development of this book. The author has attempted to provide an accurate description of the history and lifestyle of the natives and non-natives through research and talking to people over the years. But it is not uncommon for someone from another part of the reservation to have another version of a story or to spell words differently.

The maps in this book are not drawn to scale. My primary purpose for including them is to point out what comes next. Please do not read while driving. Have a passenger read the book to you. If you are alone, read when you pull over to enjoy the view.

The purpose of this book is to educate and assist you in your travels. Neither Rio Nuevo Publishers nor the author can accept responsibility or liability for any person or entity with respect to any loss or damage caused, or alleged to be caused, directly or indirectly by the information contained in this book.

ACKNOWLEDGMENTS

Many people helped me with this book over the years - especially friends I met while working at Diné College. I want to specifically thank Ursula Knoki-Wilson for what I have learned from her and for her friendship. Likewise to Mom and Dad Knoki and Jim and Caroline Bluehouse for sharing their blessings with me. To the staff in the Center for Diné Studies, Community Campus and Continuing Education, thank you for your friendship and help throughout the years. My special thanks to my good friend Lena Fowler for believing that all things are possible.

To Jim Babbitt, Ronnie Biard, Karen Berggren, Kevin Cloud Brechner, Curtis Cornelius, Brother Gerald Grantner, O.F.M., Karen Hughes, Wilson Hunter, Joe Magee, Angie Maloney, Tom McMillian, Wade Newman, Gay Nord, Ann and Pat O'Connor, Bob Rhoades, Mick Robbins, Tara Travis, Ursula Knoki-Wilson, and to my English teacher George Hardeen, thank you for your expertise and talent in making this a better book.

I would like to thank the staff at the Northern Arizona University, Cline Library Special Collections and Archives; specifically, Karen Underhill, Laine Sutherland, Diane Grua, and Bee Valvo for their advice and extensive knowledge about the photographic collections at NAU and the history of the Colorado Plateau. Likewise to Carol Burke at the Museum of Northern Arizona Photo Archives. I would also like to thank the Hopi Tribe for their review of the drive through the Hopi Nation.

A special thanks to my parents, Joe and Laura Kosik, for believing in me.

Bibliography

Ahmann, Steve, et al. "Native Uses of Plants of Canyon de Chelly." Chinle High School Science Department, Chinle Unified School District No. 24, N.D.

Anderson, Owanah. *The Good Shepherd Mission in the Navajo Nation 1892–1992.* Fort Defiance, Arizona: Good Shepherd Mission, 1992.

Anderson, Roger, et al. *Guidebook of the Black Mesa Basin: Northeastern Arizona,* New Mexico Geological Society, Ninth Field Conference, 1958.

Anonymous. "Tuba City and the Charlie Day Spring." *Museum Notes* 3, no. 11 (May 1931): 1-4.

———. "The Tsegi Country." *Museum Notes* (1934).

Ash, Sidney. *Petrified Forest: The Story Behind the Scenery.* Holbrook, Arizona: Petrified Forest Museum Association, 1985.

Baars, Donald L. *Red Rock Country: The Geologic History of the Colorado Plateau.* Garden City, New York: Doubleday/Natural History Press, 1972.

Babbitt, James. *Rainbow Trails: Early-Day Adventures in Rainbow Bridge Country.* Page, Arizona: Glen Canyon Natural History Association, 1990.

———. "Trading Posts Along the Little Colorado." *Historic Trading Posts.* Flagstaff, Arizona: Museum of Northern Arizona, 1986.

Babbitt, John. G. "The Babbitt Brothers Trading Company: An Address Before the Newcomen Society." April 15, 1967. Privately printed, 1967.

Bailey, Lynn. "Thomas Varker Keam: Tusayan Trader." *Arizoniana* II (1961): 15-19.

Barnes, Will C. *Arizona Place Names.* Revised by Byrd H. Granger. Tucson, Arizona: University of Arizona Press, 1960.

Barrs, Don. *San Juan Canyons: A River Runner's Guide.* Lawrence, Kansas, Canon Publishers Ltd, 1986.

Berggren, Karen. Park manager, Homolovi Ruins State Park, Winslow, Arizona. Personal communication, April 1995.

Bingham, Sam and Janet. *Navajo Farming.* Chinle, Arizona: Rock Point Community School, 1979.

Brechner, Kevin Cloud. Personal communication, April 1995.

Breed, William, J. *The Age of Dinosaurs in Northern Arizona,* Flagstaff, Arizona: Museum of Northern Arizona, 1968.

Broderick, Johnson H. *Navajo Education at Rough Rock.* Rough Rock Demonstration School, D.I.N.E., 1968.

Brooks, Juanita. *The Mountain Meadows Massacre.* Norman, Oklahoma, University of Oklahoma Press, 1974.

Brown, Bonnie et al. *The Complete Family Guide to Navajo-Hopi Land.* Navajo Tribe, Office of Tourism, 1986.

Brugge, David. *Hubbell Trading Post: National Historic Site.* Tucson, Arizona: Southwest Parks and Monuments Association, 1993.

Butler, Kristie Lee. *Along the Padres' Trail: St. Michael's Mission to the Navajo 1898-1939.* St. Michaels, Arizona: St. Michaels Museum, 1991.

Byrkit, James W. *The Palatkwapi Trail.* Flagstaff, Arizona: Museum of Northern Arizona, 1988.

Cerquone, Joseph. *In Behalf of the Light: The Domínguez and Escalante Expedition of 1776.* Denver, Colorado: Domínguez-Escalante Bicentennial Expedition, Inc.,1976.

Chronic, Halka. *Roadside Geology of Arizona.* Missoula, Montana: Mountain Press Publishing Company, 1986.

————. *Pages of Stone: Geology of Western National Parks and Monuments.* Seattle, Washington: The Mountaineers, 1988.

Clark, H. Jackson. *The Owl in the Monument and Other Stories from Indian Country.* Salt Lake City, Utah: University of Utah Press, 1993.

Cleeland, Teri A. *The Cross Canyon Corridor Historic District in Grand Canyon National Park: A Model for Historic Preservation.* (Master's thesis, Northern Arizona University, 1986).

Correll, J. Lee. "Events in Navajo History." *The Navajo Times* (Mar. 3, 1966): 8.

Crampton, C. Gregory. *Sharlot Hall on the Arizona Strip: A Diary of a Journey Through Northern Arizona in 1911.* Flagstaff, Arizona: Northland Press, 1975.

Dedera, Don. *Navajo Rugs: How to Find, Evaluate, Buy and Care for Them.* Flagstaff, Arizona: Northland Publishing, 1990.

Dennison, Johnson. Presentation at the Advance Navajo Cultural Orientation for Health Professionals. Farmington, New Mexico: 1994.

Donovan, Bill. "Where is Peter McDonald?" *Window Rock Scene* (Feb. 1993): 17.

Erisman, Fred. *Tony Hillerman.* Western Writers Series 87, Boise, Idaho: Boise State University, 1989.

Evans, Edna. *Tales From the Grand Canyon: Some True, Some Tall.* Flagstaff, Arizona: Northland Press, 1985.

Fireman, Bert. *Historical Markers in Arizona Vol. I.* Phoenix, Arizona: Arizona Development Board, 1957.

Frink, Maurice. *Fort Defiance and the Navajos.* Boulder, Colorado: Pruett Publishing Company, 1968.

Gillmor, Frances and Louisa Wade Wetherill. *Traders to the Navajo: The Story of the Wetherills of Kayenta.* Albuquerque, New Mexico: University of New Mexico Press, 1934.

Good, John. *Grandview Grand Canyon Trail Guide.* Grand Canyon, Arizona: Grand Canyon National History Association, 1985.

Guernsey, Samuel James. "Basket-maker caves of northeastern Arizona: report on the explorations, 1916-1917." *The Museum* (1921).

Granger, Byrd Howell. *Arizona's Names: X Marks the Place.* Scottsdale, Arizona: Falconer Publishing Company, 1983.

Grattan, Virginia. *Mary Colter: Builder Upon the Red Earth.* Grand Canyon, Arizona: Grand Canyon Natural History Association, 1992.

Grey, Zane. *The Rainbow Trail.* New York: Harper & Row, 1915.

Hardeen, George. Interview with Ben Muneta, M.D., epidemiologist, 1992.

————. "Hogans in Hospitals: Navajo Patients Want the Best of Both Worlds." *Tribal College* (winter 1994): 20-21.

Bibliography

————. "Jacob Hamblin's Vision Resulted in Settlement." *Navajo-Hopi Observer* (July 20, 1985).

Hargrave, Lyndon. "The Tsegi Country." *Museum Notes* 6, no. 11 (May 1934): 51-54.

Hamm, R. *The Navajo Detective Novels of Tony Hillerman: A Bridge Between Cultures*. (Master's thesis, Texas A & I University, 1989.)

Harrison, Laura Soulliere, et al. "Historic Structure Report Chinle Trading Post, Thunderbird Ranch, and Custodian's Residence Canyon de Chelly National Monument, Arizona." Santa Fe, New Mexico: National Park Service, Southwest Regional Office, October 1989.

Hegemann, Elizabeth Compton. *Navajo Trading Days*. Albuquerque, New Mexico: University of New Mexico Press, 1963.

Hewett, Edgar L. "Origin of the Navajo Name." *American Anthropologist* 8 (1906): 193.

Holt, Ronald. *Beneath These Red Cliffs: An Ethnohistory of the Utah Paiutes*. Albuquerque, New Mexico: University of New Mexico Press, 1992.

Hooper, C. R. "Guest Register at Willow Springs." *Outdoor Arizona* (Jul. 1977): 20-22.

Hooper, Mildred et al. "Blue Canyon: Wonderland in Stone." *Outdoor Arizona* (Sept. 1978): 17, 31, 36.

Houk, Rose. *The Painted Desert: Land of Light and Shadow*. Holbrook, Arizona: Petrified Forest Museum Association, 1990.

Indermill, Roc H. "Roadside Fever: The Social Organization of Roadside Frontage Tenure in the Context of the Navajo Beadwork Trade, 1928 to 1988." (Master's thesis, Northern Arizona University, 1990).

James, Harry C. *Pages From Hopi History*. Tucson, Arizona: University of Arizona Press, 1994.

James, H. L. "Navajo Rugs: The Regional Style." Albuquerque, New Mexico: New Mexico State Highway Department, 1973.

Jett, Stephen. "Red Rock Country." *Plateau* 37, no. 3 (1965): 80-84.

Johnson, J. "The Hash Knife Outfit." *Arizona Highways* (Jun. 1956): 2-7.

Jones, Anne Trinkle, et al. *A Sketch of Grand Canyon Prehistory*. Grand Canyon, Arizona: Grand Canyon Natural History Association, 1979.

Johnston, Lyle. *Centennial Memories: Holbrook, Arizona 1881-1981*. Holbrook, Arizona: Friends of the Holbrook Public Library, 1981.

Kelly, Charles. "Chief Hoskinnini," *Utah Historical Quarterly* (Jul. 1953): 219-226.

————. "John D. Lee's Lost Gold Mine." *Desert Magazine* (Aug. 1946): 9-11.

Kildare, Maurice. "Cave of Death," *Desert Magazine* (Sept. 1967): 30-31.

Kinnear, Willis. "House of Three Turkeys," *Desert Magazine* (May 1965): 32-33.

Kinsey, Joni Louise. *Thomas Moran And the Surveying of the American West*. Washington, D.C.: Smithsonian Institution Press, 1992.

Klinck, Richard. "Movie Making In Monument Valley," *Guidebook 24: Monument Valley (Arizona, Utah, and New Mexico)*. Soccorro, New Mexico: New Mexico Geological Society, 1973.

Lamb, Susan. *A Guide to Navajo Rugs*. Tucson, Arizona: Southwest Parks and Monuments Association, 1992.

Lanner, Ronald. *The Piñon Pine: A Natural and Cultural History.* Reno, Nevada: University of Nevada Press, 1981.

Loving, Nancy J. *Along the Rim: A Road Guide to the South Rim of Grand Canyon.* Grand Canyon, Arizona: Grand Canyon Natural History Association, 1981.

Luckert, Karl W. *Navajo Mountain and Rainbow Bridge Religion.* Flagstaff, Arizona: Museum of Northern Arizona, 1977.

MacDonald, Peter. *The Last Warrior.* New York: Orion Books, 1993.

Malotki, Ekkehart. *Hopi Ruin Legends.* Lincoln, Nebraska: University of Nebraska Press, 1993.

Mann, Timothy. *A Guide to Grand Canyon Village Historic District.* Grand Canyon, Arizona: Grand Canyon Natural History Association.

Markward, Anne. *Monument Valley Navajo Tribal Park.* Santa Barbara, California: Companion Press, 1992.

Matthiessen, Peter. *Indian Country.* New York: Penguin Books, 1984.

Mayes, Vernon. *Nanisé A Navajo Herbal.* Tsaile, Arizona: Navajo Community College Press, 1989.

McGibbeny, Joseph Howard. "The Niman Ceremony." *Arizona Highways* (Jul. 1959): 16-28.

McFarlane, Mary. *Motorist Guide to the Navajo Reservation Publications.* Gallup, New Mexico: 1960

McIlhaney, Sam. "The Blue-Eyed Navajo," *Albuquerque Journal Magazine* (Jan. 25, 1983): 12-15.

McPherson, Robert S. *Sacred Land Sacred View.* Salt Lake City, Utah: Brigham Young University, 1992.

McNitt, Frank. *The Indian Traders.* Norman, Oklahoma: University of Oklahoma Press, 1962.

Miller, William C. "Records in Rock of A 1054 A.D. Star Explosion." *The Desert Magazine* (Jan. 1963): 30.

Moon, Samuel. *Tall Sheep.* Norman, Oklahoma: University of Oklahoma Press, 1992.

Morris, Earl H. "Mummy Cave." *Natural History* (Sept. 1938): 127-138.

Muench, Joseph. *Arizona Highways* (Mar. 1963): 14-33.

Nations, Dale, et al. *Geology of Arizona.* Kendall/Hunt Publishing Company, 1981.

"National Register of Historic Places Registration Form." Window Rock, Arizona: Navajo Nation Archaeology Department, N.D.

Nelson, Mary Carroll. *Annie Wauneka.* Minneapolis, Minnesota: Dillion Press, 1972.

Nequatewa, Edmund. *Truth of a Hopi: Stories Relating to the Origin, Myths and Clan History of the Hopi.* Flagstaff, Arizona: Northland Printing, 1967.

Newcomb, Franc Johnson. *Hosteen Klah: Navajo Medicine Man and Sand Painter.* Norman, Oklahoma: University of Oklahoma Press, 1964.

Nininger, H. H. "Visitor from a Distant Planet." *Desert Magazine* (Jul. 1942): 9-11.

Bibliography

Noble, David Grant. *Wupatki and Walnut Canyon.* Santa Fe, New Mexico: Ancient City Press, 1993.

Parker, Charles Franklin. "The Kaibab and the North Rim." *Arizona Highways* (May 1957): 4-9.

Peterson, Willis. "Sixty Miles an Hour on the Hoof." *Arizona Highways* (Jun. 1956): 32-37.

Price, Theresa, et al. *A Picture Tour of Old Ganado Mission.* Ganado, Arizona: College of Ganado,1991.

Reid, Betty. "Making room for a new hotel: trading post to be cleared." *Gallup Independent* (Jan. 31, 1992): 2.

Richardson, Gladwell. "My Wonderful Country by Joe Lee." *Frontier Times* (Feb.-Mar. 1974): 6-56.

———. *Navajo Traders.* Tucson, Arizona: University of Arizona Press, 1986.

———. *Two Guns, Arizona.* Santa Fe, New Mexico: Blue Feather Press, 1968.

Richardson, Toney. "Traders at Tonalea." *Desert Magazine* (Jan. 1948): 17-20.

———. "Trail to Inscription House." *Desert Magazine* (May 1948): 14-16.

Rigby Keith J. *Field Guide: Northern Colorado Plateau.* Dubuque, Iowa: Kendall/Hunt Publishing Company, 1976.

Rusho, W. L. *Lee's Ferry: Desert River Crossing.* Salt Lake City, Utah: Cricket Productions, 1992.

Seaman, David. *Hopi Dictionary.* Northern Arizona University Anthropological Paper No. 2, 1985.

Scott, Kenneth. *Zane Grey: Born to the West.* Woodridge, Connecticut: G. K. Hall & Co., 1979.

Shinkle, James D. *Fort Sumner and the Bosque Redondo Indian Reservation.* Roswell, New Mexico: Hall-Poorbaugh Press, Inc., 1965.

Sleight, Eleanor Friend. "Fort Defiance." *El Palacio* (Jan. 1953): 3-11.

Smith, Ida. "The Mystery of the Little Trees." *Arizona Highways* (Sept. 1962): 32-35.

Stegner, Wallace. *Beyond the Hundredth Meridian.* New York: Penguin Books, 1992.

Stein, Pat. *The Basques in Arizona From Spanish Colonial Times to the Present.* Phoenix, Arizona: Arizona State Historic Preservation Office, 1991.

Suran, William. *The Kolb Brothers of Grand Canyon.* Grand Canyon, Arizona: Grand Canyon Natural History Association, 1991.

Tanner, George et al. *Colonization on the Little Colorado.* Flagstaff, Arizona: Northland Press, 1977.

Thomas, Bob. "Two Guns: A Big Tourist Draw?," *Arizona Republic* (Apr. 18, 1993): T6.

Thybony, Scott. *Walnut Canyon National Monument.* Tucson, Arizona: Southwest Parks and Monuments Association, 1988.

Trueger, Frederick D., editor. *Guidebook 18: Defiance–Zuni–Mt. Taylor Region (Arizona and New Mexico).* Soccorro, New Mexico: New Mexico Geological Society, 1967.

Underhill, Ruth. *Here Come the Navajo.* Washington, D.C.: United States Department of the Interior, Branch of Education, 1953.

Van Valkenburgh, Richard. *Diné Bikeyah.* Window Rock, Arizona: United States Department of the Interior, Office of Indian Affairs, Navajo Service, 1941.

———. "Inscription at Hwoye Spring." *Desert Magazine* (Jan. 1941): 9-11.

———. "Sacred Places and Shrines of the Navajo Part 1: The Sacred Mountains." *Museum Notes* 11, no. 3 (Sept. 1938): 29-34.

———. "Tsosi Tells the Story of Massacre Cave." *Desert Magazine* (Feb. 1940): 22-25.

Vokes, H. E. "The Goosenecks of the San Juan." *Natural History* (May 1942): 272-273.

———. "Rainbow of Rock." *Natural History* (Oct. 1942): 148-152.

———. "The Story of Shiprock." *Natural History* (Apr. 1942): 212-215.

Walters, Harry. Presentation at the *Advanced Cultural Orientation for Health and Social Service Providers.* Farmington, New Mexico: 1994.

Weatherburn, Stephen. "Bashas' in Chinle Using Navajo Labels." *Navajo-Hopi Observer* (Apr. 12, 1995).

Weaver, Donald E., Jr. *Images on Stone: The Prehistoric Rock Art of the Colorado Plateau.* Flagstaff, Arizona: The Museum of Northern Arizona, 1984.

Wheat, Joe Ben. *The Gift of the Spider Woman: Southwestern Textiles, The Navajo Tradition.* Philadelphia, Pennsylvania: University Museum, University of Pennsylvania, 1984.

Whiteley, Peter. *Bacavi: Journey to Reed Spring.* Flagstaff, Arizona: Northland Publishing, 1988.

Wicoff, Mary. "Visiting Baby Rocks, peaceful, eerie, awesome." *Gallup Independent* (Aug. 27, 1993): 11.

———. "Old Hopi Writings Marred." *Gallup Independent* (Jun. 1990).

Willson, Roscoe G. "How the Buffalo Came to Arizona." *Arizona Days and Ways Magazine* (Oct. 16, 1960): 24-25.

Wyman, Leland C. *The Windways of the Navaho.* Colorado Springs, Colorado: Taylor Museum of the Colorado Springs Fine Art Center, 1962.

Yazzie, Ethelou. *Navajo History, Volume 1.* Tsaile, Arizona: Navajo Community College, 1971.

Index

Index

Index

Index

Index

Index

Index

Index